W9-ADP-785

Why I Hate Abercrombie & Fitch: Essays on Race and Sexuality
Dwight A. McBride

In a Queer Time and Place: Transgender Bodies, Subcultural Lives
Judith Halberstam

God Hates Fags: The Rhetorics of Religious Violence
Michael Cobb

Once You Go Black: Choice, Desire, and the Black American Intellectual
Robert Reid-Pharr

The Latino Body: Crisis Identities in American Literary and
Cultural Memory
Lázaro Lima

The Latino Body

Crisis Identities in American Literary and Cultural Memory

LÁZARO LIMA

NEW YORK UNIVERSITY PRESS

New York and London

NEW YORK UNIVERSITY PRESS
New York and London
www.nyupress.org

© 2007 by New York University

Library of Congress Cataloging-in-Publication Data
Lima, Lázaro.
The Latino body : crisis identities in American literary and cultural
memory / Lázaro Lima.
p.   cm. — (Sexual cultures : new directions from the Center for
Lesbian and Gay Studies)
Includes bibliographical references and index.
ISBN-13: 978-0-8147-5214-2 (alk. paper)
ISBN-10: 0-8147-5214-4 (alk. paper)
ISBN-13: 978-0-8147-5215-9 (pbk. : alk. paper)
ISBN-10: 0-8147-5215-2 (pbk. : alk. paper)
1. American literature—Mexican American authors—History and
criticism. 2. Mexican Americans—Ethnic identity. 3. Mexican
Americans—Historiography. 4. Mexican Americans in literature.
5. Chicano movement. 6. Mexican American literature (Spanish)—
History and criticism.   I. Title.
PS153.M4L54 2007
810.9'86872—dc22   2007006121

New York University Press books are printed on acid-free paper,
and their binding materials are chosen for strength and durability.

Manufactured in the United States of America
c 10 9 8 7 6 5 4 3 2 1
p 10 9 8 7 6 5 4 3 2 1

A Caridad Ondina León
y
en memoria de Lázaro Prospero Lima
y Florencio Rigoberto Gutiérrez,
queridos

Contents

Acknowledgments

The body of this book and the material body that produced it were both nurtured and supported by many people and institutions. I take great pleasure in acknowledging them here. The genesis of this book was conceived at the University of Maryland, College Park, where Sandra Messinger Cypess, Regina Harrison, Phyllis Peres, Simon Richter, and Saúl Sosnowski were early supporters, generous readers, and exemplary academic role models. At Maryland I was also fortunate to come in contact with scholar-teachers who provoked and reeducated me about the uses of *América*, national belonging, and cultural memory in invaluable ways: Karen Christian, Peter Hulme, Linda Kaufmann, José Emilio Pacheco, Ineke Phaf, José Rabasa, and Beatriz Sarlo all fostered the intellectual climate that allowed me to engage the fields of American studies and Latin American literatures in ways that traditional disciplinary boundaries would have otherwise prevented.

I received important feedback on various incarnations of this book from the audiences at numerous conferences of the American Studies Association, the Latin American Studies Association, and the Modern Language Association and from invitations I received from colleagues to present my work at various institutions. I thank Shiva Balaghi at New York University, Zilkia Janer at Hofstra University, Luis Rebaza-Soraluz at King's College, University of London, and Jennifer Spear at the University of California, Berkeley, for helping make these particular engagements so rewarding and the company so gratifying. I also received useful feedback from the editors of the *Wallace Stevens Journal,* where an earlier portion of chapter 4 first appeared, and I thank them for permission to reprint. The assistance of the librarians and staff of the Bancroft Library at the University of California, Berkeley, facilitated much of the archival work necessary to complete this book, and I especially thank Susan Snyder for securing permissions and meeting my requests with efficiency. The staff of the Beinecke Rare Book and Manuscript Library at Yale University, the National Archives and Records Administration, the Van Pelt Library at the University of Pennsylvania, and the Canaday Library at Bryn Mawr College were resourceful and unfailingly helpful with my varied inquiries and requests. Institutional and financial support came at various stages of the project from the University of Maryland, the Penn Humanities Forum at the University of Pennsylvania, and Bryn Mawr College. At Bryn Mawr, I am grateful to Provost Ralph Kuncl for providing invaluable assistance, generous support, and thoughtful advice. I also wish to thank Director of Sponsored Research Nona Smith for facilitating travel funding to several research collections. At New York University Press, I thank José Esteban Muñoz and Ann Pellegrini, editors of the Sexual Cultures series, for supporting this project. Also at NYU Press, I have been fortunate to count on the enthusiastic support and intelligence of Eric Zinner, editorial director, as well as the remarkable efficiency of Emily Park, and Despina Papazoglou Gimbel.

Many colleagues at Bryn Mawr have been extraordinarily supportive and humanely responsive to all manner of things academic, personal, and political. I especially wish to thank Pim Higginson, H. Rosi Song, and Sharon Ullman for their intelligence, camaraderie, and the strength of their convictions when I needed it most. I must also thank Juan Arbona, Inés Arribas, Linda-Susan Beard, Duncan Black (a.k.a. "Atrios" in the blogosphere), Oliva Cardona, Jody Cohen, Anne Dalke, Jeremy Elkins, Florence Goff, Homay King, Michelle Mancini, Bethany Schneider, Kate Thomas, Michael Tratner, and Ted Wong for their intractable support and sheer good humor. My Tri-College consortium colleagues at Haverford and Swarthmore, as well those at Penn, have been intellectually receptive and always welcoming. I am particularly lucky to be able to count on the support and intellectual camaraderie of Cristina Beltrán, Israel Burshatin, Aurora Camacho de Schmidt, Edmund Campos, Roberto Castillo Sandoval, Ramón García, James Krippner, Yolanda Martínez-San Miguel, Lydie E. Moudileno, and Patricia Riley. In the field, my colleagues Arlene Dávila, Roberto Fernández, Licia Fiol-Matta, Juan Flores, Zilkia Janer, Larry La Fountain-Stokes, José Esteban Muñoz, Ricardo Ortíz, José Quiroga, Israel Reyes, Juana María Rodríguez, Ben Sifuentes-Jauregui, and Doris Sommer continue to show through example that the best of what is intellectually possible can and should transform lives for the better, *gracias*. I have been fortunate to work with some remarkable students at Bryn Mawr who inspire me with their enthusiasm, idealism, and intellectual passions. My thanks to them and especially to Omaira Alicea, Melinda Barbosa, Lucy Edwards, Danielle Kurin, Molly Mc-Tague, Miriam Ortíz, Mia Prenskey, and Yinette Sano for keeping it both real and rigorous. The wonderful students of BACaSO, Mujeres, Sisterhood, and Zami deserve my special thanks; everybody knows why.

Few established scholars will take it upon themselves to nurture a younger scholar's work, look after them, open doors, and keep those doors open as a matter of course and principle. Though humility may prevent them from speaking about how their work has transformed the fields that engage their respective projects as well as those whose work they have nurtured, it does not prevent me from doing so here: Azade Seyhan's intellectual generosity and support has made her a wonderful mentor and the measure of the ideal reader my writing aspires to reach; Nicolás Shumway's brilliance and integrity have made him an academic role model sans paragon; to both, my appreciation and gratitude. I also had the good fortune early on at Dickinson College to have my American Studies comrade and chair Lonna Malmsheimer create the conditions that allowed interdisciplinarity to work when this project required it, and I will always be thankful to her for this. Many of the writers and cultural agents whose work inspired this book have imparted their wisdom in ways that register between and beyond the pages of this book. I must especially thank Alicia Gaspar de Alba, Rafael Campo, Cherríe Moraga, and Elías Miguel Muñoz for giving so freely of their time at various stages of the project and for demonstrating in both words and deeds how moving the long arc of the moral universe in the direction of justice is a collective undertaking.

Long-standing debts of a personal sort are owed to my dear friends Dave Conway, Mark Fisher, Lisette León, Yreri Mendoza Mondragón, Salvador Miranda, Kathryn Troth Robinson, Misael Rodríguez, Nestor Tirado, and Larry Wilson, without whom life would not be as pleasurable or as rewarding. When this book was only an idea, I went to Vienna for the Universität Wien and intellectual distance but stayed for Alexander Rheingold Jonach. Carlos Gacio found me a job at the Wiener Staatsoper, which allowed me to prolong my stay for far longer than was sensible; I thank them both for introducing me to more than I can admit by keeping a promise made long ago to mention them in this book, and I do so with affection. My sincere appreciation to my dear friend John Wood Sweet for taking time from his own book to nurture my own and for providing invaluable counsel when I needed it. Alison Anderson provided essential editorial suggestions, and the book is better for it. I am lucky to count on Patrick Edward Killeen's friendship and love as one of life's few constants, and I will always be grateful for this fact. The early and sustained support of Eva Lloréns made academic and personal life in New Haven a locus of possibilities; I only wished I could have thanked her before she passed away. Missed, too, are S. Paige Baty, Haley Thomas, and Michael Powell, who inspired through example and did so much in so little time.

My family has put up with the best and worst of me long before this book gave me an excuse to be absent in body though never in spirit. My mother, Caridad Ondina León, made do with exile in two continents, four countries, and unfamiliar languages with a selflessness and strength I am not sure I could muster under the same circumstances; her love and sacrifice have ensured that I will likely never have to. My father, Lázaro Prospero Lima, and the man who raised me like a son, Florencio Rigoberto Gutiérrez, both passed away before I could share this book with them or explain why I stayed away. The best of who they were continues to motivate the best of what I do, and I am grateful to them for that and so much more. I thank my *tías extraordinarias* Felicia Troadia Gutiérrez and Justa Rodríguez for their loving support, not to mention the many meals and *batidos* whenever I have felt hungry and thirsty for home. My *primo hermano* and intellectual comrade Osiris Gutiérrez gave me the encouragement to imagine more than what was discernible in inner-city Bridgeport after arriving first from Madrid (via Havana) and then again after some years from Miami. I consider myself fortunate for being able to thank him for this and, more recently, for sharing all the fun that comes from being an honorary member of *los* Gutiérrez along with Julia, Liska, and Alex. Finally, I thank Ted Hallinan for giving corporeal substance to my optimism. His extraordinary intelligence, humor, companionship, and cooking keep my body nourished and my spirit sated, *por fin*.

Part I

Longing History

tence but because they allow him to excise Mexicans from America's past and his own present in order to imagine a country free of a people rendered unfit for national civic life. This "degraded, turbulent, ignorant, and superstitious" population is effectively deracinated of historical and cultural specificity.

The discursive resonance of "The American Congo" resided in its ability to amortize and consolidate various nineteenth-century representations of Mexican, Amerindian, and, as I will later argue, Black corporealities as prima facie indices of difference and strangeness. At face value, the habits of Bourke's subjects become racially marked through a simple tautology, with disastrously complex consequences: these people are not American because they are racially different from "real" Americans, and they are racially different because they are not American. Bourke's presumption of a normative Americanness and its conflation with whiteness inscribed colored difference as a deviation from an American norm that did not exist outside the representational logic of the interests it served. His tautology ultimately deprived his *Scribner's* citizen-readers of part of their historical memory and aspirants to citizenship of the very promises of democratic participation and inclusion that underwrite the narratives of American democracy.

In this study, I contend that what is understood today as the "Latino subject" surfaced along the literal and metaphorical divide between Mexico and the United States, a divide that fractured alliances, elided ethnic and racial identities, and disembodied subjects from the protocols of citizenship. The literal divide was a trope of nationalism, and its complicit metaphorical weight and accompanying truth claims were perpetuated in the public sphere through various print media.[3]

Bourke belonged to that first generation of Anglo-Americans who were able to naturalize a sense of belonging in a territory that extended from coast to coast. After the signing of the Treaty of Guadalupe Hidalgo in 1848, which put an end to the Mexican-American War, Mexico ceded modern-day California, Utah, Nevada, and parts of New Mexico, Arizona, Colorado, and Wyoming, as well as Texas (which had claimed independence from Mexico in 1836 as the Lone Star Republic). For Bourke and his generation, the newly acquired territories represented a cultural landscape untranslatable to monological majoritarian interests. His *Scribner's* piece, replete with high-quality engravings, gave visual evidence of a people as inhospitable to reason as the region was to Anglo-American order. As a career soldier, his authority was institutional and emblematic of how language and images began to create subaltern bodies for literary and visual public consumption after the war. As an ethnographer, he began the production of knowledge about what we today call Latinos by conflating space and race and making ethnically marked identities incompatible with national imaginings. That Latinos have appropriated similar mechanisms of identity construction for political gain is instructive of both the limits of American citizenship and the promise of democratic participation that this study charts.

The Latino Body: Crisis Identities in American Literary and Cultural Memory analyzes the conditions under which it becomes necessary to create a specific Latino subject of American cultural and literary history.[4] It tells the story of the U.S. Latino body politic and its relation to the state: how the state configures Latino subjects and how Latino subjects have in turn altered the state's appellative assertions of difference (the contemporary emphasis on "Latino" instead of "Hispanic," for example) to their own ends in the public sphere. This study accomplishes this by providing an analysis of Latino cultural, literary, visual, and popular texts that suggest that becoming historical has often been tantamount to becoming "American," and how this public metamorphosis of group ontology has almost always entailed a crisis in meaning for both Latinos and the broader culture.

The term "crisis" is meant to call attention to the cultural manifestations of historical conflict that have resulted in publicly rendered and redressed modes of being both American and Latino through narratives, images, and various other sign systems. A crisis is ultimately a narrative recapitulation that takes place either before or after the crisis event has occurred. The crisis itself eludes common locution and, in this sense, could be said to be inherently antinarrative. Narrative either precedes a crisis, as a justification or exoneration of an impending or perceived crisis, or follows it, as an explanation or attempt to make sense of a crisis moment *after* the fact.[5] Crisis identities are therefore always grounded in the recognition of a capitulation that seeks an explanation or resolution in and through narrative. Indeed, the term signals a philosophical inquiry into the structures of consciousness experienced from what could be understood as the narrative first-person point of view, the *cogito* before the *ergo sum*.

By studying a series of crisis moments, the book proposes that the current emphasis on and ostensible novelty associated with Latino identity is but a recent manifestation of a larger and unresolved cultural crisis that arose after the Mexican-American War. I contend that ever since the war the various conceits associated with American democratic participation and the unfulfilled promise of equality have created crisis moments where competing forms of cultural citizenship have vied for legitimacy and access to cultural capital.[6] Indeed, the Latino cultural production currently in the forefront of the public sphere foregrounds the most recent Latino crisis as the national culture begins to contend, as never before, with the largest "minority" group in the nation. Having inherited the unresolved Mexican question—What is the country to do with Mexicans?—the national culture is faced anew with the contemporary renderings of that older question— What is the country to do with Latinos?—rather than the more logical, exacting, though infinitely more difficult, process of identifying why Latino subjectivity has been constructed as incommensurate with the American body politic.

The discrete crisis moments I propose for consideration in this study are therefore necessarily epochal and, as I will argue, represent significant transformations in the way both majority and minoritarian cultural actors have been imagined, rendered, and conceived within the national culture. These epochal shifts are necessarily diachronic and seek to capture the way in which changes over time have required representational strategies that in some way break with previous and often entrenched modes of understanding what today we understand to be "Latino" identity negotiations. The engagement requires not just understanding how and when do Latinos enter American literary and cultural history but, more specifically, why it becomes necessary to do so in the public sphere of national contemplation.

American Publics and the Subaltern Subject

For Jürgen Habermas, the rise of the public sphere coincided with the development of literary culture as private bourgeois ideals found public expression through writing and various representational media.[7] The articulations of class-based ideologies and civic ideals that circulated in the eighteenth and nineteenth centuries through print media eventually universalized a public subject who was presumed to be representative of the broader culture. Habermas's public sphere is, of course, problematic on several grounds.[8] The presumption of equal access to public articulation of group concerns belies the ostensible democratic imperative in his conception of Modernity, since bourgeois representational agency is not representative of anything except the interests bourgeois ideology serves. For subaltern groups this has resulted in a quandary, since the enabling condition for intervention and clout in the public sphere has often meant the uncritical acceptance of bourgeois inclusionary norms.

Habermas attempts to counter criticism regarding the implicitly uncritical rendering of the Enlightenment project's universal subject by making a distinction between the public sphere of the literary (*literarische Offentlichkeit*) and the political (*politische Offentlichkeit*), that is, the representation of group-specific imaginings through literature and the mechanisms by which representations are accorded legal limits by political systems (*Structural Transformation*, 51). The conditions under which inclusion in the public sphere is permitted, granted, or denied determine how civic problems can be publicly rendered through textual and visual sign systems by making identities historical and providing context in the national imaginary.

In the chapters that follow, I study how competing forms of *being* American appealed to the ontological status of citizens (the purportedly knowable core of their being) in the public sphere. I propose that the organizing principle of Latino public-sphere identities offered context-specific strategies for cultural enfranchisement and participation in the broader body politic. Specific crisis moments have given rise to particular forms of Latino cultural engagement that have involved assimilationist, patriotic, cultural nationalist, and more recently gendered modes of *being* American. These identity modalities have characterized Latino responses to cultural crisis, political conflict, and erasure at moments of profound cultural transformations. These transformations constitute subject positions that alter the way Latinos understand themselves in relation to the American body politic and the way they are imagined as a community by the culture writ large.

Citizenship in the Public Sphere: Appellative Strategies and the Language of Loss

American calls to unity and a shared common vision arise at times of crisis, when it becomes difficult to apprehend what eludes common locution. That language leaves us at moments of culturally significant trauma comes as no surprise to anyone who has witnessed natural or human disaster, either in person or through representational media. That these calls to unity come at moments of profound national crisis and are ignored in times of relative stability make the calls disingenuous, if not outright manipulative, to scores of nationals otherwise excluded from the patriotic embrace.

This book charts the interrelated groups born out of the Spanish colonization of the Americas and the ways these groups have responded to monocultural calls to unity and nationally shared conceptions of American cultural identity. Those who were called "Mexican" in U.S. territories after the

to redress their relationship to the United States through enfranchisement and civic participation as U.S. citizens or citizens in the making, this tendency is counterproductive at best. This is not to suggest that the term is not problematic on several grounds. Foremost, it elides the very differences that make it referentially useful (as will become evident in subsequent chapters). Indeed, one of the term's principal limitations is its collusive ability to unproblematically erase a past replete with the very Latino modalities of American identity construction and nation building that it seeks to affirm as contemporary phenomena (especially in its more staunchly cultural nationalist expressions of ethnic pride).

A Different Love

The public-sphere articulations of national identity that I chart from the nineteenth century onward also borrow from and refashion the more well-known nation-building projects of Latin America in and through belles lettres, that is, the fictions that aesthetically attempted to resolve the nation's pressing crises at its founding or at moments of cultural transformation. The Venezuelan writer and intellectual Andrés Bello (1781–1865) called this process of "becoming historical" *el método narrativo*. For Bello, this "narrative method" would inscribe the nation into history through writing, by providing a cultural specificity where none had existed. Bello was concerned with history and writing as the inexorably linked progenitors of the nation. For him, language not only functioned to legitimate the nation but also constituted it through writing. He made this clear in his 1848 "Autonomía cultural de América" ("The Cultural Autonomy of America") when he stated that, "cuando la historia de un país no existe, sino en documentos incompletos, esparciados, en tradiciones vagas, que es preciso compulsar y juzgar, el método narrativo es obligado" ("when the history of a country only exists in incomplete and sparse documents, in vague traditions, which make it necessary to compel and to judge, the narrative method is obligatory").[15]

Bello's obligatory recourse to the narrative method for constituting the nation found its complement in the practice of "literature" as a form of historical writing. The narrative resolution of national conflict through narrative emplotment has, as Doris Sommer brilliantly observed, characterized the national literary traditions of Latin America. Sommer's significant book *Foundational Fictions: The National Romances of Latin America* (1991) grounds

Benedict Anderson's and Homi Bhabha's paradigm for national consolidations, or the links between "nation and narration" (Bhabha), squarely within a Latin Americanist contextual field of signification.[16] Sommer's other significant rhetorical move entailed the recognition that the heteronormative couplings that aesthetically resolved national crises around questions of race, history, and economic disparity in the emplotments of "romance" also left too many citizens outside the national patriotic embrace. Sommer, of course, employs "romance" in both its contemporary sense and the nineteenth-century use that made it "more boldly allegorical than the novel" as Latin American authors "were preparing national projects through prose fiction" (*Foundational Fictions*, 5–7). A crucial distinction has to be made, however, between Latin American nation-building projects and their articulation in the United States in the nineteenth century. As Latin American nations were creating historical identity projects after achieving independence, Mexicans living in the United States as ersatz citizens were attempting to interpolate themselves into national historical processes *in medias res*—in the middle of a National Symbolic teleology where they fettered national dreams of unity because of their linguistic difference and their publicly constructed proximity to "blackness" and the attendant question of slavery.

Nonetheless, the inexorably linked processes of nation and narration provide a window through which we can better understand the strategic identity negotiations we have inherited from inter-American nation-building projects. As Juan De Castro reminds us about these early Latin American nation-building projects, "Even for those opposed to the undeniably totalizing and totalitarian aspects of the nation, these early constructions of identity serve as cautionary examples or—in the frequent paradox—as that which by being resisted ends up defining its putative opposite."[17] If the Latin American historical romance served national interests by giving public examples of how ideal couplings could sustain national contradictions through romantic pairing for the love of nation, in this study I propose a different reading of the national allegory of love in the United States. I do this in order to understand the National Symbolic outside the passion plays of romance by which it has been articulated in much of the research and literature on inter-American nation-building projects.[18]

The conceits associated with Latin American nation-building projects through the emplotments of romance also warrant an investigation into their relevance as Latino groups have jockeyed the privileged category of "the literary" for the public articulation of ethnically and linguistically marked expressions of group identity from the end of the Mexican-American War onward. Read this way, this book is also a metaphorical national love story about the limits of historical romance, about not being loved enough, about sometimes being loved too much, and about the national spoils and excesses inherent to these two extremes. Like all potential love stories, it asks the question valiant lovers must eventually ask if they want to spend the rest of their lives with each other, or at least learn to ask if they even plan on cohabiting for any substantial period of time: Do you love me? And if so, and this is one big if, at what cost such love?

Even with a "prenuptial agreement," as was the case with the relationship the United States established with Mexicans and, later, Mexican Americans after the Treaty of Guadalupe Hidalgo, these are difficult questions indeed. Some lovers regrettably never ask them out of convenience, others because they are afraid of the answer. The relationship the treaty established between the two countries provided a series of strategies of coexistence characterized by desires, expectations, and unmet needs that have kept the relationship alive through mutual codependence. After the war of wills, the metaphorical love between the two countries began to follow a pattern of embraces and rejections, lies and deceits, and unthinkable collusions that created necessities too comfortable to abandon even after the expression of love's desire abated.

Terms of Engagement

As will become evident, the terms Latina and Latino would be difficult to understand outside the context of their relation to the United States were it not for the unifying memory of nonbelonging. As Suzanne Oboler reminds us, "Latinos have been racialized such that they experience the effects of invisibility in social and political institutions,"[19] unless, I would add, they are needed for labor or war, in which case they are welcomed into the national fold through the elusive embrace of an exhausted American dream.[20] The texts I study demonstrate that not being loved enough is just as bad as being suffocated by love in the throes of patriotic national passions.

This brings me to America. The social symbolic functions of the terms "America" and "American"—in their ability to conjure the nation-state as an imagined community—alienate Latinos, and others disenfranchised from the National Symbolic, by virtue of the myth of an American cultural history that emerges fully formed after the establishment in 1607 of the first permanent English settlement in Jamestown, Virginia. That the immigrant status of these settlers has been erased while other immigrants continue to be posited as "foreign" is a pervasive national fantasy about American cultural identity that this project seeks to redress. I do not mean to engage in a reconstruction of the myth of American origins; the Native American presence would make such a proposition moot. I do intend to interrogate the facile assumptions about cultural interaction that continue to inform our epistemic grounding with regard to a usable and abusable cultural past. Consequently, my use of the terms "America" and "American" is meant to recall a certain irony in nationalistic popular use—the terms' ability to conjure the United States as an imagined community, often by relegating interactions with Atlantic and Amerindian cultures to symbolic oblivion.

The conceptual recourse to memory throughout the study is not meant to invoke a past nostalgic longing for "truth" as it was or was not imagined. Anderson has noted that the profound cultural transformations that create national "amnesias" through historical crises also engender narrative rememberings that structure memory's relation to state identity and loss.[21] What is excised from cultural imaginings at the time of national consolidation haunts the nation in the form of countertexts that emerge from memories of loss. Anderson is referring not just to monuments or the state's memory apparatus (archives and legal record systems) but rather to the traces of loss that inhere in lived experience and manifest themselves publicly in what Cherríe Moraga calls "the memory of the body."[22] Moraga notes how the imperiled Latina body foregrounds a corporeally grounded aesthetics of memory in *A Xicanadyke Codex of Changing Consciousness* (2005):

> We are despised when we speak up; we are despised when we act out.
> . . . Whether we are lesbian or heterosexual, as self-proclaimed desirers, we become bodies of revolt, bodies in dissent against oblivion. I am reminded here of Alicia Gaspar de Alba's depiction of Malintzín, in her short story, "Los derechos de Malinche." In it, an imprisoned Malinche in anticipation of Cortez' arrival to her cell, places a *nopal con espinas* (a thorny prickly pear) inside her vagina. She awaits her rapist. She is a body in dissent against oblivion. (11)

Moraga's corporeally rendered mnemonics of history, the "body in dissent against oblivion," is an aestheticized meditation on communal memory as a publicly rendered personal antidote to cultural forgetting, a countertext to historical elision. This is precisely what Toni Morrison in the African American context has called "rememory": memory as a countertext for the re-presentation of a past in need of national reevaluation.[23] In performances of loss like those of the Mothers of the Plaza de Mayo, who silently protested the "disappearances" of their children by Argentina's military dictatorship during the "dirty war," the countertext could be a photograph, a diaper worn as a headscarf, a memory of loss evoked through a publicly enacted code. Our ability to think through the limits of the National Symbolic emerges from these countertextual forms of recording and the literal body's material relationship to the symbolic orders that constitute the body as a subject of history.

Though the body and memory are two of my principal tropes, I also invoke the juridical notion of *corpus delicti* (literally, body of crime)[24] with regard to the national body politic. This is useful because the National Symbolic categories of citizenship and the discourses of national belonging are plagued with metaphors with juridical meaning and historical weight (alien, citizen, legal, illegal, foreigner, national, immigrant, migrant). The body's legality is bound to both law and symbolic citizenship. The categorization of "illegal" bodies as they pertain to "aliens" is still meant to conjure fear in the public imagination by positing the immigrant body as a national pathogen.[25] Anthropologist Jonathan Xavier Inda has gone so far as to say that the national fear of immigrants has made the United States a "pathological nation": "nativist rhetoric implicitly figures the immigrant, the Mexican immigrant in particular, as a parasite intruding on the body of the host nation, drawing nutrients from it, while providing nothing to its survival and even threatening its well-being."[26] That defining "legal" and "illegal" bodies in the National Symbolic requires a series of hesitations should alert us to the prior motivations and actions that imbue the body's materiality with meanings that are never disinterested.

Organizing the Latino Body

This book is divided into two parts. The first, "Longing History," attempts to recover a literary and cultural historiography of Latino intervention in American cultural history from the mid-nineteenth century to the rise of the equality-rights movement of the 1960s and early 1970s. The texts I study are unified by a concerted attempt at inflecting American notions of ideal citizenship with "Latino" ethnic, linguistic, and cultural markers that are often seen as recent phenomena. These texts foreground how Latino identities responded to the crisis of symbolic and literal annihilation by becoming historical during two pivotal periods in American cultural history: the territorial consolidation of the United States after the Mexican-American War and the rise of the equality movements of the 1960s. The chapters themselves chart various couplings and modes of living together as well as the costs associated with convivial strategies born out of historical disjunctures. The epochal focus related to these disjunctures seeks to make visible significant shifts in the way people who today we would consider Latinos have reimagined themselves or been reimagined in the public sphere of the national. As such, these literary and cultural realignments tell the story of representational realignments and ruptures with previous identity modalities but not the marked continuity that has characterized the significant and steady outpour of Latino literary and cultural production in the United States.

Chapter 1, "Negotiating Cultural Memory in the Aftermath of the Mexican-American War: Nineteenth-Century Mexican American Testimonials and *The Squatter and the Don*," focuses on Mexican Americans' responses to the founding crisis that resulted when former Mexicans became "American" after the end of the war. The chapter analyzes Mexican American negotiations of citizenship, national belonging, and the strategic uses of cultural memory and amnesia in two nineteenth-century testimonials that contest the idea of a stable Mexican subject of American cultural history as propagated in much of the writing of California history: Eulalia Pérez's *An Old Woman and Her Recollections* (1877) and Catarina Ávila de Ríos's *Memoirs of Doña Catarina Ávila de Ríos* (1877). The texts are counterpoised with María Amparo Ruiz de Burton's historical romance, *The Squatter and the Don* (1885), whose author is credited with writing the first Latina novel written in English.[27] This chapter proposes that in the aftermath of the Mexican-American War, a highly symbolic public language was cultivated through print culture that rendered Mexicans as interlopers on the American landscape and cultural imagination. Focusing on broadsides, testimonials, and literary texts in the nineteenth century, I demonstrate that the publicly constructed nature of American identity through print culture made visible a public American ideal that left Mexicans outside the National Symbolic. By showing how the Mexican body ultimately became conflated with "blackness" in the public sphere, I demonstrate how "whiteness" became the organizing principle for the construction of American citizenship and identity for Mexicans in the nineteenth century. Mexican American racial passing, I argue, attempted to trump linguistic difference to create a logic of solidarity with Anglo-American culture through racialized associations. This strategy of accommodation and collusion created one of the first viable and most enduring strategic crisis identities still operative today. Though Mexican Americans and other U.S. Latinos were producing and developing collective social identities inflected with regional themes and concerns, I contend that it was not until the Chicano renaissance of the late 1960s that a discernable political agenda emerged and manifested itself for national reflection.[28] Chapter 2, "Reading the *Corpus Delicti*: Tomás Rivera's *Earth* and the Chicano Body in the Public Sphere," analyzes one of the most important texts to come out of the Chicano civil rights movement, Tomás Rivera's . . . *And the Earth Did Not Devour Him* (1971).[29] Rivera's *Earth* marked a critical turn away from the assimilative grounding in the majority of texts written and recovered before the civil rights apogee of the 1960s and early 1970s. As Manuel M. Martín-Rodríguez noted in *Life in Search of Readers: Reading (in) Chicano/a Literature* (2003), Rivera's *Earth* and the novels written by his contemporaries that followed his landmark text allowed, "for the first time in the history of Chicano/a letters, the possibility of conceiving of a Chicano/a readership at the national level."[30]

Indeed, it was the paucity of narrative models that made the Chicano movement found a public identity centered on Mexico's indigenous heritage and the greatness of Aztec civilization through the invocation of Aztlán, the mythic homeland of the Aztec in the southwestern United States. Aztlán created a logic of presence that grounded Chicano experience and being *in* the United States, thereby making Chicanos heirs to an indigenous historical tradition that antedated the Anglo-American presence in the country. Emerging out of this cultural nationalist assault on American cultural amnesia, *Earth* served as a novelized reenactment of the historical and metaphorical exclusion of the Mexican body from the American body politic. From the vantage point of the early 1970s, Rivera's novel re-created and critiqued the Cold War patriotic rhetoric of the 1950s and how the forging of America often meant both literal and symbolic annihilation for Mexicans. In order to analyze the conditions under which Latino counterpatriotic crisis identities could register in the public sphere as viable political interventions, the chapter necessarily focuses on mid-twentieth-century popular culture and the Cold War hysteria the text implicitly alludes to.

Part II, "Postmodern Genealogies: The Latino Body, in Theory," focuses on two recent crisis moments for Latino cultural identity projects born of the cultural nationalism and equality-rights movements of the 1960s. First, the institutionalization of Latino literature created the need to establish the theoretical basis for a field of inquiry that seemingly lacked the methodological apparatus to understand its modes of production, diffusion, silences, and apparent lack of temporal contiguity. If a Chicano and more broadly Latino presence existed in the United States before the Latino identity projects of 1960s, then how to explain the apparent absence of cultural and textual foremothers and forefathers? Second, this section analyzes how political inclusion and enfranchisement created the concomitant need to render visible how sexuality and sexual identity inform national conceptions of citizenship and personhood.

Chapter 3, "The Institutionalization of Latino Literature in the Academy: Cabeza de Vaca's *Castaways* and the Crisis of Legitimation," is devoted to a critique of Latino criticism's genealogical search for a Latino-specific subject of American literary history, as Latino cultural recovery projects focus on Alvar Núñez Cabeza de Vaca's *Castaways* (1542)[31] as a strategic starting point for articulating a foundational Latino subjectivity. I focus on *Castaways* because—aside from having been anthologized and considered a foundational precursor of U.S. Latino literature in the more inclusive domains of academic curricula—the text raises a series of questions about the theoretical and methodological problems inherent to "identity recovery projects," as well as our critical and ethical investment in these projects. Although *Castaways* has been traditionally considered one of the founding texts of the colonial Latin American literature canon, the research I cite about Cabeza de Vaca's chronicle is quite recent. One motive for this is to show how *Castaways* has been reread and reinterpreted during the late twentieth and early twenty-first centuries as an exemplary and founding account of a very recent phenomenon: the rise of Latino literature and the discourse of multicultural inclusion in the academy.

That this curricular inclusion came at the height of 1980s multiculturalism, and the era of the Reagan-Bush "culture wars," shows the degree to which texts like *Castaways* were presumed to do the transformative cultural work that so many in the Latino community craved. Indeed, while the curriculum was diversifying, the country experienced the first major backlash against affirmative action and the first assault on so-called political correctness. Having inherited this Latino forefather, it now becomes imperative to assess critically what *Castaways* does and for whom.

Chapter 4, "Practices of Freedom: The Body Re-membered in Contemporary Latino Writing," examines how constructions of postmodern identity projects at the end of the twentieth century began to reconfigure Latino subjectivity at the intersections of gender, ethnic, and national identities in

Luz María Umpierre's *Margarita Poems* (1987), Elías Miguel Muñoz's *The Greatest Performance* (1991), and Rafael Campo's *What the Body Told* (1996).[32] The texts in this chapter, wittingly or not, all attempt to come to terms with the contradictions inherent to Latino ethnic identities and the possibility of loving openly as well as *being* who one is "veinte y cuatro horas al día, siete días por semana," twenty-four hours a day, seven days a week, as Boricua writer Víctor Fragoso so poignantly observed shortly before his death from AIDS. The specter of loss vis-à-vis s/exile and AIDS prompted a literal re-membering of the Latino body in cultural theory and social texts. Social and representational death ceded way to an accounting of the literal death of Latinos as Latino literature entered the twenty-first century. The inclusion of these Cuban American and Puerto Rican interventions in this chapter also seeks to redress and call attention to the importance of placing Latino Atlantic communities in conversation with the important work undertaken by Chicana theoretical and cultural producers who have challenged ethnic, gender, and sexual orthodoxies in significant ways.

The conclusion, "Democracy's Graveyard: Dead Citizenship and the Latino Body," engages Alicia Gaspar de Alba's detective thriller, *Desert Blood: The Juárez Murders* (2005),[33] as a novelized testament to the latest Latino crisis moment and the possibilities it offers for rethinking human agency outside the strictures of the globalized commodification of bodies. Gaspar de Alba's novel focuses on the silence surrounding the "disappeared" and murdered women of Ciudad Juárez from the early 1990s to the present in the context of the transnational flow of capital. The globalized body of commodity capital finds a gross literalization in Ciudad Juárez, where predominantly female factory workers in *maquiladoras,* border factories, continue to be murdered and "disappeared" at an alarming rate while their Anglo-American managers cross the border into El Paso, Texas, to the safety of depoliticized homes. As a model for twenty-first-century Latino identity negotiations, the bodies of the disappeared, and the aesthetic responses to violence about the disappeared, position us within the knowable limits of the most recent Latino crisis moment and alert us to Moraga's call for a Chicana memory conceived as a living memorial to processes of continued colonization. In the process, the conclusion surveys the rhetorical repertoire of Latino identitarian strategies studied in the previous chapters and their implications for our present. I conclude with Cherríe Moraga's ethical call for understanding the Chicana body *as* mnemonic history, a living and remembering body of knowledge as articulated in her most recent work, *A Xicanadyke Codex of Changing Consciousness.*

The texts included in this study illuminate different aspects of my concerns surrounding corporeality and citizenship that have arisen in response to specific crisis moments in American cultural history. They tell a story about how unfinished historical business both founds and limits Latino demands for social and political parity. Their modes of address and redress have formulated the terms of Latino engagement with majority culture in the public sphere in order to constitute what they demand or envision as legitimate during moments of significant historical disjunctures. In the process, I risk temporal rifts in order to build bridges across times and spaces that have burdened the backs of many through historical waves of majoritarian subjection, waves of institutionalized aggression against Latinos that have sometimes barely registered in the national culture. In so doing, I hope to call attention to the dynamic, creative, and at times courageous responses to majoritarian subjection that have secured the staying power of peoples born out of the colonization of the Americas. This move requires, to paraphrase Walter Benjamin, continuous historical "illumination" in order to safeguard the memory of these disjunctures from the inimical master narratives that would efface historical accountability were it not for the ongoing accounting these texts demand.

The texts in question, like the Latino bodies that haunt them, are representative of historical moments that required collective responses to national and historical crises that, in turn, determined their mode of address and forms of diffusion in the public sphere. As such, these texts and cultural artifacts cannot transcend the history into which they are interpolated, nor can we demand that they do so. That responsibility falls on us after we read stories like the ones they are dying to tell and finally, in moving from imagining to doing, we lay our books down long enough to enact what we envision in their wake.

Coda: Red Dead Revolver, or Playing American

Reperire pax, "find peace," is a noble enough call to justice and the raison d'être of Red, the protagonist of the video game *Red Dead Revolver* (2004). But Red—pictured with this imperative call literally crowning one of his revolvers in one of the video game's scenes—attempts to find it through the pursuit and annihilation of Mexican General Diego and those of similar ilk who killed his family when he was a boy. Armed with his father's revolver as a literal and metonymic emblem of forced penetrations, Red's quest—and that of anyone playing the video game *Red Dead Revolver*—partakes of a cultural repertoire of images that have infused the American popular imagination with murderous Mexicans from the nineteenth century on. But playing American in this context is about being played. From the serial western novel, to the *Lone Ranger* radio show of the 1940s and, later, the television show of the 1950s, and its heirs in the Hollywood and spaghetti westerns, all the way to *Walker, Texas Ranger, Red Dead Revolver* continues an investment in American national identity through a folk mythology that is neither historically factual nor ethically accountable. As an exemplar of the processes by which American cultural memory and amnesia find public expression, Red—like Bourke before him—evinces the continued investment in an American national fantasy that requires continuous interrogation, resistance, and illumination. *Reperire pax,* indeed.

1

Negotiating Cultural Memory in the Aftermath of the Mexican-American War

Nineteenth-Century Mexican American Testimonials and *The Squatter and the Don*

Truce and Consequences

The "truce" that followed the signing of the Treaty of Guadalupe Hidalgo in 1848 occasioned a series of remembrances about the Mexican-American War, its prehistory, and its aftermath. On both sides of the redrawn border, the war demanded justification, description, documentation, and recollection. As previously noted, Mexico ceded to the United States modern-day California, Utah, Nevada, and parts of New Mexico, Arizona, Colorado, and Wyoming, along with its claim to Texas. Mexicans living in the newly consolidated United States found themselves classed as foreigners in places they had inhabited even before Mexico's independence from Spain in 1821. This generative crisis in meaning for Mexicans created the need to negotiate their relationship to the nation as well as the literal and symbolic functions of national belonging, citizenship, and what it meant to be an American.[1] The testimonial and narrative remembrances born of the war demonstrate how writing about its aftermath and prehistory could be just as important as how the war itself was fought.

In this chapter I explore how Mexican American cultural memory attempted to participate in an emerging, but increasingly restrictive, National Symbolic order that began to delimit ideations of ideal citizenship in the public sphere. The three principal texts I engage are two testimonials, Eulalia Pérez's *Una vieja y sus recuerdos* (*An Old Woman and Her Recollections*) and Catarina Ávila de Ríos's *Recuerdos históricos de California por la Señora Catarina Ávila de Ríos* (*Memoirs of Doña Catarina Ávila de Ríos*), and María Amparo Ruiz de Burton's historical romance, *The Squatter and the Don: A Novel Descriptive of Contemporary Occurrences in California.*[2] These texts found the discursive parameters from which to better understand both the promise and limits of what today we would call "Latino subjectivity" by insisting on making their relationship to the state historical.

The two testimonials are among those gathered for Hubert Howe Bancroft's multivolume *History of California* project (1884–1889). Critical attention to these texts has been limited; the two serious book-length works are Genaro Padilla's *My History, Not Yours: The Formation of Mexican American Autobiography* (1993) and Rosaura Sánchez's *Telling Identities: The Californio Testimonios* (1995).[3] These important and often illuminating studies offer readings of representative testimonials from the Bancroft Collection but tell only part of the story. There are texts in Bancroft's archive that are exemplary not because they offered what was expected but because of their reticence at disclosure. This is the case with Catarina Ávila de Ríos's testimonial, which graphically details the violence wrought on Western Mexican American culture as a result of the California Gold Rush. Eulalia Pérez's *An Old Woman and Her Recollections,* to date the best-known and most reprinted testimonial, is also the most misunderstood. It continues to be read as exemplary of nineteenth-century Mexican American autobiography (Padilla, *My History,* 130–39) without taking into account its complex recourse to internalized racism after the 1848 cultural and political divide.[4] Now that much archival work about the testimonials has been done, a more complete analysis is feasible.

Ruiz de Burton's *The Squatter and the Don,* published under the pseudonym C. Loyal, is an important counterpoint to the testimonials, as the novel has perhaps been too generously read alongside the likes of Cuban independence leader José Martí (1853–1895) as a critical intervention against imperialism and monopoly capitalism.[5] The novel has the honor of being one of the first fictional narratives written and published in English from the perspective of the conquered population.[6] In the novel, Ruiz de Burton sought a locus of enunciation for the reconciliation of her elite class standing and her ethnic identity as it related to the Treaty of Guadalupe Hidalgo. This strategy of ethnic accommodation, in the face of social symbolic and literal disenfranchisement, offers a compelling story about the limited possibilities Mexicans had for broad cultural and political inclusion born out of the crisis of 1848.

The elite novel and the women's testimonials from the working classes provide a picture of nineteenth-century Mexican American culture and identity negotiations that informs the present through renderings of the past. They are part of the limited repository we possess of specifically Mexican American attempts to participate in the discourse of American citizenship after the signing of the treaty. Furthermore, their gendered nature speaks to the limited possibilities for women to insert themselves into the emerging discourses of nationalism, given the constraints of their class, ethnic ancestry, and inchoate cultural identity. The texts are also connected by the search for an ethnic, class, and gender identity that could reconcile their ethnic particularisms with an increasingly restrictive understanding of what it meant to be an American at the close of the nineteenth century. By recalling a past of dispossession and the shards of collective loss, these "writers" authored a version of their American histories either by remembering historical specifics the emerging American republic was too eager to forget or by accommodating the very limitations imposed by conquest. This process of incorporating their individual histories into the American body politic necessarily entailed *becoming* historical.

"The American 1848": Racializing the Mexican American Body

With the end of the Mexican-American War came the first major incorporation of a "foreign" people into the continental and geographic fold of a country that now stretched from the Atlantic to the Pacific. The massive acquisition of Mexican territory in 1848 occasioned a growing sense of what could be understood as institutionalized cultural amnesia with regard to Mexicans who remained in the newly consolidated territories. As I will show, their history, language, religion, and cultural practices were all denied a part in legal, academic, religious, and civic discourse. Cultural forgetting, rooted in Manifest Destiny politics, attempted to erase the Mexican American presence from geographic and psychic spheres of the nation's consciousness through a racialized discourse of dispossession. As Shelly Streeby has poignantly noted, the eventual territorial victory over Mexico ultimately entailed a reevaluation of the question of race in America.[7] Following scholars such as David Porter, Michael Paul Rogin, and José David Saldívar, Streeby reminds us how their work has ultimately "called attention to the connections between the U.S.-Mexican War and the Civil War, between foreign conflict and domestic discord, and between the acquisition of a new empire and the increasingly divisive debate over slavery" (*American Sensations*, 6). Streeby credits Rogin for coining the term "the American 1848" as a type of critical shorthand that forces us to attend to how former Mexican territories and nationals were racialized as they were simultaneously incorporated into the American body politic.

The processes relating to the American 1848, and the ensuing racialization of Mexicans living in the United States, resulted in the literal and metaphorical excision of the Mexican body from the American body politic. It also created a crisis of representation for Mexican Americans who were left to negotiate, and ultimately justify, their relationship to the nation in the interstices of national belonging. As Homi Bhabha reminds us, "It is in the emergence of the interstices—the overlap and displacement of domains of difference—that the intersubjective and collective experiences of *nationness*, community interest, or cultural value are negotiated."[8] As I will show, the processes relating to national "negotiation" of cultural, racial, and linguistic diversity ultimately made the category of "difference" central to understandings of what it meant to be an American. Yet, by not recognizing difference as its own creation, the American body politic initiated a collective fiction of whiteness that is still operative today. To illustrate the embeddedness of this collective fiction, I now turn to one of its generative moments.

On January 4, 1848, almost four weeks before the signing of the Treaty of Guadalupe Hidalgo, Senator John Calhoun (1782–1850) of South Carolina appeared on the Senate floor to state his disdain for the annexation of Mexican territories to the United States. Calhoun, though an expansionist, vehemently expressed his disdain for the Mexican people in a last-ditch effort to prevent the signing of the treaty:

we have never dreamt of incorporating into our Union any but the Caucasian race—the free white race. To incorporate Mexico, would be the very first instance of the kind of incorporation of the Indian race; for more than half of all Mexicans are Indians, and other is composed chiefly of mixed tribes. I protest against such a union as that! Ours, sir, is the government of a white race. The greatest misfortunes of Spanish America are to be traced to the fatal error of placing these colored races on an equality with the white race. That error destroyed the social arrangement which formed the basis of society. . . .

Sir, it is a remarkable fact, that in the whole history of man, as far as my knowledge extends, there is no instance whatever of any civilized colored races being found equal to the establishment of free popular government, although by far the largest portion of the human family is composed of these races.[9]

Calhoun's "human family" has a clear racial hierarchy and limited familial memory. He omits or forgets the triumph of the Haitian revolution in 1804 as an attempt to establish a "free popular government." He also conveniently forgets the 1821 achievement of independence from Spain by the very "race" he denigrates, a race whose independence was encumbered by continuous aggression and provocation from the United States.[10] Calhoun's primary concern, however, was the question of slavery as related to the Mexican territories that would be annexed. Three of the twenty-three articles in the Treaty of Guadeloupe Hidalgo dealt specifically with Mexicans who would remain in the territories: Article 8 guaranteed U.S. citizenship and all its privileges, Article 9 guaranteed religious freedom, and Article 10 validated all Mexican land grants in the Southwest. Calhoun knew that these three articles could seriously complicate the balance of power between South and North; he feared that the annexed territories would be admitted into the Union as free states, toppling the South's predominantly agrarian and slave-driven economy.

Calhoun's influence was ultimately felt: only Article 8 survived intact when the treaty was ratified by the Senate on March 19. The significance of this fact cannot be overstated. By striking Article 10 completely, the Senate made voting much more difficult for Mexican Americans. Poll-tax and literacy laws meant that a man had to be at least a landowner and in many instances functionally literate to vote. Mexican Americans thus found themselves in the precarious position of having to defend their rights as citizens in territories they had inhabited even before independence from Spain. In the process, they began to seek ways to graft the ethnic specificity of their cultural history onto an emerging sense of Americanness that, paradoxically, became ever more restrictive in measure with its territorial expansion. As U.S. subject-citizens in theory but not in practice, Mexican Americans were forced to renegotiate the possibilities of being American in strategically mediated ways that sought to create a Mexican-specific subject of American history.

This was the situation during the last quarter of the nineteenth century, when Mexican Americans in conquered California were called upon to narrate their histories for wealthy San Francisco book dealer and publisher Hubert Howe Bancroft's massive project to assemble available information on California history. The interviews, or testimonials,[11] were conducted in order to solicit information for his seven-volume *History of California*. Bancroft's main interest in the sixty to one hundred or so Mexican American testimonials was to account for Mexican American participation in California's political and cultural history. Fewer than fifteen of them were from women.[12] Not surprisingly, as Padilla has noted, women's testimonials often appeared as supplementary accounts on the margins of cultural and political history (*My History*, 110–11). By including fewer than a fifteen testimonials, Bancroft also minimized the presence and importance of Mexican American women in his *History of California*. His *History* in fact attempted to narrate the newly consolidated nation with a justification of territorial expansionism that made the Mexican body an interloper in the national archive—the repository of historical memory that became his story of California. The visual and narrative testimony offered by Eulalia Pérez, one of Bancroft's most famous testimonialists, offers an emblematic example of the cultural disjuncture occasioned by the American 1848.

"Passing" as Identity Paradigm: Mass-Mediated Performances of Eulalia Pérez's Body

In 1877, Thomas Savage, one of Bancroft's principal oral historians, interviewed Eulalia Pérez, purported to be 139 years old, to collect information on the development of the mission system in California, the lives of various missionaries, the ecclesiastical and socioeconomic aspects of Christianization, and the daily management and operation of the missions charged with these tasks. Pérez's participation is striking because of her purported age and because her photographic likeness was reproduced so often that it became paradigmatic for Mexicanness. As Padilla has noted, "the anecdotes and arguments about her as a curiosity of old age are more impressive than her narrative" (*My History*, 131). Not surprisingly, her visual testimony was far better known than her textual one. I situate Pérez's figurations—in particular, the photograph that accompanied her testimonial and the engraving based on the photograph that appeared in *Frank Leslie's Illustrated Newspaper*[13]—in order to read the photograph and the reproduced image as a subject of history defined through mass-mediated performances of her body and to analyze how her body was vested with various meanings in the post-Reconstruction American imaginary.

The images of Eulalia Pérez invariably represented the photographic medium as content (the "truth" about her life), a process that aligned her image with her ethnicity. Iconic image and purported textual truth were intimately related forms of signification since they represented the Mexican body for public consumption and provided visual evidence of America's "other" racial question, the Mexican question. The renderings of Pérez's body in relation to her testimonial reveal relationships of the Mexican body to American cultural memory and amnesia, as well as to political orders and communities.

Photography has been associated with memory and loss since its inception. The nineteenth-century emphasis on portrait photography demonstrated the desire to fix an identity in the image, to have the image live after the individual's death. Jane M. Rabb notes that with the 1839 inception of the daguerreotype in France, photography began to be defined as writing with light and could be regarded as a system of notation. Rabb goes on to state that

[i]t is not coincidental that literary realism flourished after the invention of photography, earlier in France than elsewhere. As Paul Valéry observed in retrospect, "From the moment photography appeared, the descriptive genre began to invade Letters. . . . In verse as in prose the decor and exterior aspects of life took an almost excessive place."[14]

An attendant quality of the realism to which Rabb refers is the significance of photography as an ethnographic medium that sought to document the racial, social, and class conditions of the emerging nation.[15] In the United States the development of photography also coincided with the rise of industrialization, westward expansion, massive European and trans-American migration, and consolidation of the country as a geopolitical power. Arising out of and coterminous with these developments, photography facilitated the inclusion of bodies that had been considered unsuitable for elevated cultural representation in traditional painting and portraiture. Pérez's photograph can thus be understood as an ethnographic social text that helped create the category of the "Mexican," in addition to providing evidence of her advanced age and the bygone era she was asked to relate for Bancroft's history.

Discussions about the relationship of Pérez's mass-mediated image to her testimonial have been conspicuously absent. Padilla gives the photograph a full page but no critical discussion (*My History,* 132),[16] a striking omission when we consider that Thomas Savage's introduction to Pérez's testimonial made a point of offering her photographed body as a historical artifact: "The accompanying photograph gives a very correct idea of her as I found her when I took from her lips the notes which appear on the annexed thirty three pages."[17] The documentary importance of the photograph in the national historical imaginary cannot be overlooked. Photographic im-

EULALIA PERZ, 139 YEARS OF AGE.

Figure 1. Photo of Eulalia Pérez. Bancroft Library, University of California, Berkeley. Reproduced by permission.

ages like Pérez's ultimately convey meaning through the framing conditions of their recording on the negative's surface in addition to the historical evidence "taken from her lips" by Savage (see figure 1).

Benedict Anderson has noted in *Imagined Communities: Reflections on the Origin and Spread of Nationalism* (1991) the documentary importance of photography as a form of archival historical evidence:

All profound changes in consciousness, by their very nature, bring with them characteristic amnesias. Out of such oblivions, in specific historical circumstances, spring narratives. . . . The photograph, fine child of the age of mechanical reproduction, is only the most peremptory of a huge modern accumulation of documentary evidence (birth certificates, diaries, report cards, letters, medical records, and the like) which simultaneously records certain apparent continuity and emphasizes its loss from memory. Out of this estrangement comes a conception of personhood, *identity* . . . which, because it can not be "remembered," must be narrated.[18]

I would add that the photograph serves the aggregate function *not* of creating identities narratively, as Anderson explicitly suggests, but of disassociating identities symbolically in the nation's present by positing them as ghosts of the nation's past. That is why the visual referent, the photograph itself, is so powerful a medium: it does not need to be submitted to an analysis of its narrative truth claims because it disengages reason (historical cause and effect) from intuitive sentimentality (the photograph's performance of what has *already* happened in the past, of that for which it serves as "evidence"). This is especially the case in photographs like Pérez's whose function is not only historical but ethnographic as well. It is an effect of what could be understood as "photo-historical death" in that, as art historian Christian Metz has noted, "Even when the person photographed is still living, that moment when she or he *was* has forever vanished. Strictly speaking, the person who has been photographed—not the total person, who is an effect of time—is dead."[19] The visual story told in Pérez's photograph mimics her testimonial's truth-bearing qualities (the photograph is, after all, evidence of disjunctures occasioned by the Spanish to Mexican to American domination of the West *in the past*) and impregnates her body with meaning by creating a mechanically reproduced inscriptural surface.

This story written on Pérez's body can paradoxically be written out of existence in Bancroft's *History* insofar as she is posited as a relic, a memorial if you will, of the past she is called upon to narrate. I would suggest that her photograph "performs" the loss of what she relates by corporally mimicking that loss. Her inclusion in Bancroft's heterotopia is then an instance of erasure through exscription, a metaphorical writing out of history by virtue of what her body performs—the memory of loss and, ultimately, of losing.

How has the absence of scholarly discussion of Pérez's photograph and mass-mediated images affected our understanding regarding the (ab)uses of Pérez as an icon and metonym for Mexican culture? As Betty Bergland has noted,

we have witnessed a resurgence of interest in both ethnicity and autobiography, yet an examination of visual texts in autobiography has been ignored, despite the fact that photographs frequently appear in ethnic narratives. Because of the power of visual images to frame the boundaries of meaning, they serve a critical function for readers in the construction of the ethnic identity, personal and collective, and thus the construction of ethnic memory and meaning.[20]

The inscription under Bancroft's commissioned photograph is telling with regard to Pérez as a repository of Bergland's "ethnic memory and meaning." Like the political erasure of the Mexican body that Bancroft's *History* sought to effect, the inscription attempts to neutralize perhaps her most obvious ethnic marker, her name. Pérez's identity is effectively cleansed of its otherness, culturally cleansed of a nearly unpronounceable interconsonantal vowel in the English language's unaccommodating, sharp phonemic lengths. The acute accent mark that should appear over the first "e" is also omitted.[21] The missing "e," like the vanquished accent mark, points to a silent signic space, an absence too eagerly naturalized into monolingual complacency. The strange name is re-dressed and made familiar. The photograph that records the body's touch of light and the letters that seek to point to a truth about her identity beyond the image both evince a semiotic breakdown, where the signifier not only displaces the signified but attempts to efface its presence. Pérez is caught up in a narrative history where the facts relating to her name, not to mention the facts pertaining to her story, reveal the inadequacies and contradictions of the very truth claims inscribed on her body: Eulalia Perz [*sic*], the centenarian invented in Bancroft's archival history, as opposed to Eulalia Pérez, the subject of history caught in the interstices of cultural disjunctures. Much like the California history she is required to reveal in her testimonial, Pérez is posited as both relic (her decrepit body) and repository (her memories) of a social landscape that no longer exists, Eulalia as elegy.

The statement following her name, "139 years of age," situates her sideshow persona for public display. With her age stated as fact, the photograph likely indicated the passage of an era for those who viewed it: the symbolic end, or "photographic death," if you will, of the Mexican era in the Southwest—an era that must now be subsumed into American history.

The topos of Eulalia as elegy is further reinforced by her truncated and apathetic presence in the photograph. She is visible only from the waist up, in typical portrait fashion. In typical nineteenth-century photographic portraiture, the body in the frame was situated so as to engage the viewer outside the frame, with the sitter usually facing and looking at the viewer. But

Pérez's eyelids sag over her nearly unseen eyes, suggesting lethargy or resigned submission. She is looking down, eyes glancing at the viewer's left, as if in deference or indifference to the camera before her. There is no class equality between the viewer and the sitter; the photograph belongs not to her but to Bancroft's archive. Within the emerging discourse of visual ethnography, she attains the status of "specimen," by being represented in front of a barren wall that displaces her from the life she is to relate in her testimonial. The image attempts to mimic the signifiers under her name, "139 years of age" (BANC C-D 139, Frontispiece). Old and decrepit at century's end, the Eulalia Perz [sic] before the camera reinforces the socially scripted narratives of Manifest Destiny by metonymically representing the conquered, defeated body of the Other.[22]

Roland Barthes's beautiful and idiosyncratic semiological approach to photography in *Camera Lucida: Reflections on Photography* (1981) can illuminate our understanding of Pérez's photograph by distinguishing its historical value from its timeless ability to perform emotively for the viewer.[23] As Barthes's final work, *Camera Lucida* foregrounds the theoretical anxieties born of poststructuralism's "death of the subject" by positing the body as the subject's proxy. Barthes's brilliant theoretical recourse to "matter"—the photograph itself and the photographic subject *matter*—serves as an antidote to the poststructuralist exscription of personal experience from the subject *in theory* by realigning the personal to the sociocultural *in practice*.

For Barthes, the culturally codifiable moment of visual interest was what he termed the photograph's *studium*, its relationship to the environment it captures and the attendant meaning(s) behind that relationship: "It is by *studium* that I am interested in so many photographs, whether I receive them as political testimony or enjoy them as good historical scenes: for it is culturally (this connotation is present in *studium*) that I participate in the figures, the faces, the gestures, the settings, the actions" (26). Barthes distinguishes a photograph's *studium*, its possibility for serving as political testimony, from its *punctum*, its ability to "puncture," to act on us in subjective but discernible ways. *Punctum* gives the photograph special individual meaning for the viewer in addition to the formal connotations inherent in the image's *studium*. The *punctum* is the "accident which pricks" (27). The relationship between the two is part of photography's allure, especially that of photographs with explicitly "political testimony"—with historically contingent meanings. The Barthian distinction is appropriate in Pérez's case, for her image serves a culturally sanctioned function that is at once historical (*studium*) and subjective (*punctum*).

A Barthian reading begs us to ask why she might not be a willing sitter, why her eyes do not face the viewer. Her image, like her testimonial, tells a poignant story written on her body. Wrinkles are visible on all the exposed areas. She appears to be sad, pensive, tired. Her flesh sags, her body is hunched, and under her sunken breasts her right hand rests above her left hand in apparent resignation. She is not the author of her image, and she knows it, but her image poignantly registers the framing conditions of her life by raising the dead she's called upon to re-member. Paradoxically, because the "photo-historical death" arrests Pérez in time, she manages to be rescued from Savage's visit forever. As bell hooks has noted, "Photography has been, and is, central to that aspect of decolonization that calls us back to the past and offers a way to reclaim and renew life-affirming bonds. Using these images, we connect ourselves to a recuperative, redemptive memory that enables us to construct radical identities, images of ourselves that transcend the limits of the colonizing eye."[24] The photograph permits Pérez to travel and perform for us by creating a wrinkle in time that allows her to escape the ordinary fate of her caste, gender, and ethnicity, the fate of "the colonizing eye." The framing conditions of her image, preserved in the photograph, emerge and ultimately permit her to speak to us from the dead about the nature of being Mexican American at her century's end: too far from us to touch, but close enough to feel her presence, *studium* and *punctum,* the political and the personal, Perz reframed as Pérez.

Eulalia Pérez's words in *An Old Woman and Her Recollections* also seek to establish an identity where others would erase it. She begins by stating, "I, Eulalia Pérez, was born in the Presidio of Loreto in Lower California" (BANC C-D 139 Translation, 1). Her recourse to name and geography as progenitors of identity creates a strategic locus of enunciation that positions her body on an American map that looked quite different at the time of her birth. That time of coming into being, however, is as indefinite in her memory as it is on Thomas Savage's page: "I do not remember the date of my birth" (ibid., 1). She does, however, remember to mention her surname at birth, Pérez. This is significant, since she opts for her maiden name instead of that of either of her deceased husbands, Miguel Antonio Guillén and Juan Mariné. In his analysis of Pérez's suppression of surnames, Padilla notes that "Pérez's reappropriation of her given name constitutes an act of self-volition, the willing into textual permanence of her own personality and experience" (*My History,* 137).

Padilla glosses over the fact that her recourse to origins is essential to her identity construction in Bancroft's history, not because it is a self-constituting autobiographical strategy but because her father, Diego Pérez, and her mother, Antonia Rosalia Cota, were both, according to Eulalia, "pure Caucasians" (BANC C-D 139 Translation, 1). Though Pérez's trope of racial "purity" is elided in Padilla's exaltation of her birth name, it must be noted that she was not constructed as "white," despite her efforts, in the racial pigmentocracy of post-Reconstruction America. In an article in *Frank Leslie's Illustrated Newspaper* (January 12, 1878), "Eulalia Perrez, the Oldest Woman in the World," Mrs. Frank Leslie[25] writes that Eulalia Pérez's "skin was almost as dark as a mulatto's."[26] The article begins by noting that

[a]mong the remarkable objects to which the members of the Frank Leslie Transcontinental Excursion had their attention attracted, while in California last Spring, not the least interesting was the venerable lady whose name heads this article, and whose portrait is likewise given on this page. . . . While in San Francisco we had been shown the photograph of Eulalia Perrez [*sic*], of Los Angeles—the oldest woman in the world—and now finding ourselves in the close vicinity, we resolved on paying her a visit. (BANC MSS C-D 139, Frontispiece B)

Objectified and commodified for public consumption, Pérez's celebrity was likely facilitated by the photograph that sought to prove her age and, unbeknownst to her, her ethnically marked body. The daughter of purportedly "pure Caucasians" was bound by the mass-mediated racialized constructions that circulated about her racial identity. The "remarkable object" of the Frank Leslie Transcontinental Excursion becomes the site of contested meanings that compete for legitimacy.

Mrs. Leslie's article ethnically marks Pérez's environment. She mentions how she and the members of her party "were met by a very pretty and very typical Spanish girl, wearing a high comb and speaking English with a very charming accent" (BANC MSS C-D 139, Frontispiece B). As a linguistic marker for ethnic difference, the "very charming accent" of Pérez's great-granddaughter is part and parcel of the ethnic drag, the "high comb" (presumably an Andalusian high comb that supports a mantilla) that mixes Andalusian-Spanish ethnic dress with nineteenth-century Mexican and Mexican American culture. Mrs. Leslie's characterization of Pérez's great-granddaughter as a "typical Spanish girl" further complicates and erases the specificity of Mexicanness in the post-Reconstruction imaginary.

Ironically, the article creates a social symbolic representation of the very "Spanishness" (read: "whiteness") Pérez sought to connote in her testimonial, but, once taken out of its purely European context and re-created in

Figure 2. From *Frank Leslie's Illustrated Newspaper,* January 12, 1878 (BANC MSS C-D 139, Frontispiece B). The caption under her portrait reads, "Eulalia Perrez [*sic*], of Los Angeles, Cal., the oldest woman in the world."

Leslie's version of California, it is intermeshed with the coloring Pérez sought to whitewash, that "skin [that] was almost as dark as a mulatto's." The article's conflation of "Spanish" with "Mexican" likely helped graft Eulalia's Mexican body onto the "mulatto body," facilitating the polarization of the racialized identity scripts relating to the unresolved "white" and "black" issues inherent to post–Civil War American society. The "portrait" of Pérez in *Frank Leslie's Illustrated Newspaper* further reinforces the "colored" nature of the racialized Mexican body that exceedingly came to be associated with the black body (see figure 2).

The iconic and the narrative signifiers in Mrs. Leslie's article infuse

Pérez's body with meaning. Like Bancroft's inscription, *Leslie's Illustrated* also distorts her name, this time into "Perrez." The "portrait" (an engraving made from the photograph) further distorts the image by creating a smile where none existed in the photograph. Similar to the Brothers Grimm engravings of witches that accompanied their tales, Eulalia here is re-created as a supernatural, witchlike figure with eyes "shrunken to such a degree as to give the impression of having disappeared altogether, leaving only two narrow loopholes, red as fire, and uncanny to look upon" (BANC MSS C-D 139, Frontispiece B). This living-dead description of Pérez's face creates an otherworldly quality that places her as an interloper in the land of the living. Her face, her eyes, are cloaked and framed in sunken crevices and shadows. Her nose protrudes in a distorted aquiline curve that animalizes her form. Her hands are suggestively elongated, with fingernails that resemble claws. Once again, Pérez's body becomes an inscriptural surface where facts are secondary to the use value of her image.

Religion also plays an important role in the inordinately visual description of Pérez in the article: "She wore a brown rosary about her neck, and, on my referring to her being a good Catholic, said that by the crucifix she had learned the lesson of how to live and, she hoped, how to die" (ibid.). But is she not already posited as death incarnate? What lessons has she learned about living and dying that the article has not already illustrated? And in her portrayal as a practicing Catholic, what are we to make of the description in the article and engraving? Is this what "a good Catholic" looks like? As an attendant quality of *Leslie's Illustrated*'s image production through narrativity and iconicity, all that points to Pérez in the article illustrates her literal and figurative distance from the English-language public who read about her and saw her in the paper: race, religion, language, otherworldliness. The article is a diluted and truncated version of Eulalia Pérez's life that "borrows" from the testimonial she offered to Thomas Savage, a borrowing that produces effects Pérez would not have wanted.

Mrs. Leslie takes Thomas Savage's role as Pérez's interviewer for Bancroft's *History*, though she only mentions the most topical information relating to Pérez's story: age, names of family members, and how often she had married. The details, it would appear, are ancillary to the image. How Pérez was received and how she might have wanted to be received deserve further scrutiny, and I now turn to the account of her life that she offered to Savage.

According to Padilla's reading of *An Old Woman and Her Recollections*,

Pérez's account of mission life at San Gabriel is a textual tease of delays and hesitations that promises to deliver a history of the missions but revels in personal disclosures that differ from the expected accounts of a woman's place in the mission system (*My History*, 130–39). He concludes that, in both effect and affect, Pérez forestalls Savage's attempt to chart the lives of missionary men by a performance of polite intransigence that refuses to take Savage's phallic pen seriously, thereby keeping the historical weight of Bancroft's pendulous *History* at bay. The evidence provided in her account, however, does not support such a celebratory reading. Since Padilla is one of the few critics to date to study Pérez's account of mission life at length, it will be necessary to review his important contribution in order to arrive at a more nuanced understanding of her identity negotiations.

Padilla's reading of what he calls Pérez's "autobiography" does not suffi-ciently take into account the violence enacted against the Mexican and Amerindian body in the mission system, nor does he account for Pérez's economic need to assimilate into that system. Sánchez notes that "[a]s in a traditional colonial model, the missionaries created an elite within the mis-sion to police their own and to serve as intermediaries for control of the la-bor force" (*Telling Identities*, 85). Pérez, an exemplar of this "elite," attempts to pass as a "pure Caucasian" to position herself in the power structure she had learned to manipulate in her favor, at the expense of erasing her ethnic markers to the best of her ability. The pressure to assimilate was acute, since, as Sánchez notes, the mission systems were "clearly the economic centers in California" (91).

Pérez's account is nonetheless impressive, as Padilla notes, for it is one of the few testimonials that give an insider's day-to-day perspective on the mission system's prescribed gender roles, housing, division of labor, and re-ligious regimentation. Pérez's allegiance to Father José Sánchez, who pre-sided over the San Gabriel mission, wealthiest in a chain of twenty-one missions, and to the system itself is clear from the beginning of her ac-count, where she states that after her first husband's death, "Father José Sánchez lodged me and my family" (BANC MSS C-D 139 Translation, 4). She notes how Father Sánchez and Father Zalvidea "looked for some way to give me work" (5). Father Sánchez eventually procures work for Pérez after a cooking contest with two other women:

> When the meal was concluded, Father Sánchez asked for opinions about it, beginning with . . . Don Ignacio Tenorio. This gentleman pon-dered for awhile, saying that for many years he hadn't eaten the way

he'd eaten that day—that he doubted that they ate any better at the King's table. . . . The Fathers were very satisfied; this made them think more highly of me. . . . After this, the Fathers conferred among them- selves and agreed to hand over the mission keys to me. (7–8)[27]

Her position secured in the mission's distribution of labor among Amer- indians, Pérez assumes a managerial role, a fact she delights in telling Sav- age, making the role manifest to Bancroft's agent for possible inclusion in California history. It appears from what can be surmised that her moti- vation for inclusion in Bancroft's heterotopia is principally to fashion a position in the public imaginary about her importance to the mission system. After all, the system provided economic security and a degree of independence she would not otherwise have had as a widow with six children.

The extent of Father Sánchez's control over Pérez's life is clear. He con- vinces her to marry her second husband, Juan Mariné, "a widower with family who had served in the artillery" (BANC MSS C-D 139 Translation, 10). Pérez relates to Savage how she "didn't want to get married, but the Father told me that Mariné was a very good man—as, in fact, he turned out to be—besides, he had some money, although he never turned his cash-box over to me. I gave in to the Father's wishes because I didn't have the heart to deny him anything when he has been father and mother to me and to all my family" (ibid.). Her decision to marry Mariné is posited as mediated by her desire to please Father Sánchez and the possibility of financial gain, since Mariné "had some money." Mariné, of course, does not share the proverbial "cash-box" with his wife. In fact, much to her chagrin, he causes her to lose property Father Sánchez had given to her as a gift:

Father Sánchez, besides having supported me and all my daughters un- til they were married, gave me two ranches—or rather, land for a ranch and an orchard. . . . When he delivered the lands to me I was already married to Juan Mariné. Afterwards he [Juan Mariné] only turned over half of the land to me and kept the other half. (19–20)

We can only conjecture about his "family" and how they fared thanks to Pérez's industry in the mission economy.

Another important aspect of Pérez's account concerns the demise and secularization of the mission system. This profound transition began in

1825 when José María Echeandía was appointed governor of Alta California by the recently independent Mexican government. Rosaura Sánchez has noted how in Alta California "The breakdown of the old order was set in motion, thanks in no small measure to Echeandía and his introduction of discourses of liberalism, secularism, and constitutionalism" (*Telling Identities*, 97).

She notes how "Liberals saw California as a place to put into effect their liberal policies and begin the process of secularization and appropriation of mission lands, reforms that liberals envisaged already for Mexico, where the church was the largest landowner and the wealthiest corporation" (99). At the San Gabriel mission, these policies amounted to the overthrow of the mission's religio-political order. Pérez recounts how in 1833 the system began to collapse when Captain Barroso, a Mexican army officer,

> came and excited all the Indians to rebel, telling them that they were no longer neophytes but free men, Indians arrived from San Luis, San Juan, and the rest of the missions. They pushed their way into the College, carrying their arms. . . . Outside the mission, guards and patrols made up of the Indians themselves were stationed. They had been taught to shout "Sentinel—on guard!" and "On guard he is!" but they said "Sentinel—open! Open he is!" (BANC MSS C-D 139 Translation, 10)[28]

After Barroso's arrival, the Amerindians—initially described by Pérez as treated "very well" by both Fathers Sánchez and Zalvidea—ambush Father Sánchez's coach as he is about to leave for Los Angeles:

> in front of the guard some Indians surged forward and cut the traces of his coach. The Father jumped out of the coach, and then the Indians, pushing him rudely, forced him toward his room. He was sad and filled with sorrow for what the Indians had done. . . . He became ill and never again was his previous self. Blood flowed from his ears and his head never stopped paining[29] him till he died. He lived perhaps a little more than a month after the affair with the Indians, dying in the month of January, I think it was, of 1833. (Ibid., 11)

Immediately following Pérez's account of the Amerindian insurrection, nature mirrors the collapse of the San Gabriel mission: "The river rose very high and for more than two weeks no one could get from one side to the other" (11). Father Sánchez, as principal overseer, is confined to his room much as the Amerindians were subjected to incarceration and punishment under the mission's regime of control and corporeal punishment. After describing the flood, she moves further into the mission's past to a time when the system worked for the administrators and overseers of the mission. Ironically, she begins by describing the strategies of control and domination exerted on the Amerindian body. As I previously mentioned, she details these practices *after* she has offered Savage "the end" of her story, that is, after relating the death of Father Sánchez immediately following Captain Barroso's arrival:

> The punishments that were meted out were the stocks and confinement. When the misdemeanor was serious, the delinquent was taken to the guard, where they tied him to a pipe/tube or a post and gave him 25 or more lashes, depending on his crime. Sometimes they put them in the head-stocks; other times they passed a musket from one leg to the other and fastened it there, and also they tied their hands. That punishment, called "The Law of the Bayona," was very painful. (14)

After her detailed description of the mission's regime of discipline and punishment, Pérez feels compelled to excuse Fathers Sánchez and Zalvidea's role by stating that they nevertheless "were always very considerate with the Indians" (14). Pérez is sympathetic to the Christian discourse of paternalism and protection that legitimates the control and punishment exerted over the subjugated Amerindian body at the height of the mission monopoly, the control and subjection she vividly describes as occasioned by "misdemeanors." The public nature of these spectacles also functioned to discipline and deter dissenters.

As Sánchez has noted, "Discipline, order, the lash, stocks and imprisonment are all coercive strategies used to contain the resistance of the Indians, as are a rigid work schedule and ideological manipulation, but as in all colonial structures, one additional strategy is employed to enslave the Indians: the Indians themselves" (*Telling Identities*, 84). Pérez's collusion with the mission system and its protocols of domination are such that she cannot understand why the Amerindians could confine and, in effect, discipline Father Sánchez. Not surprisingly, his death is posited as the direct result of the insurrection occasioned by Captain Barroso's arrival, since, "A short while before Father Sánchez died, he seemed robust and in good health, in spite of his advanced age" (BANC MSS C-D 139 Translation, 10).

Pérez's identification with the mission system and her loyalty for Father Sánchez are intimately intermeshed in her account of San Gabriel mission life, but they are also intimately related to her conscious self-fashioning strategies.

Savage seldom includes ancillary material in his interviews, but he does include a stock poem Pérez dedicates to him at the close of their interview. He relates how she sang the following verses "while holding my hands in hers":

> *Little Thomas, who can*
> *Explain my sorrow to you,*
> *So that, charitably,*
> *You will make me well with your love.*
> *This is my intention:*
> *never offend you,*
> *Always to have for you*
> *An unreasonable passion.*
> *With great contentment*
> *And in sweet peacefulness*
> *To surrender my soul*
> *And my heart to you. (Ibid., 23)*

In the song, Pérez's "intention" to "never offend" Bancroft's agent, Savage, structures an exchange between his testimonial prerogative and the intended effect of her own self-fashioning that he has "taken from her lips" and transcribed. Her desire to be preserved by *surrendering* ("To surrender my soul / And my heart to you") and her need to fashion an identity that marks her as she wished her parents to be marked, as "pure" Caucasian, must begin to inform our own understanding of nineteenth-century identity politics and the limited possibilities for accessing culturally legitimated ways of being. Read this way, the various performances of Eulalia's body and their attendant truth claims shed light on the "assimilationist" American identity myth by demonstrating the psychic violence inherent to its "surrender." Like Savage's photograph of Pérez, the areas of darkness and light compete in a violent refraction of the social mirror that coerces the body's submission into racialized identity scripts and forms of surrender. Such mutable corporeal surrender, for such limited imaginings? Whitewashed, darkened, and endlessly recycled, Pérez's body becomes a palimpsest of competing truth claims.

Catarina Ávila de Ríos's *Memoirs*: Of "Mangled Bodies," Memory, Violence, and Gold in Alta California, 1849

[T]he large pool of blood was evidence. . . . After committing these murders, they gathered together all the mangled bodies and piled them up in the adjoining room.

—Catarina Ávila de Ríos, *Memoirs*

Catarina Ávila de Ríos was not so willing a participant in Bancroft's project. Her account of the massacre at the mission of San Miguel in 1849 makes manifest the cultural and ethnic antagonisms inherent in the interplay between memory and Bancroft's history of forgetfulness. Ávila de Ríos's testimonial is particularly challenging because of the scope of what she addresses, as well as what she leaves out. It is unusual on at least two counts. First, what she relates is in no way related to the archival information Bancroft wanted. Bancroft had entrusted Savage with the task of retrieving documents pertaining to Ávila de Ríos's husband, Sergeant Petronilo Ríos, during his service as chief commandant in the California artillery. Ávila de Ríos was asked by Savage and Don Vicente P. Gómez, his assistant, to procure these documents for inclusion in Bancroft's *History*. In his introductory remarks to her testimonial, Savage relates her refusal: they "endeavored to get her husband's papers, but she assured me and Don Vicente P. Gómez that she had none" (BANC MSS C-D 35 Translation, i [unnumbered title page]).[30] Second, what she had to say about a series of murders in December 1849 in the San Miguel mission, a gruesome crime completely unrelated to Bancroft's expressed interest in acquiring her husband's papers, was a story too compelling for Gómez not to transcribe. She related how a violent clash of cultures, occasioned by greed on the heels of the California Gold Rush, had killed nine people in the mission of San Miguel nearly thirty years earlier.

Ávila de Ríos relates how mission ownership had passed from the Church and its representatives to secular landowners like her husband after Pío Pico was named the first Mexican governor of California. Before independence, Spanish troops had protected the Church's interest, whereas the secular landowners had little or no protection from the U.S. judicial establishment. Ávila de Ríos's testimonial documents the violence and civil disorder occasioned by the arrival of Anglo prospectors:[31]

In December of the year 1849 there resided at the old Mission of San Miguel an Englishman named Mr. William Reed, the husband of María

Antonia Vallejo, a native of Monterey. This couple had living with them a brother of the wife named José Ramón, a child of their own two or three years of age, and with the wife awaiting the birth of another, for which reason there was also present with them a midwife named Josefa Olivera and with her a daughter about fifteen or sixteen years old, a grandchild four years of age, an Indian 60 or 70 years old and with the latter a grandson aged four or five. This household, as had been said, lived quietly at the mission above referred to, extending gracious hospitality to all who passed through the place, which was very frequently, *as a large number of persons were coming to the North attracted by the recent discovery of gold,* it being necessary then, as now, to pass over this route. This mission had been granted to C. Petronilo Ríos and the said Reed as owners by the last Mexican governor, C. Pío Pico. (BANC MSS C-D 35 Translation, 1; my emphasis)

Ávila de Ríos's knowledge of what she relates comes from her association with the house at the mission, since her husband, Petronilo Ríos, was co-owner with William Reed. Her recollections also point to miscegenation during the period of secularization. María Antonia Vallejo, after all, is married to William Reed and is expecting their second child. Their lives and the lives of those in the house, however, will meet a horrific end. Ávila de Ríos tells Gómez how "there arrived three or four Irishmen, accompanied by an Indian."[32] The prospectors were seeking lodging and remained at the house on the mission as guests for approximately five days. But as they were finally about to leave,

they wished to change certain gold coins which they had with them. Mr. Reed then asked his brother-in-law to bring him a canvas sack, in which he kept all his gold coin [*sic*], acquired by his own personal labor. He changed the coins for them, as they wished, and they set out, it being fairly late. They only went as far as the vicinity of the rancho de San Marcos, however, about half a league away, from which point, the night having closed in, they returned to the mission residence where they had supper in a room with a fireplace. They stirred up the fire, remaining there in conversation with Mr. Reed, the other members of the household having retired to other rooms of the house very late in the evening, when the fire had burned down, one of them went out into the corridor to split some firewood, bringing back with him the ax he had used along with the firewood. The women had not yet gone to bed, since they were found murdered dressed as they had been during the day. It is not known as to the exact time that Mr. Reed was dealt the first blow in the head, but he had his hat on, since it was cut through at the back and the large pool of blood was evidence that he had been killed there. They went to the rooms where the women were and there began to kill them wherever they were found, as evidenced by the traces of blood on the floor and the walls, where they had left hand prints. They also murdered the two children with the ax as they slept, one being the son and the other the brother of Señora Doña María Antonia, for the pillows were cut and drenched with blood.

After committing these murders, they gathered together all the mangled bodies and piled them up in the adjoining room. From there they went out to the kitchen to kill the negro who acted as cook. . . . The body of this negro was left there where it fell. They then went to the room where an Indian, who was employed as a shepherd, was asleep with his little Indian grandson and left the two bodies there. (BANC MSS C-D 35 Translation, 2–3)

Ávila de Ríos's memory of the massacre at the San Miguel mission addresses the wanton violence occasioned by historical disjunctures and the necessity of memorializing these events for Bancroft's archival history of California life. Though she claims not to possess any of her husband's papers, at least not for inclusion in Bancroft's heterotopia, she does possess endangered knowledge about California living in the mid-1800s and the violence brought on by westward expansion, replete with dates, names, and dead bodies that she will not forget.

The scene of the massacre is carefully reconstructed in Ávila de Ríos's narrative as she spares no details about the evidence of the murdered women's terror and suffering as they left red traces of their horror on the floor and wrote their pain on the walls of the house, where they left their bloodied fingerprints. A less obvious but equally suggestive comment in the testimonial reveals that Mr. Reed was also a "prospector," as he had "a canvas sack, in which he kept all his gold coins, acquired by his own personal labor." Mr. Reed's entrepreneurial wealth through the legal acquisition of gold is contrasted to the banditry of the "three or four Irishmen" and their accomplice, who do not respect Mr. Reed and, by extension, Sergeant Ríos's legal authority in the San Miguel mission.

Ávila de Ríos's willingness to offer her memories of this cultural clash might have been motivated not only by the violence wrought on the Mexican body that she wanted to memorialize but also by the violence enacted by laws that diminished Mexican and Mexican American access to some of the most basic rights of citizenship. The Compromise of 1850 serves as a case in point.

In California, after the signing of the Treaty of Guadalupe Hidalgo, "A convention at Monterey drew up a proposed state constitution" that included "the nation's first provision for married women to own property—both because that was the Mexican tradition and because, it was argued, it might attract prosperous prospective wives to California."[33] With the killing of the Reed family, it would only be logical to assume that Sergeant de Ríos would be the sole proprietor of the house he co-owned with Reed in the San Miguel mission. This would, in theory, make it possible for Ávila de Ríos to become "a prosperous prospective wife," the proprietor of the house after her husband's death with the attendant wealth occasioned by the mission's importance as an access route to the gold fields. However, by 1850, "American miners pressured the California legislature into enacting a monthly tax of twenty dollars on all miners who were not United States citizens, far more than most could possibly pay."[34] So it is likely that Ávila de Ríos's reticence to help Bancroft is also related to her frustrated attempts to profit from the gold traffic through San Miguel and to the California legislature's inability to protect the old Californios[35] from the throes of avarice, violence, and the frontier mayhem of the Gold Rush. As she states at the beginning, "This household, as had been said, lived quietly at the mission above referred to, extending gracious hospitality to all who passed through the place, which was very frequently, as a large number of persons were coming to the North attracted by the recent discovery of gold, it being necessary then, as now, to pass over this route" (BANC MSS C-D 35 Translation, 1).

The mission's strategic position in relation to the gold fields makes her display of violence and dispossession all the more poignant. Even the narrative close of her testimony is marked with a curious type of poetic justice. Both literal and figural oppressors receive what they deserve. A sympathetic judge in Santa Barbara, Don Caesar Latallaide, writes to her husband, Petronilo, asking "whether he wished the murderers [to be] brought for hanging to the place where the killings had occurred," but Señor Ríos replies that "the punishment should take place there (at Santa Barbara) as it did" (ibid., 4–5).

Bancroft and his assistants are also slighted by a polite but firm refusal to hand over her husband's memories for inclusion in his archive. After all, not only did she say she did not possess any of Sergeant Petronilo's papers;

she did not offer any of her husband's "stories" either. I believe that her reticence to help in writing Bancroft's history is directly related not only to her distrust for Bancroft's version of California but also to her need to have others remember how that history must be a witness to the violence occasioned by the Gold Rush. Ávila de Ríos appears to distrust Bancroft's historians (Savage and Gómez) because, to paraphrase Benjamin, even the dead will not be safe from the enemy unless the practitioner of history, against the enemy, "writes" the dead into the nation's memorial archives.

Writing about the Other's recourse to memory after colonial subjugation and oppression in Latin America, Michel de Certeau noted that, "[d]ominated but not vanquished, they keep alive the memory of what Europeans have 'forgotten'—a continuous series of uprisings and awakenings which have left hardly a trace in the occupiers' historiographical literature. This history of resistance punctuated by cruel repression is *marked on the Indian's body* as much as it is recorded in transmitted accounts—or more so. . . . In this sense, 'the body is memory.' "[36] If, as for de Certeau, violence is a mode of writing that memorializes on the text of the body the oppressor's inscriptions, memory for Ávila de Ríos is the inadequate but necessary antidote to physical, epistemic, and cultural violence. Ávila de Ríos's unwillingness to offer the information Bancroft wanted for his project registers one of the few moments in the extant documentary sources that we possess when the conquered Californios step back and refuse—through polite intransigence—to tell the colonizer how they, the subaltern, were colonized. This counterhistorical move is rhetorically suggestive to the degree that it forestalls historical closure by disrupting the linear imperatives of progress Bancroft ultimately wants to read in his history of western migration, Manifest Destiny, and its discursive containment in the country's historical archive of memory.

María Amparo Ruiz de Burton's novel *The Squatter and the Don* is also about violence, broadly understood as economic and class violence narratively resolved through the emplotments of romance. It confronts American indifference to the Mexican question with regard to the Mexicans who remained in the newly consolidated United States after the American 1848. It also confronts—in often unrecognized and collusive ways—the construction of American citizenship for these "Mexicans" by addressing their legal status as articulated in the treaty's original three relevant articles. Like Bancroft, Ruiz de Burton too was interested in the Mexican period in a California history she herself had witnessed and narratively historicized in *The Squatter and the Don*. In fact, her interests in the historical rendering of the

Mexican question made her a primary Californio supporter of Bancroft's project. As José Aranda notes, Ruiz de Burton was called upon by Bancroft himself to participate in his project: "Ruiz de Burton was excited about the project and saw it as an opportunity to narrativize their histories and presence in the country."[37] She even solicited contributions from the Californio elite on Bancroft's behalf but ultimately lamented their lack of participation in his heterotopia. It is her investment in Bancroft's historical imperative to document and represent the Californios and, more broadly, Mexican Americans that interests me here for what it could tell us about the importance of becoming historical for Ruiz de Burton and the class interests served by such an investment in *The Squatter and the Don*.

The Catholic Don, the Protestant Squatter, and the Romancing of Whiteness

The Squatter and the Don posits "romantic [heterosexual] love" as the ideal resolution to the historical conflict and economic violence enacted by the United States on a specific group of Californios. Unlike the testimonials gathered from a heterogeneous group, *The Squatter and the Don* focuses on the landed California aristocracy, specifically the Alamar clan, a family of Californios whose wealth was imperiled by Eastern squatters who during the last years of Reconstruction were taking the land that legally belonged to them. The Don in the title is Mariano Alamar, a patrician rancher whose wealth had been encroached upon by an Eastern squatter, William Darrell. The Darrells, well-to-do Easterners, find themselves caught in a moral dilemma involving the legitimacy of Mexican-Spanish land grants and the right to stake claims to those grants that may or may not be binding in the Reconstruction judicial system. Mrs. Darrell, nobly characterized by Ruiz de Burton, implores her son Clarence to purchase the land directly from Don Mariano and thus circumvent the moral conundrum. Clarence agrees to his mother's wishes and unwittingly falls in love with Mercedes Alamar, Don Mariano's daughter. William Darrell, however, finds out about the land purchase and cancels the wedding, much to the consternation of the families and the lovers. Without the Darrells' wealth, the Alamars are forced to confront the fact that their own wealth is succumbing to industrialization, westward expansion, modernization, and a market monopoly that cannot accommodate their ties to a *ranchero* economy. They watch as entrepreneurs such as Charles Crocker, Mark Hopkins, Collis P. Huntington, and Leland Stanford promote underdevelopment in Southern California by blocking a Southern transcontinental railroad. The families, however, are eventually reunited through the marriage of Clarence and Mercedes, thus preventing the Alamars' decline from landed aristocracy to working-class mestizo status in the class- and pigmentocracy-based Reconstruction imaginary. More significantly, Ruiz de Burton's recourse to narrative closure, her "happy ending" if you will, sought to provide an ethno-historical resolution to the rapid proletarianization of California's *criollo* elites, a naively optimistic assimilationist fiction that ultimately did not mirror the social reality it sought to document. Yet some of the most important critical analysis of *The Squatter and the Don,* and the period from which it emerged, has obviated Ruiz de Burton's recourse to racial accommodation. It is to this critical impasse that I now turn.

In José David Saldívar's classic study *Border Matters: Remapping American Cultural Studies* (1997), he provocatively notes how in a 1932 *Los Angeles Times Sunday Magazine* article, Winifred Davidson provided a titillating title for María Amparo Ruiz's own love and eventual marriage to Henry S. Burton: "Enemy Lovers."[38] Burton traveled west after being an artillery instructor at West Point at the onset of the Mexican-American War. He met María Amparo after being transferred to La Paz, capital of Baja California, where he set eyes on "the prettiest young lady on the peninsula."[39] When the United States and Mexican forces squared off in La Paz, Burton offered María Amparo and her mother, Doña Isabel, passage on the USS *Lexington* to Monterey. After several years, the "enemy lovers" finally married. Ruiz de Burton's life, however, changed dramatically in 1869, when her husband died of malaria contracted while serving as brigadier-general in the Union Army (*The Squatter and the Don,* 10–11). The most famous of the enemy lovers, it would seem, was Ruiz de Burton, whose literary career began after her husband's death, when she was left a widow at thirty-seven.[40]

Ruiz de Burton published a comedy, *Don Quijote de la Mancha: A Comedy in Five Acts, Taken from Cervantes' Novel of That Name* (1876),[41] under the name Mrs. H. S. Burton, and the anonymously published novel *Who Would Have Thought It?* (1872). *The Squatter and the Don* was published under the pseudonym C. Loyal. In their introduction to the novel, Rosaura Sánchez and Beatrice Pita note that "[t]he 'C' stood for *Ciudadano* or 'Citizen,' and Loyal for *Leal,* i.e., *Ciudadano Leal,* a 'Loyal Citizen,' a common letter-closing practice used in official government correspondence in Mexico during the nineteenth century" (11). Referring to the suggestive play of names, Saldívar asks, "Does she perform in a ritual of consensus how it feels to be a loyal citizen by constructing Alta California as a domestic land and a place where the 'actual' and the 'imaginary' meet?" (*Border Matters,* 170).

Saldívar is, of course, referring to her bicultural biography when he mentions the "actual" events the novel critiques and the "imaginary" characters that populate the novel and imbue post-Reconstruction culture with meaning for dispossessed "actual" Californios like the Alamars. For Saldívar, the novelized romance is intermeshed with Ruiz de Burton's biography, which leads him to conclude that "Ruiz de Burton functions as a subaltern mediator who is simultaneously an insurgent critic of monopoly capitalism and a radical critic of Anglocentric historiography" (ibid., 170). For Saldívar, *The Squatter and the Don* serves as an allegory of nation by presumably allowing Latinos to identify with Clarence and Mercedes as they

overcome the cultural, political and ethno-racial roadblocks placed in front of them. Thus, after Mercedes and Clarence agree to marry on September 16 (the date Miguel Hidalgo [*sic*] initiated Mexico's liberation from Spanish imperialism in 1821), the battles between Darrell and Mariano over *honor* and shame create for the young lovers a socially symbolic and transcendent purpose. These obstacles, moreover, heighten the lovers' desire for a new national symbolic, which in Ruiz de Burton's words is "capable of emancipat[ing] the white slaves of California." (175)[42]

Yet Ruiz de Burton is neither an organic intellectual nor the testimonial voice of a subaltern interlocutor for one of Bancroft's oral historians. As an elite representative of her privileged class, like the Alamars in her novel, she is important degrees apart from the role Saldívar suggests. She is directing her narrative, after all, in English to an English-speaking and presumably literate public that might more easily identify with Mariano Alamar than, say, with Eulalia Pérez. Mercedes herself, like her father, represents an elite class of Californios who could meet the protocols of "passing" with greater ease than many of the testimonialists in Bancroft's heterotopia. Saldívar's assertion that Ruiz de Burton is "an insurgent critic of monopoly capitalism and a radical critic of Anglocentric historiography" is also problematic. The "C." in C. Loyal is, after all, a genderless author whose authority is partially constructed by virtue of denying (1) that she is a woman and (2) that either the implied author or the narrator is ethnically marked.[43] With this said, I now turn to the elision of race in *The Squatter and the Don.*

Ruiz de Burton's description of Don Alamar puts him on the white side of the national divide, as one might see in the "sad gaze of his mild and beautiful blue eyes" (*The Squatter and the Don,* 64). Once his "color" is established, it is not coincidental that we are made privy to his views on the

Treaty of Guadalupe Hidalgo. His sentimental reverie sets in motion the thematic ax to be ground in Ruiz de Burton's novel, an ax that chips away at the class positioning of the Californio elite in the post-Reconstruction imaginary:

"I remember," calmly said Don Mariano, "that when I first read the text of the treaty of Guadalupe Hidalgo, I felt a bitter resentment against my people; against Mexico, the mother country, who abandoned us—her children—with so slight a provision of obligatory stipulations for protection. But afterwards, upon mature reflection, I saw that Mexico did as much as could have been reasonably expected at the time. In the very preamble of the treaty the spirit of peace and friendship, which animated both nations, was carefully made manifest. That spirit was to be the *foundation* of the relations between the conqueror and conquered. How could Mexico have foreseen then that when scarcely half a dozen years should have elapsed the trusted conquerors would, '*In Congress Assembled*,' pass laws which were to be retroactive upon the defenseless, helpless, conquered people, in order to despoil them? The treaty said that our rights would be the same as those enjoyed by all American citizens. But, you see, Congress takes very good care not to enact retroactive laws for Americans; laws to take away from American citizens the property which they hold now, already, with a recognized legal title. No, indeed. But they do so quickly enough with us—with us, the *Spano-Americans,* who were to enjoy equal rights, mind you, according to the treaty of peace. This is what seems to me a breach of faith, which Mexico could neither presuppose nor prevent. . . .

"I think but few Americans know or believe to what extent we have been wronged by Congressional action. And truly, I believe that Congress itself did not anticipate the effect of its laws upon us, and how we would be despoiled, we, the conquered people," said Don Mariano sadly. . . . "We have had no one to speak for us. By the treaty of Guadalupe Hidalgo the American nation pledged its honor to respect our land titles just the same as Mexico would have done. Unfortunately, however, the discovery of gold brought to California the riff-raff of the world, and with it a horde of landsharks, all possessing the privilege of voting, and most of them coveting our lands, for which they very quickly began to clamor. There was, and still is, plenty of good government land, which any one can take. But no. The forbidden fruit is always sweetest. They do not want government land. They want the land of the *Spanish people*, because we 'have too much,' they say. So, to win their votes, the votes of the squatters, our representatives in Congress helped pass laws declaring all lands in California open to preemption. . . ." (66–67, my emphasis)

Don Alamar's recourse to memory ("I remember") presents the personalized narrative of a "reasonable" man who has weighed the injustices of empire and found Congress, and by extension the nation itself, wanting in its responsibility and moral obligation to the "Spano-Americans," the "Spanish people." The authorial recourse, however, to "beautiful blue eyes," "Spano-Americans," and "Spanish people" is problematic to the degree that Don Alamar's soliloquy is racialized, "colored" if you will, in order to perform on the collective imagination of readers; the signifiers in question ultimately attempt to point to a single signified "white." The identification established between the implicit reader and the explicit racial markings of Don Alamar function to neutralize any racial antagonisms by blurring the color line. The creation of sociohistorical and racialized sympathy between the reader and the Alamars' plight, as representatives of their class, is the intended effect.

When Don Alamar states that "[w]e have had no one to speak for us," we can assume that Ruiz de Burton is speaking as ventriloquist for his class interests. This is precisely why Don Alamar makes such a point of mentioning the treaty; it sought, after all, to represent the "land" interests of an established Californio elite who had land to begin with (and therefore the prerequisite for voting). As someone who lived through the Gold Rush, Don Alamar's critique is directed against the institutional mechanisms (including Congress) that after the discovery of gold created retroactive laws that facilitated the arrival of "the riff-raff of the world" and "a horde of landsharks, all possessing the privilege of voting, and most of them coveting our lands."[44] Don Alamar's ostensible critique of the government's inability to secure the provisions under the treaty's Articles 8 (citizenship) and 10 (validation for land grants) is made tenable by eliding popular social symbolic representations of Mexicans as "Greasers," since he is narratively constructed as a "blue-eyed Spano-American" (see figure 3).

These social symbolic representations, however, had real and enduring discriminatory effects.[45] David Weber has noted how "[t]he 1855 legislature had passed laws prohibiting such Sunday amusements as bull, bear, and cock fights, clearly aimed at customs of the Californios" and how "the same legislature passed an antivagrancy act aimed at the Spanish-speaking

Figure 3. The representations of Mexicans as "Greasers" and a sinister element of the American body politic were commonplace in the popular press. This image comes from Cornel Frank Tripplett, *Conquering the Wilderness; or, New Pictorial History of the Life and Times of the Pioneer Heroes and Heroines of America* (New York: N. D. Thompson, 1883), 404.

which was popularly known as the 'Greaser Law' " (*Foreigners in Their Native Land,* 149). As a narrative figuration of a Californio, Don Alamar is not a "Greaser" or, as John Calhoun would have it, of "Indian" or "mixed ancestry."

If Don Alamar's critique of nation is sustainable by virtue of his deracinated Californio identity, then the religious obstacles between Catholic and Protestant in the post-Reconstruction imaginary must also be fictionally resolved in the novel. The degree of American concession over religious freedom (Article 9 of the treaty during ratification) is made manifest by William Darrell's own acceptance of "religious" difference, which he romances in a courtship that ends in marriage to Mary Moreneau. The future Mrs.

Darrell is described clearly as a white woman whose "beautiful dark eyes" melt Darrell's "pretended calmness," the hint of difference seemingly making her all the alluring to her suitor (*The Squatter and the Don*, 61). During their courtship, she is concerned about his "quick anger," since "a strong trait of character is not controlled easily" and "is more apt to be uncontrollable" (62). His assurance to the contrary, she is quick to stop his advances and proposal because she sees another obstacle: he is Protestant and she is Catholic. She asks him, "Will you go with me to church? You see, that is another obstacle; the difference of religions" (62). But William Darrell is quick to retort, "Indeed, that is no obstacle; your religion tells you to pity me." It is not her pity, however, that ultimately persuades her to marry William Darrell. He visits a priest and after a long talk promises "solemnly not to coerce or influence his wife to change her religion, and that should their union be blessed with children, they should be baptized and brought up as Catholics" (62).

This religious resolution of conflict through erotic love, the eventual "living and loving together" of William and Mary Darrell, had its historical complement in President James Buchanan's explanation regarding Article 9 of the Treaty of Guadalupe Hidalgo. Buchanan noted that

[a]fter the successful experience of nearly half a century, the Senate did not deem it advisable to adopt any new form for the 9th Article of the Treaty; and surely the Mexican Government ought to be content with an article similar to those which have proved satisfactory to the Governments of France and Spain and to all the inhabitants of Louisiana and Florida, both of which were Catholic provinces. (Cited in Weber, *Foreigners in Their Native Land*, 167)

Buchanan effectively summarizes how the coexistence of religions had been an established historical fact in French Louisiana and Spanish Florida prior to annexation. This "living together" of religious difference was the hallmark of the American republic. After all, how could a country premised on religious freedom deem it necessary to guarantee it to Mexicans in the newly consolidated territories? Buchanan's rationalization effectively neutralizes the racial connotations in the term "Catholic" without taking into account the populist renderings of Catholicism inherent in, say, the *Leslie's Illustrated* version of Eulalia Pérez's Catholicism, where it was racialized into "foreignness," "Otherness," and "other-worldliness." Like Buchanan's rationalization, Ruiz de Burton's "enemy lovers" in *The Squatter and the Don* manage to overcome historical roadblocks to love, marriage, citizenship, class, and religious affiliation.

This Is No Romance

John M. González's rearticulation of Doris Sommer's well-known "erotics of politics" has posited that the belletristic emplotments of Latin American nation-building that were narratively resolved through "romance" also found a similar resolution in *The Squatter and the Don*.[46] Following Sommer, González notes how for Ruiz de Burton, "The historical romance of Latin America provided a narrative strategy for articulating Californio citizenship within the post-Reconstruction reformation of national interests around race" ("Romancing Hegemony," 35). As I have shown, these "interests around race" are effectively deracinated in *The Squatter and the Don* to the point where whiteness and racial passing, not romance, serve as the organizing principle around which citizenship can be fully articulated. The novel deals with a particular type of Californio, not an ethnically marked subject who can interrogate the protocols of American citizenship and critique the limited possibilities for accessing cultural capital. Likewise, the "romance" around land reclamation and its concomitant association with citizenship, central to both *The Squatter and the Don* and Eulalia Pérez's testimonial, evinces a palliative strategy of accommodation through assimilation. Though land and citizenship were also two of the principal organizing features of Aztlán, and the Chicano cultural nationalism of the 1960s Chicano renaissance, their articulation in nineteenth-century cultural production revolved around a completely different set of class- and race-based goals. The centrality of land and citizenship, important to both identitarian crisis moments, involved different ends and should not obfuscate our critical vision with regard to our usable past.

The obvious bears repeating: the function of marriage as archetypal resolution to cultural conflict did not have an analogue in practice. Catarina Ávila de Ríos's testimonial certainly points to the frontier violence occasioned by the greed for gold and the devaluation of lives marked by miscegenation, as were those of María Antonia Vallejo, her husband, William Reed, and their children and family members. What is more, the texts in question do not positively identify with their Mexican roots, nor can we demand that they do so; an awareness of public-sphere conflations of Mexicanness with blackness made the option impolitic. Caught in the interstices of cultural survival, the texts' "authors" renegotiate their individual relationship to the national at the expense of their cultural ties to the Mexican milieu from which they emerged as political subjects. The narrativization of their relationship to the country as ersatz citizens transformed their bodies and the bodies of those they remember into vectors of meaning through narrative processes that rendered them historical after the crisis occasioned by the American 1848.

To invoke Foucault, the "subjugated knowledges" and, by extension, subjugated lives memorialized in Bancroft's Californio testimonials should inform our understanding of the past by virtue of the interplay of ideologies and interests that shaped those lives and knowledges. For Foucault, "Since memory is actually a very important factor in struggle (really, in fact, struggles develop in a kind of conscious moving forward of history), if one controls people's memory, one controls their dynamism. And one also controls their experience, their knowledge of previous struggles."[47] The testimonials offer incomplete but compelling memorious versions of the past that attempt to delimit Bancroft's version of California history as they point to the limited possibilities for Mexican participation in the nation's National Symbolic imaginary. How mediated or whitewashed these possibilities were, we may never be completely certain. Between the Californio version of history offered by Ruiz de Burton's elitist defense of Californio claims on American citizenship, the history offered as an image of and by Eulalia Pérez, and Ávila de Ríos's memory of a massacre, Mexican American struggles do demonstrate that the politics of race and national belonging is no romance. As I have argued, these memories of publicly rendered race-changes, violence, and dispossession are a type of historical reenactment—a literal narrative re-membering—that allowed both the testimonialists and Ruiz de Burton to rewrite their relationships to the nation by becoming historical. Like Bancroft's archive, the texts perform history by attempting to delimit those memories that will and will not be preserved.

2

Reading the *Corpus Delicti*

Tomás Rivera's *Earth* and the Chicano Body in the
Public Sphere

After Passing for Spain

José Antonio Villareal's novel *Pocho: A Novel about a Young Mexican American Coming of Age in California* (1959)[1] was considered to be the first Latino novel published in English prior to the archival work undertaken by Rosaura Sánchez and Beatrice Pita.[2] Their critical endeavors make patent the extent to which we must continually reevaluate the status of Latino literatures of the United States, as scholarship in the field has yet to catch up to the depth and breadth of what Latino writers were—and have been— writing, publishing, or both. Yet what is astounding in the development of Latino literary history from the American 1848 to the rise of the Chicano equality-rights movement of the 1960s is the uniformity of approximation to questions of cultural inclusion, ethnic identity, and entry into American civic life. Most of the texts that were written from the late nineteenth century to the 1960s followed two principal lines of strategic accommodation with Anglo-American culture; they endeavor either to assimilate or to celebrate heritage traditions while asserting a racial commonality with Anglo-American culture in the broader hopes of eventual cultural inclusion. As a representative text of this first tendency, Ruiz de Burton's *The Squatter and the Don* provides a narrative meditation on inclusion in American civic life and the possibility for participation in the American body politic through racialized association with whiteness. Eulalia Pérez's class-marked testimonial partakes of the same identitarian slippage between Mexican and white, despite her subaltern positioning, and suggests that, irrespective of social standing, the appeal of the assimilative model did not discriminate on the basis of class. This structural proximity to whiteness rendered in representational media is part of a broader racialized "illusion" that critic Rosa Linda Fregoso has analyzed. Adopting Carey McWilliams's well-known term for illusory whiteness, Fregoso writes, " 'Fantasy heritage' named the selective appropriation of historical fact, the transformation of selected elements of history . . . into a romantic, idyllic past that repressed the history of race and class relations in the region."[3]

The discursive futility of this assimilative appeal for social and political parity through whiteness likewise engendered the late-nineteenth- and early-twentieth-century development of a mythic recourse to whiteness that attempted to disassociate the Mexican question from the Anglo-American preoccupation with race, through what has come to be known as "the myth of the Spanish Southwest." Put prosaically, descendants of Mexicans in the southwestern United States often created a public identity that aligned their linguistic and ethnic particularisms with Spain, not with Mexico. Passing for Spain, the trumping of an ethnically marked and *racialized* Mexican identity for a European *national* identity, became one of the principal strategic conceits associated with the politics of Mexican American cultural *convivencia*—the coexistence of culturally distinct groups—in the American Southwest. The celebration of Spain as the harbinger of civilization in the Americas attempted to slight Anglo-American social, political, and economic superiority with the moral authority of the Old World and the "civilizing" accomplishments of the Spanish while still maintaining a structural proximity to whiteness.[4]

It is not surprising to note that the literary production written in Spanish in the United States did not seek a structural proximity to "whiteness" as understood within the geographic spheres of the nation. Much of the extant literary material from the late nineteenth century to roughly the first quarter of the twentieth century written in Spanish from the U.S. Southwest appeared in newspapers and partook of an exilic mentality that, according to Nicolás Kanellos, posited "the idea of a Mexican community in exile, or a 'México de afuera' (Mexico on the outside), in which the culture and politics of Mexico could be duplicated [while in exile in the United States] until Mexico's internal politics allowed for their return. The 'México de afuera' campaign was markedly nationalistic and militated to preserve Mexican identity in the United States."[5] Staunchly antiassimilationist, these writers were primarily concerned with Mexican politics since they understood themselves to be Mexican even if they were living in the United States. Much of the belletristic work from this "Mexican community in exile" published in newspapers and chapbooks, through language and thematics, made its relationship historical to Mexico but not necessarily to the United States.

It is important to note that similar "exilic" identity paradigms were also operative in other parts of the United States. Cuban and Puerto Rican Atlantic communities in the Northeast from the late nineteenth century to the early part of the twentieth, and whose cultural ties to the United States were politically determined and coterminous with their Mexican and Mexican American counterparts in the Southwest, also manifested their cultural identities in relation to their country of origin *as* exiles but not as citizens or cultural citizens of the United States. The unresolved geopolitical specter of 1898, the first war the United States directed against a foreign power after the territorial consolidation of 1848, obviated a direct understanding of their public identities as anything other than Cuban or Puerto Rican. Indeed, José Martí, writing from Philadelphia and New York for much of his productive writing life, was primarily concerned with Cuba much the same way that the early Puerto Rican *independistas* and later nationalist were concerned with affirming a distinctly Puerto Rican identity as independent from the United States.

It was, however, writers of Mexican ancestry who were bound to the United States through historical circumstances and geopolitical restructuring that established a relational dynamic that demanded national accounting and inclusion. As was the case with Ruiz de Burton, this inclusion in the realm of the literary was historical and racialized around associative whiteness. Raymund A. Paredes has gone so far as to suggest that "between the start of the Mexican Revolution of [1910] and the coming of World War II, Mexican-American literature continued along established lines of development. Historical and personal narratives, short fiction, poetry and folklore predominated, with New Mexico continuing as the center of activity. Among the most visible characteristics of New Mexican writing was a growing and exaggerated emphasis on its Spanish heritage."[6]

Not surprisingly, the few major authors from the period who found a public-sphere venue for their work through publishing in presses with national distribution were often firmly invested in affirming cultural and racial "bloodlines" either to Spain or to the historical specificities of the

American 1848. For example, Nina Otero-Warren's important book *Old Spain in Our Southwest* (1936), one of the few Mexican American texts to be published in the thirties by a national publisher, ultimately reified the primacy of whiteness in the construction of social selves through the celebration and evocation of a Spanish heritage that was continually threatened with an imminent extinction attributable to Anglo-American cultural encroachment and incivility. Indeed, as Héctor Calderón has recently noted in *Narratives of Greater Mexico: Essays on Chicano Literary History, Genre, and Borders* (2004), "Before the contemporary Chicano period . . . a set of discursive and cultural practices were set in motion by native [New Mexican] writers and scholars which were marked by an emphasis on a beautiful, empty landscape, folkloric customs and religious rituals, aristocratic pretense, and an idyllic 'Old Spain in Our Southwest' to the exclusion of the real historical and social conditions of the majority of New Mexicans."[7]

Curiously, the more progressive literary work of Jovita González (1903–1983) in *Caballero: A Historical Novel* (published in 1996 but written c. 1938), as well as her folkloric *Dew on the Thorn* (published in 1997 but written between 1927 and 1940), was never published in her lifetime, despite the author's hope to the contrary.[8] Even Américo Paredes, whose foundational pioneering work helped found the field of Chicano and Latino studies with his folk classic, *"With a Pistol in His Hand": A Border Ballad and Its Hero* (1958), could not get his now highly regarded novel, *George Washington Gómez: A Mexicotexan Novel,* published until 1990 even though it was written over fifty years before its eventual publication. The first major reconfiguration of the fantasy-heritage model of racial accommodation through "passing for Spain" was to come from the financially and critically successful novel *Pocho.*

Villareal's novel marked a turning point away from strategic appeals to cultural and political enfranchisement in the development of what today we call Chicano literature. *Pocho* both mediated and continued the possessive investment in whiteness evinced in both assimilationist and early-twentieth-century heritage celebrationist narratives, but it further complicated the Mexican question by naturalizing the immigrant status of Mexicans in the privileged sphere of the literary. Where the broader tradition of writing by Mexican Americans asserted a referential and geographic logic of presence, *Pocho* made Mexicanness intelligible to the majority culture by affirming—through a novel written in English, by a Mexican, about Mexicans in the United States—that Mexicans were not part of the geographic integrity of the country.

The novel narratively stages the generational tensions between Juan and

Richard Rubio, an immigrant father and his native-born son, who confront the necessity of assimilation. The young Richard abandons heritage traditions in favor of an American identity he can only assume, the novel would suggest, by joining the U.S. armed forces.[9] In the last chapter, Richard bids farewell to his family as he embraces his future by joining the navy and serving his adoptive country during World War II (1939–1945): "he lay in an upper berth listening to the chatter of his new companions, thinking little of the life he had left behind—only of the future, and suddenly he was afraid he might be killed. If it came, he would not be ready for it—no, he would never be prepared to die, but he could do nothing about it. He would come back, he thought, making himself believe it for a moment" (*Pocho*, 186). The novel ends with a less than ambiguous "he knew that for him there would never be a coming back" (187). As the son of Mexican immigrants, Richard joins the navy for the patriotic service of country even before being drafted. Yet through either the metaphorical death of Richard's Mexican past or the possibility of the literal death of his material body, Villareal's text suggests that being willing to die for the adopted country represents one of the few possibilities open to Pochos at midcentury for becoming American through patriotic loyalty.[10]

By consolidating and affirming the National Symbolic's amnestic renderings of the Mexican question during the mid-twentieth century, *Pocho* signaled the beginning of a broader crisis in meaning for Mexican American equality projects. The prominence and popularity of *Pocho* at midcentury further complicated the claims to whiteness enacted by the likes of either Ruiz de Burton or the narratives of a neo-Spanish identity—however impolitic or unsuccessful these ultimately were—by positing the Mexican body, whether born in the United States like Richard or not, as an (im)migrant body. Whereas the previous narrative traditions both assumed a geographic presence in the territories colonized by the United States, along with a concomitant appeal to racial parity, *Pocho* obviates the Mexican historical and cultural presence in the United States by making Mexicanness legible to readers through the discursive limits set by the (im)migrant status of Mexicans. Whereas the racial assimilationist and fantasy-heritage celebrationist affronts on the national culture understood their embeddedness in the geographic parameters of the country, *Pocho* reframed the Mexican question as an extranational concern: Mexicans were implicitly posited as a foreign imposition in search of inclusion through the largesse of the national culture.

This is not to deny the very real Mexican immigration that took place, especially after the Mexican Revolution (1910–1920), and continues to take place in ever increasing numbers: first through migrant worker accords sanctioned by both Mexico and the United States (which I will discuss later) and more recently through the illegal Anglo-American practice of head-hunting for undocumented workers to occupy jobs few U.S. citizens are willing to accept. It is to say, however, that *Pocho* discursively effaced the very history that texts like *The Squatter and the Don* so emphatically wished to assert: the cultural coexistence of Mexicans and Anglo-Americans from, at the very least, the consolidation of the U.S. territorial assimilation of almost half of Mexico in 1848.

By the time of *Pocho's* publication in 1959 by the Doubleday publishing empire, the Mexican body had already been represented as an interloper on the national landscape. Indeed, the so-called Sleepy Lagoon Case and Zoot Suit Riots had by the early 1940s saturated public media across the country with accounts of Mexican Americans depicted as "dark and greasy," "sinister and grotesque," and, as Arturo Madrid put it in his important analysis, "foreign and therefore suspicious."[11] However, a much earlier institutional antecedent had already created the national perception that Mexicans, citizens or not, were foreign. The immigrant and illegal ideation of the Mexican body in the national imaginary had already been sanctioned with the creation of the U.S. Border Patrol in 1924 through an act of Congress. The Border Patrol and its first outposts *on* the Mexico-U.S. border reinforced, through law and force, the illusion of territorial impermeability that is still a fixture of current debates about "illegals." *Pocho,* as mainstream mid-twentieth-century avatar of the Mexican question, facilitated the historical elision that posited the Mexican subject as recent arrivals and thereby as "foreign." In so doing, the novel solidified the immigrant status of both Mexicans *and* Mexican Americans as a national given guarded against historical reflection. That Mexican nationals were encouraged to join the U.S. armed forces during times of war in order to speed their entry into American civic life as potential citizens makes patent the extent to which the Latino body has been understood as an expendable commodity in the broader body politic.

During times of war the American patriotic embrace across the Mexican border (and the colonized territories outside the contiguous frontiers of the country) has suffocated potential citizens to death in the throes of national patriotic passion. Stating allegiance to the country, so the story goes, by supporting its will through force enables the citizen, or citizen-to-be, to structure a relationship to the national culture premised on the mutuality of need. The country enforces its will through the material bodies of those who presumably wish the will of the country to prevail. But loving the alien like a national is a fiction premised on the assumption of the equality of death for both, the equal treatment of both either at home or at war. Proportionately speaking, the lie that tests the fiction of equality (of death) resides in the corporeal evidence before the nation at times of conflict and war: more Latinos die than do Anglo-Americans or Blacks.[12] So patriotic obeisance, Latinos have learned, is a promise filled with limited dividends and tortured returns.

The crisis proportions of the material deaths of Latino bodies through war and other forms of national subjection would find emblematic expression in Tomás Rivera's 1971 novel, . . . *And the Earth Did Not Devour Him*.[13] *Earth* was able to consolidate this crisis by presenting the literally ravaged Chicano body as evidence of a broader national crime in the public sphere of signification for reflection, judgment, and national rememory. It was through the evocative renderings of this crisis in Rivera's *Earth* that Mexican American literature ceded way to what became a politicized Chicano literature, setting the stage for the rise of what has come to be understood as "Latino literature." I turn now to a political and contextual consideration of Rivera's scene of writing in order to situate the importance and emergence of *Earth*.

The Cultural *Corpus Delicti* and the Chicano Body as Evidence

Reflecting on the nature of art and evidence in criminal photography, Walter Benjamin argued that photographs of crime scenes call for political responses because they conjure the onus of responsibility, the perpetrator or perpetrators of the crime, the questions surrounding motivation, not merely an aesthetic judgment. Benjamin was referring to the work of Eugene Atget in his much-discussed essay "The Work of Art in the Age of Mechanical Reproduction."[14] His observations resonate with anyone who has studied contestatory art or narrative because subjugated knowledges, in images, writing, or any other cultural recovery attempt, refuse to be understood outside the logic of contextual fixity. In much the same way that forensic science determines meaning by calling attention to circumstances, subjugated knowledge projects resort to the culture industry for the articulation of specific goals en masse—in the public sphere of signification— that lay claim to their embeddedness in history. In Rivera's *Earth* the evidentiary evocation of loss and the history that produced it surfaces as an indictment of the literal and symbolic annihilation of Chicanos at home and at war. It is in this sense that the novel enters the public sphere of signification to make Chicano identities historical in relation to the use value accorded to these bodies by the national culture writ large. Like the texts analyzed in the previous chapter, *Earth* narrativized the past for historical contestation and national reevaluation. *Earth* offered a narrative of Chicano cultural participation that charted the lives of Chicano migrant (not immigrant) workers during America's "Age of Prosperity" in the post–World War II era. That the novel was written and published during the early 1970s is significant because it presented a version of the Chicano past that attempted to consolidate support for the emerging discourses of the civil rights and equality movements of the late 1960s and early 1970s from a decidedly Chicano perspective. The Chicano movement intervened in the national scene with symbolic representations of collective histories of dispossession during an age characterized by a Cold War rhetoric of patriotism that had coalesced the discourses of national belonging into scripted notions of American identity through fictions of equality, national allegiance, and the promise of political participation.

Earth's significance as an intervention in the public sphere is also important because the text posited the Chicano body as the *corpus delicti* of the national "crime" wrought on it through the collective experiences of national subjection, dispossession, and disenfranchisement.[15] In *Earth,* the national crime is written on the Chicano body and memorialized in the novel's description of burned bodies, tortured bodies in the fields, itinerant "bracero"[16] bodies, and bodies lost in war. *Earth* had received the first Quinto Sol National Chicano Literary Award, for 1969–70, several months before its actual publication.[17] Quinto Sol's designation as a "National Chicano" organization also conditioned how the text was to be received publicly. Within a year *Earth* was translated into English three separate times,[18] demonstrating a demand for a public account of Rivera's *corpus delicti.*

It is important to note that *Earth* attained symbolic capital in the public sphere when other narratives about the plight of Mexicans who immigrate or migrate—to or through the United States—failed to do so. Important texts by established Mexican authors had been dealing with the theme of (im)migrant workers for many years prior to Rivera's *Earth.* Canonical narratives such as Agustín Yáñez's *Al filo del agua* (1947, translated as *The Edge of the Storm*), Carlos Fuentes's *La región más transparente* (1958, *Where the Air Is Clear*), and Juan Rulfo's "Paso del Norte," in his *El llano en llamas* (1967, *The Plain in Flames*), to name but a few, were all unable to consolidate a diasporic Mexican identity.[19] Yet Rivera's *Earth* was able to engage in a dialogue with the operative discourse of national belonging in the public sphere at a propitious historical juncture.

The text appeared at a historical moment when César Chávez and the California grape industry boycott had been saturating the public media since the strike began in 1965. Indeed, the 1960s first brought Chicano and Black bodies to the homes of middle-class television viewer-voters. As early as 1960 Edward R. Murrow's Thanksgiving Day documentary, *Harvest of Shame,* had given visual and emotive texture to the plight of migrant workers as he narrated with indignation the now known phrase he quoted from a southern farmer, "We used to own our slaves. Now we just rent them."[20] By the time Chávez's strike began, it attracted national media attention—in Spanish, English, and international media outlets—and aroused interest in a wide range of Chicano issues through print and television. The sociohistorical context that led to the rise of a contestatory Chicano identity and ensuing equality movement helps situate *Earth's* importance during this period of national transformations in the way news was reported and discussed. But before engaging *Earth,* I turn to the Mexican question the text revisits from the vantage point of Rivera's scene of writing in the early 1970s: the Cold War of the mid-twentieth century and the concomitant forms of nationalism that *Earth* wishes to submit to rememory.

Chicano Incursion into the Public Sphere

Even before Murrow's important documentary, George Stevens's 1956 epic movie, *Giant,* starring Elizabeth Taylor, Rock Hudson, and James Dean, had brought the Mexican question to the national consciousness.[21] The movie was based on Edna Ferber's best-selling novel of the same name.[22] Ferber's novel tells the story of Texas, as a state of the Union and a state of mind. Her biographer, Julie Goldsmith Gilbert, noted how Ferber claimed to have been obsessed with Texas: "I could not put Texas out of my mind. Improbable events, incredible people, fantastic incidents boiled up out of Texas. The effluvia penetrated every corner of the United States. The inner urge to try to pin down on paper this incredible form of civilization called Texas became irresistible."[23] It is clear from Gilbert's biography that Texas was irresistible to Ferber because it represented the human costs and contradictions associated with vast capital accumulation and conspicuous consumption. As a metaphor for postwar American culture, *Giant* registered how racial and ethnic strife were part of the constitutive nature of what, for Ferber, it meant to be a Texan. "Texas is as big as the Texan minds are small," she was quoted as saying, and after the publication of *Giant*, "Texas was after her hide" (Gilbert, *Ferber*, 187). Dallas critic Lon Tinckle chastised her, "Miss Ferber, you aren't writing Uncle Tom's Cabin," and goes on, "What she says about voting practices and political combines in South Texas is almost daily verified in the news; and her resentment of the exploitation of Latin-Americans [sic] will find an echo in most Texas minds. But it is deplorable that Miss Ferber has made of race discrimination a sensational and implausible factor in her plot. . . . This is sentimental cheating" (ibid., 189). Just whose sentiments are being cheated or by whom was not of concern to many of her detractors.

The theme of racial exploitation in the novel was central to the movie version of *Giant*. Indeed, if it appeared to many that the novel was too concerned with race relations, the movie not only did not shy away from this but affirmed it on a national scale as it played from coast to coast to packed movie houses. *Giant* was the first Hollywood studio epic to include what we would today consider a Chicano theme. The movie stars Elizabeth Taylor as Leslie Lynnton, the daughter of a wealthy Maryland family who is being courted by Texas ranch owner Jordon "Bick" Benedict (Rock Hudson), as well as by a ranch hand, Jett Rink (James Dean). Bick eventually wins out, but when Jett strikes oil he uses his newfound wealth to get even with Bick for taking Leslie from him, by buying all the land surrounding the Benedict estate. After many years Bick disowns his son, Jordon Benedict III (Dennis Hopper), when he marries a Mexican, Juana (Elsa Cárdenas).

Meanwhile, Bick's daughter, Luz Benedict (Carroll Baker), becomes the mistress of aging millionaire Jett, who uses her to exact revenge for his loss. When Jett insults Juana Benedict, her husband defends her honor but is beaten up by Jett's henchmen. Faced with his own prejudices, Bick defends his son and publicly humiliates Jett. In a climactic confrontation with a racist diner owner ("No blacks or Mexicans served here," reads the placard in the diner), Bick proves to his wife and family that he has recapitulated and accepted his Mexican daughter-in-law and mestizo grandson by brawling with the diner owner after he insults Bick's mestizo grandson. Bick loses the fight but wins the heart of his family for ostensibly doing the right thing. Bick's eventual acceptance of his mestizo grandson and Mexican daughter-in-law demonstrates the degree to which miscegenation was a real social obstacle. Bick is shunned by both elite and working class—as the fight between Bick and the owner-cook of the diner makes clear—for his "progressive" ways.

The Chicano theme manifests itself early in the film when Leslie questions Bick about the historical specificities that had made him rich: "We really stole Texas, didn't we, Mr. Benedict? I mean away from Mexico. . . . It's all in the history books, isn't it? Isn't that how Mr. Austin came down with three hundred families—it says—and the next thing you know they're up and claiming it from the Mexicans?" (*Giant*). Leslie's metaphorical raiding of America's cultural library and her perspicacity regarding historical specificities make her an ideal reader of Chicano cultural history. Her character also shows the extent to which Texan wealth was the result of the dispossession occasioned by the arrival of Stephen Fuller Austin in Texas in 1821. Her criticism suggests that if everything in Texas is big, as the title implies, then so is Texan greed.

Though the film focuses ostensibly on the love story between Leslie and Bick, it also portrays the profound racial and ethnic strife that obsessed Ferber enough to write her American epic. Critic Charles Ramírez Berg suggests that the movie's star appeal allowed its attack on "some of the key principles of dominant ideology," like "patriarchy, [and] the imperialistic bent of America's westward expansion."[24] The public airing of such questions, so rare in mainstream Hollywood productions even in the present, was a poignant appeal for national self-reflection.

In one of the movie's most cinematographically beautiful and somber moments, Ángel Obregón (Sal Mineo), whom Leslie had saved from death as a child, is returned to Texas for burial after he is killed during World War II. Ángel is buried in a "Mexican" cemetery as Leslie helplessly watches in despair, amid the dust and tumbleweeds that add to the environment of humility and poverty the film plainly wishes to evoke. The boy she helped save is the man being buried after fighting for a country that would deny him burial in an "American cemetery," that is, a white cemetery.

Ángel's burial also points to what could be understood as a Mexican subject position in the National Symbolic that is imbued with what Russ Castronovo has referred to as *necro citizenship*.[25] Necro citizenship refers to the way the biological event of death serves as a metaphor for the social death of the nation's unwanted citizenry, or citizenry in the making, when the state attempts to deny citizens entry into civic life and the political realm. Ángel's death exposes how the Mexican American body is still within the state's reach even after death. The affective ties that the living have to those who are materially gone make the relationship of the dead to the state paradoxically political. By figuratively killing the subaltern Mexican American body again, by sending Ángel to a peripheral burial space, the state neglects the way affective ties to the dead create forms of personhood that congeal around feelings of love, loss, and remembrance for the living. In this sense love achieves its emancipatory potential because, by publicly expressing loss, the subaltern exposes the deadly duplicity behind the patriotic embrace. Ángel is buried in a Mexican cemetery to remind the living, his extended family and community, that they are an expendable commodity. But in this second state killing, which reaffirms the subject's second-class cultural citizenship, the dead achieve a postmortem materiality that allows them to haunt the nation through the mourning rituals enacted by and for the living. Mourning here is about communal rememory, the re-presenting of the dead's materiality as a countertext to historical elision. In *Giant,* Ángel's character is strikingly reminiscent of Private Félix Longoria, a Mexican soldier whose body was recovered but whose family was refused a viewing in a white funeral home in 1949.

Private Félix Longoria of Three Rivers, Texas, was killed in the Philippines near the end of World War II. When his remains were returned for burial, the director of the Rice Funeral Home in Three Rivers refused because "the whites would not like it."[26] Longoria's widow met with the founder of the American G.I. Forum,[27] Hector P. Garcia, who helped call national attention to what the local Mexican American press had been reporting all along. When Senator Lyndon Johnson intervened, after much public outcry from Garcia as well as the Three Rivers Mexican American community, Longoria was given burial in Arlington National Cemetery. The Longoria affair, like the death of Ángel in *Giant,* which appears to reference it, points to the persistence of segregation even after death that marks the Mexican subject as a subaltern in the broader body politic. This necro citizenship, the reanimation of the materially dead body that the nation conjures only to kill again, requires constant rememory in the public sphere of signification.

In his final analysis of the film, Ramírez Berg concludes that the broader message and any possibility for cultural critique were subservient to the film's mass appeal as an epic starring Hollywood's most important actors ("Bordertown," 43). I would add that the movie was produced for a mainstream audience who had already naturalized the Mexican as a foreign presence in the country. Ángel, rescued from his first death by Leslie, was already dead as a political subject since he owed his survival to the benevolence of a national who had brought him back to life to begin with.

Chicano critics were, and continue to be, apprehensive about social texts like *Giant* that have been disparagingly termed *chicanesca* productions.

Francisco A. Lomelí and Donaldo W. Urioste, for example, noted in their influential early work *Chicano Perspectives in Literature* (1976) that "the uniqueness of Chicano reality is such that non-Chicanos rarely capture it like it is. For this reason, we propose the latter's efforts to be termed *literatura chicanesca* because it only appears to be Chicano. Therefore, it must be kept in mind that the perspective is from the outside looking in."[28] The assertion comes from what these critics understood to be the Mexican American distrust of all those not considered to be in the know, those outside looking in, even if they were sympathetic to the plight of Chicanos. In an increasing Cold War climate of "red fear," the possibilities for public debate about national belonging and what it meant to be an American, not to mention basics such as access to education and working conditions for Chicanos, were relegated to regional but rarely national press coverage.

It was during the late 1960s and early 1970s that a public dialogue could be staged about the Mexican question. Tomás Rivera would eventually come to fill a significant cultural void and imbue it with meaning by remembering the 1950s and giving "evidence" of the Chicano body's relation to American patriotism, greed, exploitation, and the cultural amnesia *Giant* had presaged. But I am getting ahead of myself. Before I can recount Rivera's recourse to the *corpus delicti*, I need to set up the scene of the crime. That scene in Rivera's text is the America of the Cold War, the early 1950s, and the cultural happenings that fetishized versions of America's past for public consumption to fashion an ideal patriotic citizenry.

The Scene: The "Freedom Train" as Traveling Ideology and the Consolidation of an American Patriotic Ideal

Rivera's scene of the cultural crime had been fomenting after World War II, when U.S. identity became increasingly defined in relation to its Other, the Soviet Union. An emerging patriotism required a symbolic rendering of what America should be in the future by imbuing the past with meaning on a national scale. Bringing to the masses a selective and representative version of the past, or at least the dominant culture's version of what was worth remembering, was what William Coblenz had in mind when he envisioned the "Freedom Train."

In his study of American cultural memory, historian Michael Kammen credits Coblenz with the idea of creating a mobile museum capable of bringing America's historical memory to the people.[29] As assistant director of the Public Information Division of the Department of Justice in 1946,

Coblenz's lunch hours at the National Archives made him realize that America, incarnate in displays and on paper at the Archives, would never be accessible to the majority of Americans. Kammen relates how Coblenz's fascination with documents pertaining to the Nazi surrender, including Hitler's will, translated into a sense of the historical awareness that he felt Americans should have with regard to the role of the United States as a superpower and the importance of diffusing America's discourses of "freedom" and patriotism to the American masses (*Mystic Chords*, 574). He envisioned a mobile museum on a train that would visit the far reaches of the country, bringing America to the people.

Attorney General Tom C. Clark took to Coblenz's idea, stating that he believed it was a "means of aiding the country in its internal war against subversive elements and as an effort to improve citizenship by reawakening in our people their profound faith in the American historical heritage" (ibid.). With President Harry Truman's approval, and the backing of both government and private sector, it was announced that the tour would begin September 17, 1947, the 160th anniversary of the signing of the U.S. Constitution. In an overt literalization of what Lauren Berlant has called the "National Symbolic,"[30] the final documents assembled for the traveling museum-train included the Bill of Rights, the Emancipation Proclamation, the Mayflower Compact, Washington's Farewell Address, Lincoln's Gettysburg Address, and the log of the USS *Missouri* with the documents pertaining to the Japanese surrender that ended World War II.[31] The Freedom Train's mission was the "reawakening" of American cultural memory, or at least memorious re-creations of an idealized and narrativized American past for the sake of America's citizens.

The Freedom Train conditioned American patriotism with a public relations campaign that included a specially commissioned song by Irving Berlin, "Freedom Train," recorded by Bing Crosby and the Andrews Sisters, as it visited forty-eight states and received more than 3.5 million people. *Reader's Digest* and *Life* included guides for visitors, and local radio stations played recordings of the "Freedom Pledge" to coincide with the arrival of the train. "Freedom Pledge" recordings comprised "familiar voices" from the entertainment industry, including Ronald Reagan (Kammen, *Mystic Chords*, 579). The stylized, sleek, metallic, red, white, and blue Freedom Train, replete with evidence of America's greatness in the copious body of documents, was a traveling memorial about what should ostensibly be remembered. It served as a traveling monument of selective memory that necessarily involved a collective forgetting, a concomitant cultural amnesia with regard to America's (ab)usable past. As traveling ideology, the patriotic embrace that the train offered to all in theory was rejected by those whose lived experience made them know better, even as the country sleepwalked through history with the sounds of the "Freedom Pledge" lulling its citizenry to political slumber and, sometimes, to death.

Langston Hughes's poem "Freedom Train" (1947) poignantly resemanticized the patriotic embrace as a death grip tied to an ideal capable of seducing but incapable of achieving its promise:

> *I read in the papers about the*
> *Freedom Train.*
> *I heard on the radio about the*
> *Freedom Train.*
> *I seen folks talkin' about the*
> *Freedom Train.*
> *Lord, I been a-waitin' for the*
> *Freedom Train!*
> *Down South in Dixie only train I see's*
> *Got a Jim Crow car set aside for me.*
> *I hope there ain't no Jim Crow on the Freedom Train,*
> *No back door entrance to the Freedom Train,*
> *No signs FOR COLORED on the Freedom Train,*
> *No WHITE FOLKS ONLY on the Freedom Train.*
> *I'm gonna check up on this*
> *Freedom Train.*[32]

Hughes's poem offers a counterdocument to the historical records aboard the train that ostensibly attempt to unite America's citizenry, "out of one, many." The legible signs that point to restrictive ideations of freedom ("FOR COLORED" or "WHITE FOLKS ONLY") make the "Freedom Pledge" incommensurate with the lived reality of scores of nationals excluded from the promise of freedom in a Black vernacular that registers the constitutive irony inherent to American citizenship: abstract citizenship loves all nationals; the lived experience of subjugated and racialized subjects prove otherwise. Through the contestation of officiating public-sphere pronouncements ("I read in the papers," "I heard on the radio") and synesthesia ("I seen folks talkin' about the / Freedom Train!"), the poetic voice achieves the rememory of lived experience as a form of national reckoning: "I'm gonna check up on this / Freedom Train." The synesthesia itself establishes the lie of the purported national "freedom for all" by privileging sight over official speech. The poetic voice registers a reality quite different from the doubletalk concerning national freedoms: if seeing is believing, it suggests that such national talk is cheap.

The calls to American unity after World War II that were enacted and performed nationally by the Freedom Train, and made ubiquitous through the publicity it garnered, were an attempt to consolidate the discourses of national belonging around state-sanctioned modes of identification. During this period the House Un-American Activities Committee (HUAC), which had been formed in 1938 to uncover Nazi subversion, redirected its focus toward uncovering communists, communist sympathizers, and all manner of subversives and "evil" that might undermine American national interests. The fear of communism created a patriotic xenophobia that led to some of the most blatant abuses of government power in modern U.S. history. HUAC, chaired by Republican Wisconsin Senator Joseph McCarthy, sought to investigate the alleged communist subversion of American life and created a climate hostile to anything deemed "un-American" and foreign. McCarthy's aptly termed "witch hunts" occasioned a cultural hysteria that affected most facets of public life and modes of being.

HUAC's ability to terrorize is a familiar story. As Ellen Schrecker has observed, the anticommunist crusade "used the power of the state to turn dissent into disloyalty and, in the process, drastically narrowed the spectrum of acceptable political debate."[33] National appeals to civic engagement through patriotism censured any significant possibility for national critique. Not surprisingly, Blacks, leftist Jewish American intellectuals, and Chicano migrant workers could all be subsumed under an umbrella signifier: un-American.[34]

Through the early to mid-1950s, the Cold War discourse of citizenship and national belonging was propagated through various cultural media such as radio, television, popular periodicals, and both popular and highbrow literature. Kammen writes,

When *American Heritage*[35] first appeared, its Cold War rhetoric was prominently displayed. Popular fiction, such as A. B. Guthrie's *The Way West* (1950), emphasized traits of national character that had graced the pioneers: leadership, integrity, courage, and above all a bold love of freedom. Scholars and intellectuals were scarcely immune. Writing shortly after the appearance of Guthrie's Pulitzer-Prize-winner, Perry Miller viewed American literary tradition as a weapon in the struggle

71

against communism. "Through the American novel and play," he declared, we could "communicate with free men everywhere. Because this is a literature of criticism in the name of fundamental man [*sic*], it is a literature of freedom." (*Mystic Chords*, 573)

The calls to unity through patriotism and the ascribed commonality of desire for freedom left untold stories outside the discourse of nationalism. It is the dissonant story of Mexican Americans and their relationship to this history that makes *Earth*'s historical revisiting of the period significant.

Like the Freedom Train, Rivera's nameless migrant workers in *Earth* traveled through the American heartland. The Freedom Train's mission was to bring patriotic sentiments to a presumably freedom-loving populace; *Earth* functioned as a counternarrative to the national patriotic embrace that left so many outside the throes of the national patriotic fantasy. With *Earth*, the Bill of Rights' claim to equality as a distinct marker for the United States as an imagined community was to be put to the test of evidence on the body of the social crime, the un-American Chicano body. The Chicano body becomes a site of endangered knowledge and American identity negotiations in *Earth*, the surface on which Rivera could reenact the scene of the national crime. But before the reenactment of the crime, first to the crime remembered.

The Crime: The Chicano *Mea Culpa* Discourse in the Public Sphere

When the Chicano civil rights movement began to gain media attention in the mid- to late 1960s, the discursive effect of the coverage resulted in a collective amnesia that posited Chicanos as a minority group demanding citizenship rights for the first time. The June 29, 1970, issue of *Newsweek* featured a story about the Chicano civil rights movement titled "Tío Taco Is Dead"[36] (an allusion to Uncle Taco, a Mexican Uncle Tom). *Newsweek* ran the Chicano story next to its continuous coverage of the Charles Manson California murder trial. Manson's calm and sardonic facial expression appeared in a photograph next to the "Tío Taco" article, an irony we can only register in retrospect.

The *Newsweek* article began thus:

It is impossible to ignore the handwriting on the wall—the enormous, angular jottings that spill over imaginary margins. Across the peeling faces of neo-Victorian buildings, on littered sidewalks, anywhere where there is a decent-size blank space, young *chicanos* scrawl their names, their slogans, their dreams. Often the graffiti ends with the mystic *"con safo,"* a charm-like incantation that is supposed to protect the scribbling from defacement. On the ash-gray bricks of one nameless liquor store deep in the heart of East Los Angeles barrio, someone has written a footnote to American history. "Tío taco is dead," it says. "Con safos." (22)

The article mentions literal and metaphorical writing on the national wall of public meaning that is "impossible to ignore." The defacing of private property by Chicanos when they "scrawl their names, their slogans, their dreams" is how they also write a "footnote to American history." Alongside the footnote there appears order amid the disorder ("littered sidewalks"): "Con safos." Con safos, that "mystic . . . charm-like incantation,"[37] appeals publicly to other Chicanos to respect the message: *littera scripta manet,* the written letter abides indeed. The connotation is clear: do not forget the fact that "Tío Taco is dead," that is, do not forget that Chicano submission to the dominant culture is a thing of the past.

However, outside the main social text of national meaning, the Chicano movement is posited as a mere footnote to American history. The article notes that "Chicanos are caught in a curious limbo, suspended between two cultures, torn between assimilation and ethnic isolation" (22). The Chicano condition can be traced to a cultural cause:

Given the plight of the Mexican-Americans, the only surprising thing about the *movimiento chicano* is that it took so long to get started. This was due, in large measure, to the fact that the overwhelming majority of Mexican-Americans are devout Roman Catholics. "The emphasis the church places on misery and penance and suffering does nothing but buttress the condition we're in—and it's one hell of a condition," says José Gutiérrez. (23)

Newsweek not only found a narrative confirmation of Chicano inferiority that placed the burden of their plight on their own collective shoulders by blaming "their" religion; it also found a Tío Taco of sorts to confirm, repeat, and quote it. The article perpetuated a dominant cultural reading that requires representing ethnic disempowerment as an effect of an ethnic cultural cause. Exculpating the dominant culture from the "plight" of the Chicano, the *Newsweek* narrative related presumably verifiable historical facts by stressing the complicitous role of the Roman Catholic Church in the life of its all too willing martyrs. But the discourse of self-blame also symbolically exculpated the dominant majority by stressing that the "Mexican-American" problem was self-imposed because it was generated through cultural dependence on the Church. The Chicanos themselves had to resort to their collective agencies; after all, they were in "one hell of a condition."

The article also racializes Chicano identity into preestablished ethnic hierarchies. It notes that there are two types of Mexican Americans. Those who arrived before the Mayflower, "Spanish Americans, as they prefer to be called, founded California and gave Los Angeles its name." They "live in rural communities scattered across New Mexico and Colorado, relatively cut off from the mainstream of American life." Those who are not Spanish are "made up of more recent immigrants from Mexico and their descendants" (23). The myth of the Spanish Southwest, what I have earlier called "passing for Spain," is perpetuated in the article by an elegiac sentimental prose that represents the "Spanish American" people as "cut off from the mainstream of American life." Could there be any American life other than "mainstream"? It would appear not, as evidenced by the recent arrivals, who are posited as out of the mainstream by virtue of color, language, religion, and politics. In the article both "groups," despite their self-naming strategies, appear out of touch with the American way.

Newsweek's coverage of the *movimento chicano* reveals a profound lack of historical awareness about Chicanos, one still deeply ingrained in the National Symbolic order of things. The nineteenth-century Chicano discourses of national belonging had not—and to a great extent still have not—been engaged in the public sphere on a scale commensurate with their historical importance. Like the early Mexican American cultural interventions and appeals to citizenship discussed earlier, the fundamental mode of being American continued to be exacted along the national racial divide where Chicanos were and to a great extent continue to be interstitially located: "immigrants" on the fringes of national belonging.

The article never discusses, for example, the various formal and informal bracero accords between the United States and Mexico, which year after year brought Mexican workers over the border, especially during war. Meier and Ribera note that the braceros have been a permanent fixture in the United States from as early as World War I. They divide the bracero program from World War II through the 1960s into three principal periods of formal accords between the two governments: "The first, during World War II, began in August 1942 and ended in December 1947; the second ran from February 1948 to 1951; and the third, from 1951 to December 1964, was initiated largely because of the labor needs during the Korean War."[38] They relate how the scarcity of manual labor in the United States during key periods made "illegal" crossings not only possible but essential to various sectors of the national economy. This was the case, for example, in El Paso on October 13–18, 1948:

> Early in October the INS was informed that the cotton would rot in the fields without braceros to pick it; as a result, the Texas border at El Paso was opened to Mexican nationals from October 13 to 18. Despite Mexican government efforts to prevent its citizens from crossing into Texas, including the use of troops, nearly 7,000 . . . streamed across the border. As they crossed, they were placed under technical arrest by INS representatives and "paroled" to local United States Employment Service centers. Loaded into trucks of the growers' agents with the approval of USES, they were then taken to labor camps. . . . the United States, after taking several muddled positions, expressed regret for this El Paso incident, but only after the cotton had been picked! (Meier and Ribera, *Mexican Americans,* 183)

The state-sanctioned exploitation of the aptly named USES made patent the extent to which public discourse about the Mexican question had relegated such un-American actions to the depths of cultural amnesia. The selective memory surrounding the Mexican question gave rise to the need to vest the Chicano experience with the symbolic accounting of the cultural *corpus delicti.* The literal and symbolic Chicano body on whose surface the cultural crime is inscribed forms the basis of my analysis of Rivera's *Earth* as I turn to the body of evidence and the evidence on the body.

The Scene of the Crime: Novel Crimes in Tomás Rivera's *Earth*

Earth's appearance in 1971 symbolically re-created the scene of the social crime committed against Chicanos by offering a narrativized antidote to American cultural amnesia on the Mexican question. This narrative reenactment of the crime was significant to the degree that it consolidated the discourses of national belonging around the question of cultural participation. Perceived as "illegals," "goons," and "greasers," *Earth*'s nameless characters and its narrative form re-created a year in the life of various migrant workers under the aegis of a unifying narrative voice. As I have argued, the importance of *Earth* is also related to its appearance during the height of the civil rights movement. By 1971, the Chicano movement had secured a locus of enunciation in the public sphere that enabled it to establish a dialogue with the culture industry at large. As I noted earlier in my discussion of some of the canonical texts from Mexican literature that deal with the plight of immigrant workers, the braceros eventually return to Mexico. *Earth's* action, however, is grounded on the U.S. side of the divide, as are the braceros that populate the text's narrative terrain. The question of the nameless characters' legal or "illegal" status is deferred indefinitely, creating a further geographic logic of presence lost after the institutionalization of the Border Patrol discursively posited the Mexican subject as an "illegal" subject, an image given narrative form with the popularity of Villareal's *Pocho*. The question then shifts from the "Mexican question" proper (What to do with the "illegal" or recently arrived Mexicans?) to discourses of privileged citizenship for the majority culture and an ambiguous terrain of cultural citizenship for the racially and ethnically marked Chicano. *Earth's* reenactment of the scene of the cultural crime is therefore important in its relational dynamic between the body and the earth, national belonging and history, citizenship and the state.

The image of the land and land rights had been pivotal to Chicano identity politics since the 1848 divide. The unfulfilled land-grant promises of the nineteenth century—recorded in such texts as the Treaty of Guadalupe Hidalgo and narrativized in *The Squatter and the Don*—made land and land reclamation a central preoccupation for Chicanos. At the national level this had specific repercussions.

Reies López Tijerina organized a separatist movement called the Alianza Federal de las Mercedes (Federal Alliance of Land Grants) in 1963. López Tijerina demanded the return of the ceded territories, and on July 4, 1964, he led a sixty-two-mile march from Albuquerque to Santa Fe, New Mexico, where he presented Governor Jack Campbell a petition demanding an act of the state legislature to investigate the Chicano land grants in New Mexico. López Tijerina was eventually jailed for attempting a citizen's arrest on a forest ranger at Kit Carson National Forest. According to López Tijerina, the ranger was "trespassing" on "private" land.[39] In California in 1965, César Chávez had brought public attention to the migrant farm workers' plight by organizing a strike against the California grape industry. In Denver, the "Plan espiritual de Aztlán" (the Spiritual Plan of Aztlán),[40] as heir to López Tijerina's confrontational politics, became the Chicano movement's manifesto as it attempted to make public the collective Chicano response to the question of land dispossession and the institutional divestiture of Chicanos. The Plan, adopted at the 1969 Chicano Youth Conference in Denver, advocated reclaiming Mexican lands ceded to the United States. The importance of López Tijerina and César Chávez lay in their ability to consolidate an agenda around land reclamation and workers' rights. *Earth*, however, reenacts Chicano civil rights prehistory. It attempts to come to terms with the conditions that led to the Chicano civil rights movement, and with the Chicano absence from the scene of writing and culture, through stylized recourse to memorial snapshots from the period it charts. As such, it seeks to document fictionally the 1950s lived experience of discrimination and what the text portrays as the literal annihilation of Mexican Americans by narrativizing the abuses enacted against the Chicano cultural body. *Earth*'s reenactment of the cultural scene is also a reassessment of the fundamental questions that informed the Chicano civil rights movement: citizenship, land, nationalism, religion, and cultural identity. The diachronic nature of the narrative allows *Earth* to examine Chicano history, its development, and its transformation from resignation to revolutionary engagement. By situating the scene of the crime in the past, it allows the community of readers to remember that past at a moment of profound cultural disjunctures, at the height of the Vietnam War.

The Body of the Crime: Civic Representation and the Memorialization of Loss

Earth is divided into twelve principal narrative units that symbolically reframe a year. Each unit is prefaced with a related vignette. There is an introductory section, "The Lost Year," as well as a concluding section, "Under the House," each with its own vignette. The narrative structure, as well as the brevity of the units that weave through the lost year in syncopated staccato rhythm, make the text difficult to situate within the confines of a defined tradition of literary genres. It is most often referred to as a "novel," though its brevity makes the designation seemingly a stretch. Its designation as a "novella" would also prove problematic because there is no central story to speak of, given the plurality of voices that intervene as snapshots of migrants' lives and suffuse the novel with its narrative textures. All this has complicated the standard generic designations that can be accorded to the text.

Furthermore, the text cannot be understood within the logic of the postmodern pastiche since such an association would align it with a European tradition (specifically, French new novel of the 1960s), thereby decontextu-alizing the necessary grounding and contextual fixity it demands as a pub-lic intervention about braceros in the post–World War II American scene to which it anchors itself.[41] Reading *Earth*, then, requires the suspension of generic formulae so that we can attend to the Chicano reality to which it alludes as testimonial evidence of a body of people who have stood outside historical representation.

The narrative revolves around an unnamed boy who functions as the central unifying character by virtue of his presence in several units as witness to the plight of his community. The characters who populate the vignettes, many of whom are unnamed, could be understood to represent a broader collectivity of migrant workers and their travels, travails, and at-tempts to break free from the circular confines of the itinerant work that would define who they are in relation to the national order of things were it not for the narrative acts of witnessing and retelling. The novel's tempo-ral location is significant, though it has been the cause of some confu-sion.[42] The jacket of the 1994 bilingual edition, for example, states that the novel "documents the lives and peregrinations of the Mexico-American mi-grant workers of the 40's and 50's." Yet, as I detail below, the "Lost Year" in question is approximately a year during the Korean War (1950–53), as can deduced from the direct mention of the war made in the text.

The introductory vignette, "The Lost Year," begins with a conundrum about the difficulty of nomination and subject individuation:

> That year was lost to him. At times he tried to remember and, just about when he thought everything was clearing up some, he would be at a loss for words. It almost always began with a dream in which he would suddenly awaken and then realize that he was really asleep. . . .
>
> It always began when he would hear someone calling him by his name but when he turned his head to see who was calling, he would make a complete turn and there he would end up—in the same place. This was why he never could discover who was calling him nor why. And then he even forgot the name he had been called.
>
> One time he stopped at mid-turn and fear suddenly set in. He real-ized that he had called himself. And thus the lost year began. (Rivera, *Earth*, 83)

The opening section makes manifest the difficulty of situating a subject position from which to speak one's identity in the context of a collective

READING THE *CORPUS DELICTI*

recourse to memory. The difficulty of nomination as a metaphor for *being* ultimately foregrounds the importance of a collective identity over and above an individual identity. The question of individual over collective identity is resolved in this section by having the proper name remain unknown to the reader even though the character knows, finally, that he has been "calling himself." This calling himself, what Louis Althusser famously called "interpellation" to refer to how the state apparatus delimits individual agency by naming subjects rather than allowing for self-nomination, makes self-individuation an act of agential self-creation. In this sense, calling himself into being is a collective assertion of communal identity for the unnamed character and the collectivity he is made to represent. The year that has been lost, the year "he tried to remember," is slowly recovered through an act of memory and the narrative historical recording of "the lost year" that will diachronically inform Rivera's present.

The opening unit, "The Children Couldn't Wait," sets the scene of the crime in the fields, where migrant workers, adults and children, are subjected to working conditions that resemble a penal colony. The heat is so extreme "that the bucket of water the boss brought them was not enough" to satiate their thirst (*Earth*, 86). The nameless boss "didn't much like the idea of their losing time going to drink water because they weren't on contract, but by the hour. He told them that if he caught them there again he was going to fire them and not pay them. The children were the ones who couldn't wait" (ibid.). After the boss notices that one child keeps going for water far too often to meet the imposed work schedule, he decides to scare him with his rifle: "What he set out to do and what he did were two different things. He shot at him once to scare him but when he pulled the trigger he saw the boy with a hole in his head. And the child didn't even jump like a deer does. He just stayed in the water like a dirty rag and the water began to turn bloody" (86–87).

The referential quality of this scene sets the parameters from which to read Rivera's *corpus delicti*. The literal body of evidence is laid out for public view in this section. The child, who would have come of age at the height of the Chicano civil rights movement, functions like a specter of meaning for *Earth*'s readers in 1971. The child is a victim of the boss's crime, and like the broader social crime to which the scene refers, there is no proof by which to hold the boss accountable except for the historical rememory of what this fictionalized murder says about the very real killings of Chicanos at home and at war. The child who is murdered at home, like those who were dying abroad in Rivera's present during the Vietnam War, also makes visible the degree to which Chicanos began to construct a social reality that discursively rendered them as soldiers at war with their own country. As we shall see in what follows, Rivera thereby establishes a parallel between his narrative, set during the Korean War, and his present scene of writing, during the Vietnam War, in order to trace a broader trajectory of Chicano participation in a war ravaging the United States at home and abroad.

George Mariscal in his documentary history of Chicanos and their participation in the Vietnam War states that Mexican American and Latino deaths were higher than those of other groups. Though "[t]he armed forces had abandoned the use of the category 'Mexican' in 1949 in response to objections to the term by Mexican American advocacy groups," making it "virtually impossible to know how many Chicanos served in Viet Nam," it is clear that Latinos suffered the brunt of the national losses:

> Two of the surnames that appear most often on the wall of the Viet Nam Memorial in Washington, D.C., are Johnson and Rodriguez [*sic*]. These two names tell us something about the composition of the U.S. military during the war. . . . "Johnson" combines the Caucasian and African American sacrifices. It locks into a single name the black/white opposition that structures virtually all discussions of race relations in the United States. "Rodriguez" stands for the Latino experience during the war. . . . "Rodriguez" functions as a third term or supplement that disrupts and complicates the black/white dichotomy. (*Aztlán and Viet Nam*, 3)

The ironic structural alignment with whiteness that made "Mexican advocacy groups" shun the term "Mexican" haunts the Vietnam War Memorial nonetheless with the "third term or supplement": Rodriguez. Still, Rodriguez—sans accent mark—figures as the name that the national wall of meaning both registers and effaces; it is the lingering historical haunting of a presence too unwilling to disappear.

The issue of national accountability regarding death and Chicanos is made evident when the Chicano body at war is contrasted to the effects of the war at home. This is the case in the second unit of the novel, "A Prayer." In the prefatory vignette, a nameless mother visits an *espiritista* ("psychic") to inquire about her son, who has been sent off to the Korean War. "Well you see, I haven't heard from my boy in over two months. Yesterday a letter from the government arrived telling me that he's lost in action. I'd like to know whether or not he's alive. I feel like I'm losing my mind just thinking about it." The psychic replies, "Have no fear sister. . . . He's just fine. . . . He'll be returning already next month" (*Earth*, 89). The psychic's prediction proves to be a false hope, an ultimately treacherous antidote to the mother's despair.

In the unit proper, the mother's prayer is imbued with sentimentality and despair: "Dear God, Jesus Christ, keeper of my soul. This is the third Sunday that I come to implore you, beg you, to give word of my son. I have not heard from him. Protect him, my God, that no bullet may pierce his heart like it happened to Doña Virginia's son, may he rest in God's peace" (90). The unnamed mother's fear, that her son will end up pierced in the heart by a bullet like Doña Virginia's son, memorializes loss as a collective experience. The mother remembers Doña Virginia's son and can only hope that her own son will return: "bring him back from Korea," she implores, "safe and sound. Cover his heart with your hands. Jesus Christ, Holy God, Virgen de Guadalupe, bring him back alive, bring me back his heart. Why have they taken him? He has done no harm. He knows nothing. He is very humble. He doesn't want to take anybody's life. . . . Here is my heart for his. Here is my heart. Here, in my chest, palpitating. Tear it out if blood is what you want, but tear it out of *me*. I sacrifice my heart for his. Here it is. Here is my heart! Through it runs his very own blood" (90).

The unnamed mother's narrative supplication provides a poignant haunting where desperation's only addressee is a seemingly vengeful god. Rivera's historically situated reader knows what the mother cannot understand: that it is the state that has literally lost her son's body and taken his life. To die for the country, like Doña Virginia's son, is unfathomable to the nameless mother who cannot understand the politics of the war abroad. Her son, unlike Richard Rubio in *Pocho,* "was very afraid to go" to war like the many Chicanos who were realizing how their subaltern standing at home did not warrant the possibility of dying for a country who treated them as human chattel (90). Bring me the body, the text seems to implore, in a literalization of the juridical habeas corpus, the literal "have you the corpse?" "Yes," Rivera's text seems to reply, the body of evidence is all around you.

For an ideal reading public of young Chicanos, this scene begged to be read in the context of U.S. involvement in Southeast Asia in a narrative foreshadowing of the costs associated with loyalty to an abstract state incapable of recognizing the war at home. The narrative positioning of the two opening units suggests that the Chicano young are the most susceptible to the war raging abroad and the war raging within the nation's borders. Though it is often observed that war is exceptional in human experience, in that killing is sanctioned in war but criminal in "peacetime," the events in the two opening units suggest otherwise by positioning the Chicano body as an imperiled historical subject never at peace from the war at home. The opening units draw a parallel between the novel's explicit present, the Korean War, and its implicit present, the height of the Vietnam War.

The number of dead young bodies as expendable commodities in *Earth* is astounding. In the eighth vignette, "The Little Burnt Victims," the narrative voice registers the tragedy of the García family with the evidentiary detachment reminiscent of a police report. It begins, "There were five in the García family. Don Efraín, Doña Chona, and their three children: Raulito, Juan and María—seven, six, and five." The narrator relates how after arriving a their home in a chicken shack they were "excited over a movie about boxing they had seen" (120). The father takes out the boxing gloves "he had bought for the children and [makes] them put them on," though the mother does not want the children to get hurt (120). But Don Efraín insists that, aside from play, the children will "at least learn how to defend themselves"; he even harbors the hope that "one of them will turn out good with the glove, and then we'll be set *vieja*" (120).

The following day the children "were left to themselves in the house when [the parents] went to work because the owner didn't like children in the fields doing mischief and distracting their parents from their work. . . . At about ten o'clock that morning, from where they were working in the fields they noticed smoke rising from the direction of the farm. . . . When they arrived the Garcías' shack was engulfed in flames. Only the eldest child was saved. The bodies of the other children were charred in the blaze" (120–21).

The narrative lists a dialogue between two unnamed speakers talking about the tragedy in a series of summative statements set off by quotation marks that further render the testimonial character of the unit visibly macabre. The description of the five-year-old, María, by unnamed interlocutors makes the relationship between production and corporeality visible:

"And you know what?"
"What?"
"The only thing that didn't get burnt up was the pair of gloves. They said they found the girl all burnt up with the gloves on."
"But I wonder why the gloves didn't get burned up?"

"Well you know how *those people* can make things so good. Not even fire can destroy *them*." (121, my emphasis)

The charred remains of the child ("one of them will turn out good with the glove, and then we'll be set *vieja*") are curiously compared with the use value of the boxing gloves that survive because "those people" can produce enduring products, but not the conditions that can allow the future, the children, to thrive. "Those people," as unnamed as the majority of the characters that populate the lost year, also refer to a broader collectivity who control—in the parlance of an outmoded but ever more necessary form of critique—*the means of production* that allow objects to survive rather than people. The scene puts in relief how the Mexican (American) subject is profoundly enmeshed in the movement of labor and capital and how the material bracero body is determined by the work that allows the structures of oppression to thrive.

The narrative units about dead children and the young (the murdered thirsty child, the unnamed mother's son, the charred children) make the relationship between the Chicano future and Rivera's scene of writing clear: there is a war at home that will imperil any Chicano future that remains re-signed to the material losses the national culture enacts on the young, the future of Chicanos in the United States. The Garcías' work and the children's living conditions are part of the broader social text that Rivera's narrative writes on the public conscience of the early 1970s. The cultural irony is written on the bodies of the Chicano young. Rivera's literal positioning of the evidence of the crime in the context of the national *corpus delicti* suggests that the Chicano body is being written out of the symbolic and material American imaginary since both work and war lead to the same ends, exscription. Then, how to remember the dead?

A mother's grief: the love for her dead son. A father's loss: how to remember his only child, the proverbial end of his line. The implications of the possibilities for "gendered" forms of grieving, implicit in my opening sentences, point to the cultural specificities of the patronym within Chicano culture, and *Earth*'s recourse to gendered forms of remembrance makes this gendered grieving manifest in the eleventh unit, "The Portrait." In this unit, a photograph restorer comes "from up north," like all Anglo salesmen, who arrive when they know the workers have money (136). The salesman tells Don Mateo, "Well, sir, see, you give us a picture, any picture you may have, and we will not only enlarge it for you but we'll also set it in a wooden frame like this one and with inlays, like this—three dimensional, as they say" (136). Don Mateo's interest is piqued since he only has one photograph of his son who died in Korea. Don Mateo tells the salesman, "It's the only picture we have of him. We took it right before he left for Korea. Poor m'ijo, we never saw him again. See . . . this is his picture. Do you think you can make it like that, *make it look like he's alive?*" (137, my emphasis). The photograph, as material proof of the life of a loved one, is a memorial and a commemorative material artifact for the father. He wants a simulacrum of his son's presence: "make it look alive." It is a double loss for the father in that it marks the end of the patronymic lineage in addition to the material end of his beloved son. The salesman offers to dress Don Mateo's son in a uniform, much like the uniformed photograph the son had promised to send Don Mateo, "with the American and Mexican flags crossed over his head" (137).

Don Mateo accepts and pays the salesman. He and his wife wait for several weeks but neither the salesman nor the photograph arrives. After endless waiting, there is a discovery: "Some very heavy rains had come and some children who were playing in one of the tunnels leading to the dump found a sack full of pictures, all worm-eaten and soaking wet. . . . Don Mateo was so angry that he took off to San Antonio to find the so and so who had swindled him" (138). Don Mateo, it would seem, might concur with Leslie, Elizabeth Taylor's character in *Giant*, about Texan size and greed. But Don Mateo's trip to San Antonio pays off. He finds the "so and so" and makes him reconstruct his son's image: "I put him to work right then and there. The poor guy didn't know how to begin. He had to do it all from memory" (139).

Don Mateo's revenge regarding the body of the crime, his son's absence, and the symbol of that absence in the photograph, is instructive to the extent that he holds the salesman accountable for the crime. Making the salesman "do it all from memory" involves a reverse remembering, where the traditionally subjugated Chicano inverses the structures of coercion and submits the salesman to the orders of Chicano cultural memory. The image of Don Mateo's son, however mediated by loss and remembrance (both his own and the salesman's), will provide a visual referent about the dead, the circumstances surrounding the death (the son dressed in a uniform the father never saw), and the possibilities for reversing the orders of exploitation that Don Mateo manages to traverse so well. The war abroad, and Don Mateo's son's participation in that war, motivate the Chicano subject into action and the possibility of agential transformations in the public sphere. Unlike the unnamed mother's recourse to communing with her dead son through a psychic, Don Mateo does not resort to prayers.[43]

Earth's reenactment also stages a dialogue with the question of religiosity as it pertains to the Chicano community and the dominant public perceptions that circulated about Chicano Catholicism. The *Newsweek* article that noted the importance of "misery and penance" for the "devout" Mexican American "Roman Catholics" conditioned the public terms of engagement with Chicanos in the public sphere. But where the *Newsweek* article explicitly placed the blame on Chicano religious beliefs, *Earth* mediates the generational split between martyrdom and agency.

According to Ramón Saldívar, the titular unit of the novel, "And the Earth Did Not Devour Him," engages these very issues. Saldívar notes that, "haunted by his inability to understand why a beneficent God would allow disaster to strike unremittingly a good and innocent people, the boy finally brings himself to do what he could not do earlier [in the narrative]: deny and curse God. This rejection of the traditional ideology of acceptance and submission that his Catholic faith has taught him allows him now to elevate his own creative will to a higher sphere of existence and thus produce his own story."[44] The unnamed boy's end of innocence, however, is sedimented in the unit "A Silvery Night," when he seeks to invoke the devil, since the figure of the devil "had fascinated him as far back as he could remember" (104).

In this section, the allusion to the proverbial bite of the apple from the tree of knowledge is clear. The boy's end of innocence is also the end of guilt: guilt conceived as the heavy weight of tradition versus the discourse of cultural accommodation, *Newsweek*'s assertion that "chicanos are caught in a curious limbo, suspended between two cultures, torn between assimilation and ethnic isolation" (Littell, Biffle, and Davis, "Tío Taco Is Dead," 22). As a cultural analogue for Rivera's ideal readers, this unit reenacted public discourses about Chicano religion and identity and served as a call to cultural action. When the boy curses the devil, he is disappointed because the repercussions he has feared prove to be unfounded: "He swore at him using all the cuss words that he knew and in different tones of voice. He even cursed the devil's mother. But nothing. Nothing nor no one appeared, nor did anything change. Disillusioned and feeling at moments a little brave, he headed back for the house. The sound of the wind rustling and the leaves of the trees seemed to accompany his every step. There was no devil" (*Earth*, 106).

I would suggest that the boy's end of innocence be understood in diachronic relation to the present from which Rivera writes, his scene of writing. In the unit "And the Earth Did Not Devour Him," when the boy curses God he does so out of anger born of deception. He feels deceived about religious notions of protection and security that are unfounded, as evidenced by the bodies around him: "he felt hate and anger when he saw his mother crying for his uncle and his aunt. They both had caught tuberculosis. . . . He became even angrier when he heard his father moan outside the chicken coop. . . . At times he heard his father start to pray and ask for God's help. At first he had faith that he would get well soon but by the next day he felt the anger growing inside of him. And all the more when he heard his father and mother clamoring for God's mercy" (108–9). He finally curses God after the body of evidence around him has proved that belief in the discourses of protection is unreliable. This, I would suggest, has a metaphorical analogue to Rivera's writing scene. The boy's religious end of innocence is the metaphorical rendering of a broader concern for "protection" understood at the national level. Rivera's polyphony of voices, after all, points to the cultural *corpus delicti*, the bodies that imbue *Earth* with meaning by literalizing the proof of the national crime that requires profound interrogation and national self-reflection.

The final section, "Under the House," reinforces this image of cultural engagement with the national crime at the public level. The unnamed voice in this closing section goes under a house and lies on the earth in a crawl space where the foundation of the house and the earth meet. His reverie replays the episodes in *Earth* from beginning to end in an elegiac stream of consciousness. His remembering under the house invokes images of the nation as he is caught between the foundation of the metonymic nation, the house, and the earth. Those living above finally realize he has been under the house for an unspecified amount of time:

> He had to come out. Everyone was surprised that it was him. He didn't say anything to them, just walked away. And then he heard the woman say: "That poor family. First the mother and now him. He must be losing his mind. He's losing track of the years." Smiling, he walked down the chuckhole-ridden street leading to his house. He immediately felt happy because, as he thought over what the woman had said, he realized in reality he hadn't lost anything. He had made a discovery. To discover and rediscover and piece things together. This is this, that is that, all with that. That was it. That was everything. He was thrilled. When he got home he went straight to the tree that was in the yard. He climbed it. He saw a palm tree in the horizon. He imagined someone perched on top, gazing across at him. He even raised one arm and waved it back and forth so that the other could see that he knew he was there. (152)

This final scene is emblematic of the text's concerns with cultural reenactment at the public level. The boy emerges under catcalls about his sanity or lack thereof. That the unnamed woman says, "He must be losing his mind. He's losing track of the years," is ironic insofar as he has been doing the opposite, imbuing the past with meaning through rememory, remembering the details of the cultural crime. The boy's engagement with a community of ideal readers is also made manifest in his desire to imagine someone "gazing across at him." This imaginative leap of faith, like a metaphorical bridge between the novelized present and desired future, conditions the boy's final farewell to his past, his arms waving in the air, "so that the other could see that he knew he was there." Yet this form of farewell is also a greeting; it is as much a good-bye to the culture of dispossession as it is an affirmation of a future of public engagement and national participation, imagined.

Forms of Farewell

Earth's reenactment of the scene of the cultural crime is also an engagement with the scene of writing as a form of public remembrance, a historical moment of articulation that needs a narrative closure in Rivera's present about the Chicano past. *Earth*'s reenactment of the Chicano question in the early 1950s seeks to account for the absence of participation of Chicanos from the public sphere. In the process, the text becomes an emblem of the period it was able to consolidate through its recourse to memories of belonging, dispossession, and finally engagement.

That *Earth* consolidated a broad national constituency around the Mexican question, while other narratives of migrant workers could not, makes patent the extent to which the geopolitical fixity of *Earth* demonstrated a broader need to ground and center the Mexican question within the boundaries of the United States. The memorious evocation of dead bodies, burned bodies, absent bodies, and bodies lost at war ultimately signaled the need for a national discussion on and about Chicanos that facilitated the emergence of some of the first multicultural gains for Chicanos, as well as other Latino groups, by claiming a coterminous history with the broader Anglo-American culture.

Earth's reinscription of the geographic presence of Chicanos in the United States was an implicit indictment of the social symbolic amnesia that patriotism's calls to unity had elided for a national narrative of freedom that served as the structuring but unfulfilled promise of American democracy for the presumably "foreign" Chicano subject. In no uncertain terms, Rivera's text offers evidence about the Chicano body as an expendable commodity that serves the interest of a dominant majority both at home and abroad. In so doing, *Earth* performs an American haunting that envisions necessary action after narrative rememory.

Part II

Postmodern Genealogies

The Latino Body, in Theory

3

The Institutionalization of Latino Literature in the Academy

Cabeza de Vaca's *Castaways* and the Crisis of Legitimation

Adrift in American Literary History

Each age must write its own books; or rather, each generation for the next succeeding. The books of an older period will not fit this.

—Ralph Waldo Emerson, "The American Scholar" (1837)

New York Times reporter James Brooke noted how on January 9, 1998, in Española, New Mexico, "an Indian commando group stealthily approached a bronze statue here of the first conquistador, Don Juan de Oñate. With an electric saw, the group slowly severed his right foot—boot, stirrup, star-shaped spur and all."[1] This four-hundred-year-delayed retaliation was carried out in response to Oñate's 1598 declaration of war on the Acoma Indians. The Spanish had "punished" the Acoma insurrection by cutting off the foot of every captured Acoma warrior. The literal display of agency, symbolically redressed by the "Indian commando group," was "designed for maximum political effect" (Brooke, "Conquistador Statue," A10). The Amerindian "commandos" sought to reenact a historical moment of violence for symbolic effect. By demonstrating how the reenactment of traumatic events allows a people to renegotiate their terms of engagement with national culture by refusing to forget the literal human costs of nation, the

Amerindian "commandos" sought to resemanticize both the past and how that past should be understood in dialectical relation to the present and the future. Oñate's arrival in present-day New Mexico was facilitated by the literal and cultural mapping by Alvar Núñez Cabeza de Vaca in *Los naufragios* (1542),[2] literally "shipwrecks," along with the account he provided of his eight-year travails through what today is the southwestern United States after his shipwreck off the Florida coast in 1528. Indeed, Cabeza de Vaca's chronicle of shipwreck, ethnographic documentation, and westward migration from the Florida peninsula to California has served not only Oñate and subsequent Spanish explorers but also Chicano and Latino critics, who, like the Española commandos, are sacking the cultural archives to recover and reimagine a Latino past for present needs. Without the presumption that Latin American and American literature have two very different objects of study, the usable past is being read in direct relation to present concerns about Latin American, Latino, and American cultural and literary identity.

Not surprisingly, critics in Chicano and, more inclusively, Latino writing have begun to address Cabeza de Vaca's *Castaways* as a complex text that can no longer be unproblematically associated solely with colonial Latin American literature by virtue of what this sixteenth-century explorer had to write, witness, and say about the cartographic construct now called the United States. In what follows, I critically engage the "place" of *Castaways* in inter-American literary and cultural history by focusing on how Cabeza de Vaca's literal and metaphorical body has been vested with various meanings, and how these meanings have sought to create a locus of enunciation for Latino subjectivity. In so doing, I question some of the paradigms of cultural interaction and accommodation that have embraced Cabeza de Vaca as a founding literary "forefather," ancestor to the Chicano and Latino struggles of the late 1960s and early 1970s and paragon of multicultural identity negotiations.[3] In the face of such a claim, it becomes necessary to analyze what his work does and for whom.

Critical Maneuvers: Genealogies of the Latino Subject's Body

Writing in the early 1970s, Luis Leal, in his now classic essay "Mexican American Literature: A Historical Perspective," provocatively states that "[t]o consider Chicano literature as a part of *American literature* is an object too idealistic, at least for the time being, for socially Chicanos are considered a group apart" (my emphasis). Leal goes on to note that "we shall consider Chicano literature here to be that literature written by Mexicans and their descendants living or having lived in what is now the United States."[4] Despite acknowledging the idealistic nature of the project, Leal sets the geographic parameters for studying Chicano literature by suggesting that it begins with the literary-historiographic deconstruction of American literary culture. He advocates what Ralph Waldo Emerson posited as each generation's obligation to "write its own books," since those "books of an older period will not fit this."[5] For Leal, this rewriting entails revisioning a Chicano past that begins with what he calls the "Hispanic Period," "characterized by prose writings of a historical or semihistorical nature including many descriptions left behind by explorers of the region where the majority of Chicanos now live" ("Mexican American Literature," 22). He reminds us that foremost among these is "the Relaciones of Alvar Núñez Cabeza de Vaca" (ibid.).

Leal wrote the essay for the first issue of *Revista Chicano-Riqueña*, a journal that set the tone for Chicano creative and scholarly writing and, more broadly, for Latino writing under the name *Americas Review* until the late nineties. Like Emerson's insistence on revisioning what is "American" as something apart from its Continental European other, Leal's strategic positioning of Cabeza de Vaca's text as Chicano writing clearly intends to situate Chicano literature within what is now the United States and to problematize the nature of national belonging, literary affiliation, and America's relationship to Chicano writing. If Chicano literature cannot "for the time being" be considered part of American literature because Chicanos are "a group apart," Leal sets out to defamiliarize the United States as a stable cartographic unity by establishing the contingent and fluid nature of the United States as an imagined community.

Leal was not the first to make this position tenable, but he was able to consolidate a literary-cultural project with definite beginnings at a time when Chicano, not to mention Latino, writing was in a precarious position with regard to the academy. Leal was echoing critic Ray Padilla's assertion that "all work prior to 1848 can be treated as pre-Chicano Aztlanense materials."[6] Padilla's assertion reminds us that the end of the Mexican-American War did not mar the trajectory and continuity of Chicano culture. His invocation of Aztlán reinforces the ties between geography as a place of origin and as a place from which to legitimate a cultural enterprise, a place to stand and speak Chicano culture.[7]

For both Leal and Padilla, becoming Chicano is therefore part of a broader historical process determined by cause and effect relations in and among peoples of the United States. The historicist positions elaborated by these scholars and the colonial narratives they included as examples of Chicano literature from their vantage point in the early 1970s, when Chicano and ethnic studies programs were beginning to emerge and garner institutional funding, were indeed integrated into the canon of Latino literary studies. However, early "Chicano Aztlanense" literary and historical materials were not as immediately relevant as the corpus of texts that formed what Philip Ortego ebulliently called the 1971 "Chicano renaissance" of literary and cultural production.[8] The emergence of a Chicano consciousness, and the militancy that secured a national audience, created a rich variety of literary expression that was immediately relevant to Chicanos. Texts like Rivera's *Earth,* which I discussed in the previous chapter, ushered in a wave of Chicano voices that expressed the lived experiences of their communities through literature (especially the poetry of social protest),[9] the plastic arts, and other culture industries. It was a propitious time for the creation and institutionalization of Chicano studies. As heir to Lyndon B. Johnson's well-known call for national "affirmative action," Chicanos (like their Black counterparts) and the history of their relationship to the United States were for the first time mandated into the curricula as both subjects and objects of study. With the earlier Civil Rights Act of 1964, Voting Rights Act of 1965, and Johnson's call for an "all-out war on poverty," the country saw major gains in "minorities" entering elite colleges and universities by the early 1970s.

Yet the years of the Reagan-Bush ascendancy between 1980 and 1992 saw a national retreat from the ethical mandates of Johnsonian affirmative action. Not even a decade old, Chicano studies, institutionally housed in various programs or more exceptionally in their own departments, were called on to invigorate their "academic quality" and rigor at the expense of community programing and support and recruitment of Latino students. Luis R. Burrola and José Rivera's analysis of Chicano studies programs notes how by the early 1980s these programs were seen as insufficiently professionalized and lacking methodological sophistication.[10] It was during this period that the theoretical use value of diversity in the academy increased as the actual entry of diverse student bodies into the academy decreased. Apropos of this disparity between theoretical and actual inclusion of diverse student bodies, Lisa Lowe has noted,

> Exploiting the notion of "multiculturalism," the university can refer to the study of ethnic cultures in its claim to be an institution to which all

racial and ethnic minority groups have equal access and in which all are represented, while masking the degree to which the larger institution still fails to address the needs of populations of color. For example, though many universities have begun to reappraise their curricula in the humanities, adding texts by non-Western or female authors to their Western civilization courses, there are fewer Black students attending college today than in 1975.[11]

For Lowe, academic "multiculturalism" became a safe—if not altogether de-politicized—proxy for the very real inclusion that communities of color craved. Not surprisingly, as public education subsidies diminished in measure with the rise in corporate tax breaks, universities began to demand professionalization and "real world" knowledge for students. In both public and private universities the scarcity of resources threatened the least protected academic units, and programs and departments that housed endangered-knowledge projects (Latino and Chicano studies, African and African American studies, feminist and gender studies) were the first to suffer.

It was during this period that it became necessary to "theorize" Latino literary and cultural studies to justify and legitimate their disciplinary objects of study. "Justification" for a founding paradigm gained currency in the academy at a time when the country was experiencing the first major assaults against affirmative action during the so-called Culture Wars.[12] With the institutionalization of Chicano literary studies in the West and Latino literary studies in the East, there came the need to found and explicate the theoretical basis and justification for a field of inquiry that seemingly lacked the methodological apparatus to understand its modes of production and diffusion, silences, and apparent lack of temporal contiguity. If a Chicano and, more broadly, Latino presence existed in the United States before the Latino identity projects of the 1960s, then how to explain the apparent absence of cultural and textual foremothers and forefathers? The answer to this question would find expression in a beautifully written—but deeply problematic—essay by one of the premier scholars of Chicano and Latino literatures, Juan Bruce-Novoa's "Naufragios en los mares de la significación: De *La Relación* de Cabeza de Vaca a la literatura chicana" ("Shipwrecked in the Seas of Signification: Cabeza de Vaca's *Relación* and Chicano Literature").[13]

In this foundational essay Bruce-Novoa boldly asserted that Cabeza de Vaca's *Castaways* founds Chicano literature, thereby mining anew the investment begun by Leal and Padilla in a genealogy of Chicano writing as the necessary strategic starting point for its inclusion in American litera-ture, as a decidedly American object of study: "those of us who toil in the malleable field of Chicano criticism have utilized Leal's position to our ad-vantage because it provides us with a historical base for what many con-sider to be a phenomenon too recent to be taken seriously at the level of national literature, or even established regional literatures" (3). He goes on to state that "one of the strategies that literary criticism incorporates to privilege certain canons is the theory of genealogical origins—the tracing of literary heritages to a remote antiquarian lineage" (ibid.). Bruce-Novoa's strategic rereading of *Castaways* posits not only that it is one of the found-ing texts of Chicano writing but also that the narrative of Cabeza de Vaca's plight is analogous to Chicano writing in that it is an interlinguistic and multicultural text.

For Bruce-Novoa, the similarities between Cabeza de Vaca's plight and Chicano struggles in the United States make Cabeza de Vaca a de facto Chi-cano engaged in multicultural struggle:

> Those initiated into Chicano culture will now recognize the similarity with ANCdV [Alvar Núñez Cabeza de Vaca]. In fact, the similarities are astounding: leaving a native land in search of riches in a territory mostly unknown except for the hyperbolic legends surrounding it; the disillusionment felt upon facing the harsh and humiliating truth of the reality encountered; the loss of original cultural context in exchange for a new one which is hostile and alienating, capable of reducing the immigrant to slavery. Through a slow apprenticeship, great hardships, and mimesis, immigrants begin to improve their social position. . . . frequently immigrants must take jobs the local citizens do not care to engage in because they are difficult, dangerous, or even illegal. Often-times the jobs require the workers to travel from one place to another. . . . In addition immigrants are forced to learn a new language. . . . In moments of crisis the immigrants seek refuge in the memories of their native land. (20–21)

In this rendering of the Chicano body, the subject in question is anach-ronistically posited as a "transnational" and aligns the immigrant—never understood as a migrant for Bruce-Novoa—with the plight of most any transnational. Such a dilution of Chicano specificity with what can be understood to be the transnational flow of people and capital makes the connections between Cabeza de Vaca and Chicanos technically true but suspect by virtue of the applicability of these experiences to most any immigrant group.

Not surprisingly, other critics were not as accommodating or convinced by this genealogical project, however mediated and envisioned by Bruce-Novoa for the sake of strategic *conveniencia*. Héctor Calderón and José David Saldívar, for example, were quick to note that a "Spanish chronicler of the area which was later to form the northern regions of the viceroyalty of New Spain, like Cabeza de Vaca or Coronado writing in the sixteenth century, regardless of whatever sympathies he may have had for Native Americans, is not a Chicano but a Spaniard."[14] Their assertion raises the logical question: What does a sixteenth-century Spaniard have to do with Chicano writing? The position of these critics, however, does not take into account the project's implicit formulation: that subject integrity and identity are as malleable as the discourses that create them. By understanding subject formation as an effect of power, a genealogical reading of *Castaways* questions national belonging and its relationship to writing insofar as the "stable subject of discourse" is an effect of writing and the institutions that legitimate "literature" as a privileged purveyor of culture. For Bruce-Novoa, Cabeza de Vaca's "alterity" is the enabling precondition for agency in the face of subjection:

> In the final analysis, our essence is in the legacy of an alterity in search of its own center from which we can relate all under a stable and vital order without forgetting that at any moment our ship can sink, leaving us once again shipwrecked in the seas of signification. In that sense *we represent the true American dream.* That is to say, the most disturbing thing about Alvar Núñez Cabeza de Vaca and his descendents is that they reveal in their alterity the inherent instability of any identity system, and they make out of it a virtue and a source of great pride. ("Shipwrecked," 22, my emphasis)

That in "[t]he final analysis" Chicanos for Bruce-Novoa represent the "true American dream" remains highly problematic for many reasons, not least that he confounds ontology—Chicanos' purported essence, if such a thing could ever exist outside of discourse—with epistemology—how we know what we know about the discursive systems that attempt to define the Chicano subject. Even more challenging in this assertion is the blind spot that accords Chicanos a "true" identity: claiming that Chicanos represent the "true American dream" reinscribes the very naming strategies and assertions of difference that make "the American dream" a nightmare to scores of nationals considered to be "illegal." The interpellation "you are a true Chicano" is as dangerous as "you are not a true American." Though I will say more about this later, for the moment I will pause to resituate the argument from the vantage point of the critical mediation between the genealogical critics (Bruce-Novoa's elaboration of Leal et al.) and the constructivist position held by Calderón and Saldívar; whereas the former purports that lines of origin determine the subject's identity, the latter purports that meaning is contextual and therefore historically determined.

Francisco Lomelí attempts to come to terms with these two conflicting positions. For Lomelí, "Cabeza de Vaca feels himself oscillating between two worlds after his extensive contact with various Indian groups, as if he were a transformed person, no longer only Spanish."[15] He distinguishes Bruce-Novoa's and Leal's genealogical projects:

> To Juan Bruce-Novoa, this explorer intimates what a third culture would become, and by extension, what a Chicano would be. To Luis Leal (1973), the psychological impact had less importance within the extant socio-historical forces as defined by the geopolitical interplay between Mexico and Anglo America. Instead, regionality and consciousness of race played primary roles in determining Chicano literary history. Therefore, the only requirement for a work to be considered under this rubric was for it to be written by a person of Mexican descent, no matter how remote or recent. ("Po(l)etics," 227–28)

Lomelí asks a crucial question that I will later address in my analysis of *Castaways*: "In the process of erecting demarcations and parameters, one pivotal concern has emerged: How to grapple with the politics and poetics of reconstructing and/or appropriating a literary past. In doing so, is there in fact a danger of historical imperialism by adopting a work or author that supposedly pertained to another set tradition, or to no tradition at all?" (228). Yet despite his own caveat, Lomelí concludes that rereading this literary past is essential: "Reclaiming it is not only viable, but necessary, even if it involves appropriating it," since "it seems obvious that Chicanos did not spring up like mushrooms in the 1960s nor from the ashes of nothingness, by extension of that logic neither have their writings" (230–31). He points out that "there is ample evidence of literature produced by peoples of Mexican descent even before the term Chicano—or for that matter, Mexican American—existed." He concludes that "[a]ppropriation, consequently, becomes an indispensable methodology of revisionism and a medium for reconstructing origins, antecedents and background, all within a framework focusing on regional expression in the shadows of memory" (231).[16] Lomelí's contribution to the debate has affirmed Leal and Bruce-Novoa's position. The essay was written for the important Recovering the United States Hispanic Literary Heritage Project (RUSHLH), and Lomelí's conclusions have had clear repercussions insofar as they have legitimated the genealogical search for origins "in the shadows of memories." Just whose versions of American cultural "memories" are to be salvaged, reconfigured, or (re-)created from the "shadows" remains to be seen. However, it appears that Lomelí's position has attained de facto legitimacy in Latino literary studies. *The Latino Reader: An American Literary Tradition from 1542 to the Present* (1997), which on its dust jacket purports to be "the first anthology to present the full history of this important *American literary tradition*" (my emphasis), situates the beginnings of Latino literature precisely with *Castaways.*[17] In the editors' "Introduction: An American Literary Tradition," Harold Augenbraum and Margarita Fernández Olmos state that

one can say that Latinos are linked, directly or indirectly, to their precursors, the early Hispanic explorers in the southeastern and southwestern United States, in having to chart a course through a treacherous and often bewildering landscape. For contemporary Latino authors, however, the frontier is the literary culture of the United States, where they have been struggling to gain their rightful place. (xi)

It would appear that the "rightful place" Augenbraum and Fernández Olmos refer to is both literal and metaphorical, as it implies a literal place (America) as well as a cognitive space (identity) from which to speak in the context of American literature as Latinos and Americans at once. They assert that Cabeza de Vaca serves an "important symbolic function," since

Cabeza de Vaca's metamorphosis into a being neither European nor Indian, a cultural hybrid created by the American experience, converts the explorer into a symbolic precursor of the Chicano/a. Not entirely identified with either Mexican or Anglo society, the Chicano/a, like Cabeza de Vaca, undergoes a cultural adaptation and transformation that makes him or her the ideal New World American. S/he can change her/himself to fit the situation and celebrate that change—in other words, s/he can make a virtue of necessity. (xv)

For Augenbraum and Fernández Olmos, the displacement of Latinos from the American literary culture and landscape necessarily involves remembering that they came from the place now called America. However, I am troubled by their notion that "the Chicano/a, like Cabeza de Vaca, undergoes a cultural adaptation and transformation that makes him or her the ideal New World American." First, the assertion assumes that the becoming an "American" is not reciprocal but rather a process of accommodating to majoritarian ideology, hardly an "ideal" alternative in the face of cultural erasure and national subjection. Second, the argument comes dangerously close to assimilationist paradigms that do not question whether it is plausible, or even possible, for individuals to assimilate and "make a virtue of necessity." Quite simply, irrespective of "necessity," some bodies cannot assimilate by virtue of their corporeal markers of difference. Augenbraum and Fernández Olmos simply echo what Bruce-Novoa considers Cabeza de Vaca's greatest asset: the "alterity . . . that permits [Cabeza de Vaca] to be the intermediary between two exclusive codes" ("Shipwrecked," 13).

Bruce-Novoa's sacking of the literary-historiographical archive and Augenbraum and Fernández Olmos's acceptance of the critical legacy of *Castaways*[18] are significant because they established the parameters from which to legitimate a literary project at a moment when Latinos were facing a direct assault in and outside the academy. By the anthology's publication in 1997, the gains of the early 1970s were eroding as profound attacks on Latinos were being carried out in the courts of law and public opinion. The crisis surrounding the Latino body and its future in the United States was related to initiatives attempting to limit Latino political power by attacking the most vulnerable: immigrants. These initiatives gained a stronghold of support first in California and later throughout the country with legal assaults against Latino health care, education, and the conditions of possibility for entry into civic life through education. The most notable in the battleground state of California consisted of Proposition 187 (introduced in 1994 to deny medical and public services to undocumented immigrants), Proposition 209 (referendum passed in 1996 outlawing "preferential" treatment based on race, color, ethnicity, or national origin), and Proposition 227 (introduced in 1998 to eliminate bilingual education), to name a few of the more prominent.

The cultural climate of crisis for Latinos, where hiding or passing (neither possible in most cases nor ethically desirable) seemed the only alternative for the undocumented, was occurring in the 1990s precisely when the curriculum was diversifying to reflect the historical realities of the populations the country had mined as work fodder but barred from civic life through educational roadblocks. While Chicano and Latino studies programs were busy legitimating their fields and areas of inquiry, the work the Latino community craved was largely in the hands of those with the fewest resources: community advocates and Latino groups and organizations.[19] At a time when diversity was gaining a stronghold in the academy and the nuances of race, ethnicity, and language were complicating the National Symbolic's ability to explain itself as a cohesive national entity, assaults on Latinos and other people of color assured the majority culture that things would continue to be black and white, as they had always been assumed to be.

Indeed, texts like *Castaways* were embraced by many Chicano and Latino scholars because they offered "proof" to students and readers that Latinos were not a recent phenomenon in the United States, even though new waves of Latino immigration made it appear so. In the process, texts like *Castaways* could assure Latino students that they too could be embraced by the state much the same was as Cabeza de Vaca had been assimilated into the emerging Latino literature canon, which—purportedly—was the American literature canon. As Lisa Lowe has noted, the institutionalization of ethnic studies and literature "provides a material base within the university for transformative critique," but "any field or curriculum that establishes orthodox objects and methods submits in part to the demands of the university and its educative function of socializing subjects into the state" (*Immigrant Acts,* 40). Lowe's caveat is instructive. The genealogical investment in Cabeza de Vaca, for example, as a Latino forefather disengaged the academy from the ethical dimension of representing the "Other." Safe from their writing present, these critics could refer to colonial texts that made the theoretical inclusion of Latinos in the American literature canon plausible, at the expense of eliding the practical dirty work that cultural politics demands of committed cultural producers. This is not to suggest that academicians working with endangered-knowledge projects or their communities have to assume roles they are unwilling or unable to fulfill. It does mean that, when engaged with such projects, we need a clear understanding of what is at stake and who stands to benefit from disseminating the complex stories endangered-knowledge projects are literally dying to tell.

As I have already noted, Cabeza de Vaca's purported "metamorphosis" and ability to serve as an intermediary between two cultures—which presumably enabled him to "pass" for an Amerindian—foregrounds problematic identity practices that posit assimilation as a paradigmatic solution to subaltern cultural displacements. Notable is the multicultural celebration of Cabeza de Vaca's ability as an outsider in the New World to become an "other" body, in and through discourse, by virtue of the tales he weaves to his explicit reader (Charles V) about what led Amerindians to believe that he was a trader, shaman, leader, demiurge.

In what follows I present a cautionary reading of Cabeza de Vaca's *Castaways* in order to create a dialogue between those critics who have invested heavily in reading the text as a foundational precursor of Latino writing and those who do not see the dividends of such an investment. My reading analyzes the discursive function of hunger and bodily integrity in *Castaways* as a trope for the strategic incorporation (assimilation) and eventual digestion (consumption) of Amerindian culture through the printed word. In so doing, I question *Castaways*'s function as a foundational text in Latino studies, especially as it relates to the genealogical critics' investment in such an enterprise. I do this in order to foreground an ethics of reading that would help us understand how serving as cultural brokers of Cabeza de Vaca's form of multiculturalism requires reproducing the very strategies of political evasion we presumably seek to undermine. In the spirit of such a critique, it behooves me to provide a close reading of the celebrated strategies of passing that made Cabeza de Vaca such an appealing and astute reader of the cultural displacements he endured, strategies that can tell us something about both the promise and limits of cultural coexistence.

Castaways's Critical Legacy: The Body in the Text, the Text on the Body

Latin Americanist readings of *Castaways* have traditionally focused on the text's "demystification" of Spain's colonization of the New World by means of Cabeza de Vaca's purported defense of the Amerindians. This image of a benevolent Cabeza de Vaca has until very recently held among critics who subscribe to Beatriz Pastor Bodmer's influential reading of *Castaways* in her *Discursos narrativos de la conquista* (first published in 1983 and translated in 1992 as *The Armature of Conquest: Spanish Accounts of the Discovery of America, 1492–1589*):

> Alvar Núñez's new perception of his own identity, expressed in the *Naufragios* by the metamorphoses he experiences as a conquistador-narrator during his long journey, goes hand in hand with a radical change in his

view of reality. This is especially true in relation to the most important component of American reality: the natives.[20]

For Pastor Bodmer, this process of "metamorphosis" goes "hand in hand with a radical change in his view of reality" occasioned by the element of reality that leads Cabeza de Vaca to transform his own identity: the Amerindian subject. This metamorphosis leads Pastor Bodmer to conclude that his position is an example of a pro-Amerindian rhetoric that "parallels the critical thinking of Las Casas," who acerbically critiqued the colonization of the Americas and the abuse it wreaked upon the native inhabitants (ibid., 144).

Rolena Adorno has further reinforced the reading of Cabeza de Vaca as a Lascasian figure extraordinaire.[21] She goes as far as to suggest that his treatment of the Amerindians had a direct effect on Spanish imperial policy, since he "advocated peaceful conversion of the natives and demonstrated that good treatment of the Indians produced results that served both the well-being of native populations and the economic interest of the Spaniards" ("Discursive Encounter," 220). This celebratory image, however, reinforces the very imperial strategies of domination that *Castaways* purportedly "demystifies" by exculpating an expansionist agenda rather than questioning its tropes of control, domination, and eventual colonial rule.

José Rabasa offers a more measured reading that takes into account how the text performs colonial maneuvers.[22] Like Pastor Bodmer and Adorno, he notes that, at the very least, "Cabeza de Vaca portrays himself as a benevolent colonial official" (*Writing Violence,* 35). However, Rabasa is quick to caution that by exalting Cabeza de Vaca we run the risk of "reiterat[ing] the belief in the natural subordination of Native Americans to Spanish rule" (ibid.). He goes on to assert that benevolent readings of Cabeza de Vaca "manage to critique imperialism while retaining a redeemable view of Spanish colonialism in exceptional individuals" and asks, "Have we been seduced by Cabeza de Vaca into an uncritical participation in and reproduction of the culture of conquest?" (ibid.).

Rabasa's reading is in consort with Tzvetan Todorov's consideration in *The Conquest of America: The Question of the Other* that Cabeza de Vaca's "position is quite close to that of Las Casas."[23] However, whereas Todorov's analysis suggests that Cabeza de Vaca's accommodation and assimilation are part of the ecumenical subject's superiority, Rabasa critiques this assumption as an example of hermeneutic colonialism. For Rabasa, Cabeza de Vaca's exaltation of his competencies as a reader of Amerindian cultures restores to his explicit reader a sense of Spanish superiority through *ingenio*: his ability to assimilate to his surroundings as a precondition for future incursion into the lands he charts. As Rabasa makes clear, Cabeza de Vaca's claims for the accuracy of his incursions have been in question ever since Gonzalo Fernández de Oviedo y Valdés, whose *Sumario de la historia general y natural de las Indias* (1526)[24] questions Cabeza de Vaca's New World experiences as related in *Castaways*. Rabasa's critical caution makes patent the extent to which *Castaways* must be held up to critical scrutiny by suggesting that the semblance of verisimilitude and humane transformation magisterially performed in *Castaways* does not amount to a discursive truth outside the text.

In an important critique that refutes Pastor Bodmer's thesis about the text's demystification of Spanish imperial ideology, Juan Francisco Maura cautions that Cabeza de Vaca's intentions were not philanthropic or benevolent, much less anti-imperial.[25] Maura's research in the Archivo Ducal de Medina Sidonia has led him to conclude that Cabeza de Vaca's purported Christian philanthropy is a fiction that bears no relation to his actions. His failed journey left him with nothing but his ability to relate the expertise behind his eight-year ordeal in the New World; his only claim to authority was the memories he packaged and "sold" ("Escalvas españolas," 191). Cabeza de Vaca's account of his travails, then, sought to position him and his knowledge over an inhospitable territory ripe for settlement and imperial exploitation: "I have wanted to tell this [story] because, apart from the fact that all men wish to know the customs and actions of others, those who may at some time have to do with these people should know about their customs and stratagems, which may be of no little use in such cases" (*Castaways*, 83). For Maura, "si su fin era conseguir un favor del monarca, tendría que sazonar su 'relación' con palabras como oro, esmeraldas, así como una detalladísima descripción de la las gentes, tierras y costumbres de las personas con las que se encontró" (if his purpose was to find favor with the monarch he would have to season his "account" with words like gold, emeralds, as well as with a detailed description of the people, lands, and customs of those he encountered) ("Escalvas españolas," 193).

On his return to Spain, Cabeza de Vaca "became connected to a brotherhood of travelers, chroniclers, and officials who exchanged information about America as they made their complicated claims" to land and positions of prestige in the service of Spain (Pupo-Walker, preface to *Castaways*, xx). These strategic associations eventually led Charles V, on March 18, 1540, to grant Cabeza de Vaca the governorship of Río de la Plata, with "the titles of Adelantado, Governor, Captain-General, and Officer of the Peace in those possessions" (ibid., xxi).[26] Spanish expansion in the Río de la Plata area was degenerating at the time. Violent confrontations with Amerindians characterized the governorship of his predecessor, Pedro de Mendoza, and the crown sought a firm hand on the Amerindians. Maura asserts that Cabeza de Vaca's appointment was expressly to "sojuzgar a los indios rebeldes e imponer su autoridad frente a sus compatriotas" (to subjugate rebellious Indians and impose his authority before his countrymen) ("Escalvas españolas," 188) and that he had an iron seal made to brand the bodies of slaves who were to be under his "care" (ibid., 188, 189).

Cabeza de Vaca's literal mark of ownership on the Other's body is significant when we consider that throughout *Castaways* his body is constantly being marked by the Amerindians and the environment they inhabit. His appeal as a proto-Chicano resides precisely in his ability to become an/Other body, to pass as an Other, markings and all. Instead of the traditional colonial rendering of the Amerindian body as an object subjected to Spanish imperial demands, Cabeza de Vaca represents his own body as that of a penitent constantly being subjected and marked by his captors' needs. But just how does Cabeza de Vaca discursively vest his body with meaning? And what paradigms of subjectivity are we advocating when we posit such a seductive self-portrayal that we wish him to be a Chicano "forefather"?

Fashioning Technologies of the Self: Cabeza de Vaca's Body, Becoming

Cabeza de Vaca's tale of shipwreck, wanderings, and misadventures centers on evading the loss of bodily integrity and security in the absence of "home" and all that is familiar. The theme partakes of a long tradition of the wanderer—from Odysseus to Moses and more recently to texts of (im)migrant displacements, as Bruce-Novoa suggests in his reading of *Castaways*—where a protagonist fights many odds in order to return home.[27] This metaphorical and literal homeward quest is essential for Cabeza de Vaca, since it will signal the restoration of order, unity, and status, the opposite of his naked ruminations through the American environment.[28] His eventual return to Spain and the longed for accouterments of monarchical favor mean that he will no longer be a foreigner, slave, or guest at the mercy of the host's will. Cabeza de Vaca's narrative imbues his body with meaning by relating what his body endured in America. His story conjures his absent body for his explicit reader: what his eyes have seen, what his body has ingested, what his hands have touched, what his heart has felt—the mortifications of a penitent in the service of his lord, the king of Spain.

Unlike most other New World eyewitness accounts of conquest and exploration, Cabeza de Vaca's recounts not how many bodies he subjected to imperial rule but how his own body was altered and marked by his experience. His failure, and that of the men he set sail with, to "conquer and govern the provinces that lie between the river of Las Palmas and the tip of Florida" puts him in a precarious place where he must refashion his loss as a triumph and vest his testimony with authority (*Castaways*, 5). To this end, Cabeza de Vaca must narrate the survival of an urbody, a superior and resilient body. His corporeality will take center stage as he weaves a narrative of misfortunes reminiscent of biblical suffering and redemption. His body, after all, unlike those of most of his compatriots, will survive and endure like a New World Jesus.[29] The corporeal cost of his survival, however, in the scene of reencounter at the end of *Castaways*, reinforces the extent to which his body has been defamiliarized and resemanticized by his New World experience. I turn to this scene now to retrace its emblematic and reiterative quality, its ability to replay itself throughout *Castaways* as Cabeza de Vaca "passes" through various registers of meaning and identities.

Cabeza de Vaca relates how at the end of his eight-year quest he finally saw "traces of Christians," and realizing "that we were so close to them, we offered many thanks to God Our Lord for being pleased to rescue us from so sad and miserable a captivity" (*Castaways*, 110).[30] He appealed to his "stronger and younger" companions to go ahead and search for the Spaniards, but they refused, "excusing themselves on the grounds of exhaustion and toil" (ibid.). He then walked ten leagues in a day, with Estebancio "the black" and eleven Indians, in search of the Christians. The eventual meeting is fraught with corporeal misreadings occasioned by his "marked" body. The Spanish "were thunderstruck to see me so strangely dressed and in the company of Indians. They went on staring at me for a long space of time, so astonished that they could neither speak to me nor manage to ask me anything" (ibid.).

Cabeza de Vaca's corporeal markers of difference, his dress and sun-bronzed dark skin,[31] inhibit the Spaniards' ability to properly read his body. The Spaniards have to recover from their "astonishment" in order to "speak" to their fellow Christian, who looks like the "Indians" with whom he has arrived. The Spaniards must recognize familiar linguistic utterances that mark Cabeza de Vaca as a fellow Christian, who is also marked as an

"Indian" by his appearance and dress. The binary Christian/Indian is resemanticized, and the reencounter serves as the framing scene of the text, since it plays out for the last time the reiterative conflict around Cabeza de Vacas becoming an "Other" so convincingly that he risks losing any stable reference marker to his Spanish identity. Cabeza de Vaca's identity paradox is made manifest in this scene: he could not have survived without successfully "passing" as an Other, disidentifying as a Spaniard.

The process of disidentification with the signifiers of his subject position as a Spaniard begins at the onset of his estrangement from Spanish authority at the start of his narrative. After unsuccessfully attempting to retrieve fellow Spaniards whom the Amerindians had accosted, Governor Pánfilo de Narváez decides to separate the makeshift barges they had been using on the Mississippi in the hope of finding their way back to Cuba or, at least, reaching land. Narváez orders that each barge attempt to reach land by whatever means necessary and begins to row away from Cabeza de Vaca's barge. Narváez's barge had the "healthiest and strongest" men, and Cabeza de Vaca and the men in his barge "could not follow or keep up":

> When I saw this I asked him to give me a line from his boat to help me follow him, and he answered me that if they themselves reached land that night, it was as much as they could do. I told him that in view of the little chance we had to follow him and do what he ordered, he had better tell me what his orders to me were. He answered that this was no time for some to give orders to others, that each must do what seemed best to do him to save his life, and that was what he intended to do. (37)

The tow-line Cabeza de Vaca hopes will unite his barge with that of the "healthiest and strongest" men is a link that cannot hold, for the governor's leadership collapses under what "each must do" to save his life. Cabeza de Vaca's call for unity in adversity casts a heroic aura over his actions. After all, it is his barge that will reach land and survive the ensuing travails, while Narváez and the men on his barge disappear as quickly as the leadership that brought them there.

With no alternative but to establish an identity apart from the hierarchical order under Narváez, Cabeza de Vaca moves important degrees away from his role as "treasurer and chief officer of justice" (5) and into a self-constituting position, a self that he must discursively fashion to survive. Distinguishing himself from Narváez's cowardice and lack of leadership establishes the narrative pretext for fashioning the hero he must become under the circumstances. This becoming will entail a literal transformation by the elements that will mar his body and the hunger that will drive his search for satiation. Cabeza de Vaca's hunger is both a literal quest for food and a metaphorical search for home, conceived as both a place to be (Spain) and a condition of being (Spanish subject).

His metaphorical hunger for home is constantly threatened by his literal hunger for food. Nevertheless, his wanderings are clearly mediated by the possibility of financial gain and of joining the explorers who return home with more than stories of conquest and colonization. Their initial departure under the orders of Charles V "to conquer and govern the provinces that lie between the river of Las Palmas and the tip of Florida" is fraught with bad omens (5). After leaving the port of Sanlúcar de Barrameda (in Santo Domingo), the fleet of five ships and approximately six hundred men arrive in Cabo de Santa Cruz (Cuba) for supplies. Here they lose two ships, sixty men, and twenty horses after a storm (9). The weather keeps them from leaving Cuba until a storm finally drives the ships off the coast and onto the coast of Florida "into the mouth of a bay" (Tampa Bay). After several forays from the beach, they encounter Amerindians and "small amounts of gold" that they understand from "signs" is to be found in abundance further inland. This incursion into the thick of American territory manifests the extent to which returning home without booty becomes too daunting for Cabeza de Vaca and his men:

> there were many among us who, besides great fatigue and hunger, had sores on their backs from carrying their weapons in addition to the other things they had to carry. But when we saw that we had arrived at the place we desired, and where they had told us there was such abundance of gold, it seemed to us that a large part of our weariness and hunger had been lifted from us. (20)

Still optimistic about finding gold, the crew are taken farther inland. Despite their weariness and hunger, their imperially mandated goal of finding gold is presented as the driving force behind their actions. Curiously, it never occurs to Cabeza de Vaca that even if they were to find gold, they would be hard-pressed to transport it, or even find their way back, given that they were both lost and shipless. This scene is discursively significant for it sets up from the onset the narrative ex culpa for going farther into the deep recesses of uncharted American territory. It is told as if to suggest to his explicit reader that he and his men were only following the prerogatives of the mission, thereby displacing any direct responsibility for getting lost for the ensuing eight years.

Once the responsibility is displaced, the decision to penetrate the Florida jungle becomes mediated by both the body's centrality to the fruition of the mission and its relationship to the American environment. The mission per se loses importance in measure with the growing significance of the body as a tool for completing it: the recognition that not just any body is capable of meeting the exigencies displaces the mission proper onto the body proper. From this point onward, Cabeza de Vaca will relate how his body's survival is a blueprint for a specific class of Spanish subject: the fortune-seeking adventurer in search of upward mobility in the ranks of empire who can now depend on his body as a commodity. He will accomplish this through fashioning a malleable body, in and through writing, that identifies in significant ways with the American territory and its inhabitants while remaining loyal to the prerogatives of Spanish colonization.

"Hunger Never Gave Me a Chance to Choose": Food, Identity Negotiations, and Going Native

In Western culture, food is both central to identity negotiations and a symbol for assimilation. Maggie Kilgour notes that from Greek antiquity onward, "to eat the food of others is to become one with them, and so to be alienated from one's true home and identity; so, too, according to Augustine, the Israelites lost their identity with God when they 'had exchanged the glory of the imperishable God for idols and all kinds of make-believe, for representations of perishable man, and of bird and beast and reptile, in fact, for that Egyptian food for which Esau lost his birthright.'"[32] The book of Genesis recounts how forbidden fruit is forbidden knowledge and is the cause of the original fall from grace: to eat is to know, and knowing is fraught with danger. In *Castaways*, the danger of going native by knowing the Other too well (identifying completely with the Other) is mediated by food, one of the central metaphors for cultural interaction in the text.

As Cabeza de Vaca's quest for food continually demonstrates, what he consumes affects both his literal survival and the more nuanced commodity exchanges that ensure his body's integrity through commerce. His hunger also demonstrates that the Spanish autonomy and mastery over the American environment, so prevalent in relations of exploration and conquest, is a myth by stating through ravenous example that his survival depends on the environment and his captors. Indeed, Kilgour has noted, "The need for food exposes the vulnerability of individual identity, enacted at a wider social level in the need for exchanges, communion, and commerce with others, through which the individual is absorbed into a larger corporate body" (*From Communion to Cannibalism*, 6). Cabeza de Vaca's recounting of how he was forced to become a "medicine man," as he penetrates the larger Amerindian body politic that he must interact with in order to survive, makes the association between hunger, food, and commerce clear:

> On that island that I have described they tried to make us into medicine men, without examining us or asking for credentials. . . . The way in which we cured was by making the sign of the cross over them and blowing on them and reciting a Pater Noster and an Ave Maria; and then we prayed as best we could to God Our Lord to give them health and inspire them to give us good treatment. God Our Lord, and His mercy, willed that as soon as we made the sign of the cross over them, all those for whom we prayed told others that they were well and healthy; and because of this they gave us good treatment and went without food themselves in order to give it to us. (*Castaways*, 50)

Cabeza de Vaca's uncredentialed entry into Amerindian culture as a medicine man garners him a reputation that will benefit him in more ways than one. This is but the first of a series of "healings" that metonymically position the Amerindian body in a state of infirmity, in need of "health" and assistance. Furthermore, it creates the narrative fiction of power over these bodies, a power that, he suggests, "God Our Lord, and His mercy, willed." His relation of the events produces an associative effect of privilege by suggesting that, despite his misfortune and suffering, "God Our Lord" favors his servant enough to bring about these healings. The Christians in turn receive the favor of the Amerindians in the form of both hospitable treatment and food. Indeed, the Amerindians go without food themselves in order to feed the Christian healers since they are so successful.

Once his reputation is established, Cabeza de Vaca's "trade" as a medicine man allows him easier access and coexistence with other Amerindian communities as well: "the people offered us many prickly pears, for they had heard of us, and how we cured folk" (66). God's will, then, is posited as that which keeps Cabeza de Vaca alive. His livelihood is related to the success facilitated by divine intervention: "The Indians told me that I should go and heal them, for they loved me and remembered that I had cured them during the time of nut gathering and that they had given us nuts and hides in return" (72). The association he establishes between being favored by God and success as a healer could not be more evident than in his relation of the raising of the Amerindian Lazarus figure:

> when I came near to their settlements I saw a sick man whom we were going to heal, who was dead, for many people were around him weeping and his house had been pulled down, which is a sign that its owner has died. And when I got there I found the Indian with his eyes rolled up and without any pulse and with all signs of being dead, as it seemed to me, and Dorantes said the same. I took off a reed mat with which he was covered, and as best I could implored Our Lord to be pleased to give health to that man and all others who had need of it.
>
> And after I had made the sign of the cross and blown on him many times, they brought me his bow and gave it to me, and a bag of crushed prickly pears, and took me to heal many others. . . . And that night they returned to their homes and said that the man who was dead and whom I had healed had stood up in their presence entirely well and had walked and eaten and spoken with them, and that all those whom I cured were healthy and very happy . . . and in all the land no one talked of anything else. (72)

The biblical narrative of Lazarus of Bethany relates how, because of his resurrection of Lazarus, Jesus's authority threatened to displace the Pharisees' control over the Jews who were coming to believe in Him:

> He cried with a loud voice, "Lazarus, come forth!" . . . Then many of the Jews who had come to Mary, and had seen the things Jesus did, believed in Him. But some of them went away to the Pharisees and told them the things Jesus did. Then the chief priests and the Pharisees gathered a council and said, "What shall we do? For this man works many signs. If we let him alone like this, everyone will believe in Him, and the Romans will come and take away both our place and nation." (John 11:43–48)

The point of contact between the biblical story and its appearance in *Castaways* is the implicit association Cabeza de Vaca makes between himself and Jesus. Pupo-Walker states that "[w]ith this chapter, Cabeza de

Vaca's authority as narrator and leader becomes more pronounced" (*Castaways*, 143n. 40). The verisimilitude of Cabeza de Vaca's miraculous raising of the Amerindian is achieved by stating, in no uncertain terms, that "in all the land no one talked of anything else." Cabeza de Vaca's "miracle" legitimates his position among the Amerindians to his explicit reader by demonstrating how they came to believe in him and his abilities. Furthermore, in the commerce economy of survival, he suggests that as a healer he is able to eat and survive by exploiting the role he says he has been thrust into, and by being a better "medicine man" than the Amerindians themselves. After the resurrection of the Amerindian, after all, he is rewarded with both the Amerindian's "bow . . . and a bag of crushed prickly pears."

It is worth noting that if food is the reward for the healings that assure Cabeza de Vaca's survival, then it is not surprising that "prickly pears"[33]—so essential to his subsistence—are the one alimentary constant he consistently alludes to. He is a connoisseur of these fruits, which he describes as being "the size of an egg, . . . red and black" and of "very good taste" (56). They become a metaphor of incorporation for the American natural environment and the identity negotiations that assure his transition from slave to healer in his corporeal economy of survival:

> During the whole time we were eating prickly pears we were thirsty, and to relieve this we drank their juice and squeezed it into a hollow that we made in the ground, and when it was full we drank to our hearts' content. The juice is sweet and the color of syrup; the Indians do this because they have no other vessels. There are many kinds of prickly pears and some among them are very good, though all of them seemed good to me and *hunger never gave me a chance to choose* among them or to give the least consideration to which were best. (65, my emphasis)

Despite Cabeza de Vaca's constant hunger, he can distinguish the "kinds of prickly pears" that "are very good" from those he has to ingest for basic subsistence. He takes pleasure in relating the taste ("sweet") and color ("of syrup") of their juice insofar as they serve him not only as food and drink but also as satisfaction to his palate. His description of the prickly pears bears a direct relation to his faith as constructed discursively by echoing the covenant that the Gospel of John promises for those who have faith in God's Word: "He who comes to me shall never hunger, and he who believes in me shall never thirst" (John 6:35). The prickly pears become a metaphor for Cabeza de Vaca's identity negotiations as a Christian subjected to the American environment he must identify with. As he delivers his relation to the king of Spain, he is also recounting how his enterprise is sanctioned by God, despite the limitations of lesser men like Narváez. As a distinctly American food, the prickly pear becomes a symbol for "going native" through the incorporation of an Other's foodstuff: "hunger never gave me a chance to choose" ultimately signals how the need for subsistence determines social relations and how "guests" must assimilate if they are to survive the "host" environment.

If going native means identifying in important ways with the environment and the people who inhabit it by relinquishing the markers of the Spaniard, then the inverse process of disidentification with the people and their surroundings is underscored by the other "foreigner," Mala Cosa, "Bad Thing." Pupo-Walker has noted that "Cabeza de Vaca's description of this figure resembles other representations of the Devil by many chroniclers of the Indies" (*Castaways*, 143n. 41). Yet, curiously enough, the similarities between the devilish Bad Thing and the penitent Cabeza de Vaca are striking. They are both "outsiders," "medicine men," who interact with the Cutalchiche Amerindians enough to inspire awe, but through very different means:

These and other Indians told us a very strange thing . . . that there was in that land a man whom they called Bad Thing, and that he was small in stature and had a beard, though they could never see his face clearly; and that when he came to the house where they were their hair stood on end and they trembled . . . and then that man entered and took whatever he wanted from them and gave them three great slashes in the side with a very sharp flint a handbreadth wide and two long, and that he put his hand into those slashes and pulled out their entrails, and that he cut off a piece of intestine a handbreadth wide, more or less, and threw it into the fire; and then he would cut them three times on the arm, the second cut being at the elbow, and then he would dislocate it; and soon after that he would set the arm in its place again and lay his hands on the wounds. (73–74)

Like Cabeza de Vaca, this bearded outsider who arrives from nowhere is capable of healing the Amerindian body. The surgery performed by Bad Thing is narratively suggestive of the desire literally to know the Other, but without a frame of reference the Amerindian subject, like the reader, is left wondering what to make of the encounter. Nonetheless, a contrast between Cabeza de Vaca and Bad Thing may help establish the narrative context from which to situate this scene. Unlike Cabeza de Vaca, Bad Thing intervenes with the Cutalchiches without reciprocity: he heals those he has performed surgery on, but they were not in need of surgery to begin with. Cabeza de Vaca's surgical prowess, however, is posited as a benefit to the Amerindian body since his "patients" are purported to be ill:

> they brought me a man and told me that a long time ago he had been wounded by an arrow in his right shoulder, and he had the point of the arrow over his heart; he said that it gave him great pain, and that he was always ill because of it. I touched him and could feel the point of the arrow and saw that it had pierced the gristly parts of the chest; and with a knife that I had I opened his chest as far as that place and saw the arrow point was wedged in crosswise and extremely hard to remove; I cut again and put the knife-point into the wound and at last removed it with great difficulty.
>
> It was very long and was made of deer bone; using my medicinal skills, I took two stitches, and after I had made them he bled very freely, and I stanched the blood with scrapings from a hide, and when I had removed the arrow point they asked me for it and I gave it to them; and the whole village came to see it, and they sent it farther inland so that the Indians who lived there could see it. . . . And next day I cut the two stitches for the Indian, and he was cured and there was no sign of the wound that I had made, except for something like the line on the palm of a hand; and he said that he felt no pain or any kind of discomfort. (93–94)

This incident, which takes place after he has had considerable practice "healing," refers to the first and only time in *Castaways* that Cabeza de Vaca performs surgery. The afflicted Amerindian body is vested with the language of suffering, a "pain" caused by an arrow too close to the heart that makes the sufferer "ill." This literal mark on the Amerindian body is presented as the outward sign of an inter-Amerindian conflict that *Castaways* remains silent about. Since we do not know the specifics of the injury, we are left to assume that the Amerindian body, lacking name and rank, is a casualty of the tribal wars Cabeza de Vaca refers to occasionally. We do know that the mark of suffering is ultimately a sign of the instability of the Amerindian body politic that Cabeza de Vaca penetrates, infiltrates, and suffuses with meaning: the afflicted Amerindian body is at once deficient (unhealthy) and dependent (submissive) on Cabeza de Vaca's ability to cure. So it is not coincidental that Cabeza de Vaca's one attempt at surgery is so fraught with danger. The danger of losing his authority as a medicine man if he fails, coupled with the danger of operating so near the heart, imbues his reportage with both sentimentality and courage. Not refusing his role as surgeon makes his "success" all the greater. After all, he risks his reputation for an unknown injured man. Perhaps deriving confidence from his prior successes, Cabeza de Vaca narrates how he outperforms Bad Thing's diabolical ability to penetrate the Amerindian body and heal it so there is "no sign of the wound." Whereas Bad Thing's performance demonstrates mastery over the Amerindian body, Cabeza de Vaca's display of surgical competence is posited as an obvious benefit for the community, all the while implicitly pointing to the lack of indigenous competence over their own bodies.

An important epistemological precedent is set here as Cabeza de Vaca demonstrates how, despite his initial enslavement, he has fashioned a social role that invalidates indigenous knowledge by virtue of his superior competence over the Amerindian body. Narratively, this is one of the most important anecdotes in the text. By relating it, he creates an identity that relies on the emerging self-sufficient subject. In his case, this is the explorer who can aspire to monarchical favor even when returning home empty-handed except for his knowledge of the environment and people he has come in contact with. Through writing, that is, *Castaways* the text, he can authorize both his competency and his subjectivity through the fiction of absolute mastery over the Amerindian body. The removed deer bone becomes an artifact that points to his artifice; an artifact-symbol of his superior skill as well as a referent of his prowess that the Amerindians sent "farther inland so that the Indians who lived there could see it."

This visible display of Cabeza de Vaca's competence stands in stark contrast to Bad Thing's cultural incompetence. Bad Thing's ability to know the Other literally through his mastery over the Amerindian body is counterpoised with his inability to understand discursively the protocols of interaction with the Other. The Cutalchiches inform Cabeza de Vaca that "they offered [Bad Thing] food," but he "never ate" it (74). Bad Thing's appetite seems to be at odds with his hosts' offerings, and his less than gracious behavior signals his inability to assimilate by refusing identification with Amerindian cultural form (accepting food as accepting the host). By not eating, Bad Thing remains forever an outsider in Cabeza de Vaca's hierarchy of cultural interaction. He assures the Cutalchiches that "if they would believe in God Our Lord and were Christians . . . they would have no fear of him [Bad Thing], nor would he dare to come and do those things to them. . . . as long as we stayed in the land he would not dare to appear in it" (74). Having established trust with the Cutalchiches, he describes how they "rejoiced greatly over this and lost a large part of the fear they had" (ibid.). In relating this scene, he reinforces his mastery over the Cutalchiches by suggesting that his word, like his hands, can appease and heal them.

Cabeza de Vaca's identification with Amerindian food also allows him to distance himself from the anthropophagic savagery of other Spaniards. The degenerated bodily and cultural integrity reflected in the actions of those Spaniards represents the epitome of disorganization. Not surprisingly, the only instances of cannibalism in *Castaways* refer to the men from Narváez's barge, who had made it to land. After seeing an Amerindian "who had barter goods," Cabeza de Vaca realizes that these are from other Christians. He relates how "upon seeing this I sent two Christians with two Indians to show those people to them. . . . They too were coming to look for us because the Indians who were there told them about us; and these were captains Andrés Dorantes and Alonso Castillo with all the men from their boat" (44). After reuniting, they attempt to repair a barge, but it sinks, so they resolve to wait out the winter on the island (Galveston Island). But

> there came a time of cold and storms so severe that the Indians could not gather their roots and could make no use of the creeks when they fished . . . and five Christians who were encamped on the beach came to such straits that they ate one another until only one was left, who survived because there was no one left to eat him. . . . The Indians were so indignant about this, and there was so much outrage among them, that undoubtedly if they had seen this when it began to happen they would have killed the men. (46)

The Amerindians are clearly in the same dire straits, but it is the Christians who are posited as savages.

Peter Hulme, referring to representations of Amerindians by Europeans, called cannibalism "the mark of unregenerate savagery. . . . Cannibalism is the special, perhaps even defining, feature of the discourse of colonialism."[34] Traditional colonial analysis of cannibalism as a metaphor for savagery cannot account for its appearance and reversal of roles in *Castaways*.

A traditional reading might analyze how colonial discourse attempts to subdue and subsume the Other for the Other's own good and to lay bare the functions and designation of "cannibal" as an imperial strategy to dominate the Other. In *Castaways*, however, I would suggest that the inversal of the role comes about as another example of Cabeza de Vaca's disidentification from the Spanish authority that was responsible for the plight the Spaniards found themselves in. Reduced to savages, these Christians are disdained by the Amerindians, who cannot conceive of such a practice. Like Bad Thing, the Christian cannibals are posited as incompetent readers of the cultural menu before them. They incorporate the wrong substance into their bodies rather than identify with the possibilities for survival offered by the "barter" system that brought news of those very Christians to Cabeza de Vaca in the first place, as well as the possibility of proper satiation from hunger through commerce. Falling under the sign of Saturn, the Roman god of harvests who devoured his own kin so they would not supplant him, the Christian cannibals feast on each other in a figurative attempt to keep the American environment outside themselves, in the hope of maintaining their subject integrity.

The classic distinction between "inside" and "outside" becomes literalized by the Christian cannibals to the degree that maintaining their subject integrity, by keeping all that is "foreign" outside, ultimately occasions their death. This point is further reinforced when Cabeza de Vaca relates how he heard the story as it "passed from hand to hand . . . and thus is the means by which the end of all that fleet can be seen and known, and the particular things that happened to each man" (59). The disorganization among the men from the Narváez expedition is exemplified in the (lack of) leadership of Pantoja, "who had become lieutenant," and treated the men

> very badly; and Sotomayor, the brother of Vasco Porcallo, from the island of Cuba, who had come in the fleet as an officer of high rank, was unable to bear it. He rebelled against him and gave him such a blow that Pantoja died of it; and so they gradually died off. And the others dried the flesh of the ones who died, and the last to die was Sotomayor; and Esquivel dried his flesh and, by eating it, survived until the first day of March. (58)

Cabeza de Vaca's relation ("passed from hand to hand") of the Spaniards' hierarchical strife further indemnifies him from complicity with the Narváez expedition; any culpability for the mission's utter failure is the result of the leadership of those loyal to Narváez. Clearly, the Spaniards' autoincorporation and digestion equal survival but degeneration in the eyes of the Amerindians and, one expects, in those of the explicit reader. What I have called Cabeza de Vaca's "disidentifications" from the Christian cannibals, Narváez, and the authority of the men loyal to him does not mean that he identifies with the Amerindians to the degree that canonical readings of *Castaways* would suggest (Pastor Bodmer, Adorno, Bruce-Novoa, Lomelí, and Augenbaum and Fernández) by positing Cabeza de Vaca as a Lascasian figure. I am in consort with more recent skeptical readings (Rabasa and Maura) that suggest quite the opposite. As I have argued, Cabeza de Vaca's identifications with the Amerindian social and body politic are an epistemological commodity that will serve the interests of empire. His disidentifications involve disassociating himself from some Spaniards, but never from the prerogatives of Spanish conquest and colonization, through a series of performances that allow him to pass as an Amerindian when he needs to. His *ingenio* separates him from the leadership of the Narváez expedition that was so poor at "reading" the American environment and its peoples. He clearly states, "I have wanted to tell this because, apart from the fact that all men wish to know the customs and actions of others, those who may at some time have to do with these people should know about their customs and stratagems, which may be of no little use in such cases" (83).

This statement is in fact a reiteration of the purpose for his narration given in his prologue to Charles V, that "my account could testify to my good will and be of service to Your Majesty. . . . Since the report of it is, I believe, advice of no little use to those who in your name will go conquer those lands and bring them to the knowledge of the true faith and the true lordship and service of Your Majesty" (4). Conquest, land, and faith: in short, Christianity in the service of empire.

In the "Service of Your Majesty": *Castaways* and the Amerindian Body in the Colonial Imaginary of Villagrá

Cabeza de Vaca's knowledge of the Amerindian peoples' "customs and stratagems" during his travails through New Mexico, offered to the king, was in fact valuable in the conquest and colonization of the American Southwest and the literature that charts this process. His text inspired the legend of "the seven cities of Cibola" and served as the historical basis for Gaspar Pérez de Villagrá's 1610 *Historia de la Nueva México* (*History of New*

Mexico), which chronicles the conquest of New Mexico by Juan de Oñate (c. 1550–1625). Oñate's exploits began approximately fifty-six years after the first publication of *Castaways* and were hyperbolically celebrated by Villagrá, his procurador general and an eyewitness to the expedition. Villagrá's *History of New Mexico,* dedicated to King Philip III,[35] is one of the earliest epic poems written in New Spain and "may claim the distinction of being the first published history of any American commonwealth."[36] The text covers the actual establishment of New Mexico by Juan de Oñate from 1598 to 1601, and chronicles the Oñate expedition's incursions through the New Mexican landscape and the attendant clashes with the Amerindians, specifically the Acoma tribe.[37] From the prologue, Villagrá establishes the need to secure the practices of empire through writing, since "[n]o greater misfortune could possibly befall a people than to lack a historian properly to set down their annals" (Espinosa, 35). Writing will entail for Villagrá the preservation of Spanish "cultural memory" as antidote to cultural oblivion, "for history not only brings before us those who are absent, but it resurrects and breathes life itself into those long dead. . . . I take my pen, the first to set down these annals, more in response to that sense of duty I feel than in confidence in my ability" (ibid.).

Villagrá's *History of New Mexico* has been accorded the status of a historical document with the truth claims the designation carries: "it is a literary recreation that not only holds strictly to the historical events and their chronology, but introduces a very bare minimum of fictional material" (Encinias et al., introduction, xx). The assertion, aside from literalizing Villagrá's stated intentions, obviates a series of facts that ignore the historical conditions around the text and the text's supporting suppositions about the Amerindian and Spanish characters that infuse the poem with historical meaning. Texts like Cabeza de Vaca's *Castaways* are accorded a truth-bearing quality that is purportedly distinguishable from those rare moments where "fictional material" is said to be inserted. Indeed, in the editors' introduction to Villagrá's *History of New Mexico,* Encinias, Rodríguez, and Sánchez state that "[i]f one discounts the almost necessary fictionalization of the Acoma world, to which the narrator had little access, *Historia de la Nueva México* interpolates no fictional passages" (xx).

If this is the case, then Villagrá relates a truncated world indeed. Relegating the Acoma to the status of fictional, while purporting to tell the "real" events lived by the Spanish, makes the Acoma peripheral in a history populated by individuals whose "reality" is the only one worth relating, recording, and remembering. Aside from the representational violence enacted on the Amerindian body, the assertion produces through writing a self-constituting Spanish subject whose imperial prerogatives do not have to be justified since the Spanish subject is presumed to be both arbiter and producer of meaning. The additional advantage perpetuated by this position would be that the question of Spanish historicity is forestalled indefinitely: the account of Oñate, and by extension the Spanish historical figures that occupy the poem, are not subjected to inquiry regarding the truth value of their claims. But were not the Acoma Amerindians from New Mexico? Are we to assume that Villagrá's poem is only about the Spanish? A reading of Cabeza de Vaca's "truth claims," perpetuated in and through *Castaways*, will situate these rhetorical questions.

Cabeza de Vaca is immortalized in the third canto of Villagrá's *History of New Mexico* as "the memorable Cabeza de Vaca." In the canto's opening epigraph Villagrá relates "How, by themselves, the Spaniards began the discovery of New Mexico, and how they entered, and who were those who first began and undertook the journey" (Encinias et al., 18). Villagrá's recourse to origins sets the stage for crediting Cabeza de Vaca's importance as forefather of the conquest and colonization of New Mexico, along with the ideology of empire perpetuated in *Castaways*, one that also informed Villagrá's rhetoric in his *History of New Mexico*. The beginning of the third canto also functions as a memorial to *Castaways*'s Spanish founding fathers, who in turn are posited as symbolic figures in Villagrá's *History of New Mexico*, as Cabeza de Vaca's narrative is grafted onto Villagrá's epic. The events in *Castaways*, most notably the healings and the resurrection of the Lazarus figure, are recounted and nuanced in ways that demonstrate just how successful Cabeza de Vaca was in constructing a mythic persona as one favored by God, a persona Villagrá is all too willing to adopt.

Villagrá's poetic voice recounts the more singular events in *Castaways* and the divinely favored lot of these

> *men most singular*
> *In the most fierce and raging storm*
> *Of all their miseries and trials sharp,*
> *Through them the Highest Power chose to work*
> *. . . Among those nations barbarous*
> *Not only healed for them their sick*
> *Their lame, the paralytic, and the blind,*
> *But also gave life to their dead*
> *Merely through blessing and their holy breath*

> *. . . Poultices, treacle, medicine*
> *Which only in the miraculous pharmacy*
> *Of God all-powerful could well be found.* (Ibid., 19)

The effect of privilege bestowed by God on Cabeza de Vaca attains de facto status in Villagrá's *History of New Mexico.* The Amerindians, however, are labeled barbarous, effectively neutralizing the complex identity (dis)identifications that allowed Cabeza de Vaca to survive.

The culminating event of the poem, the battle of Acoma peñol (Acoma Rock) in Canto XXXIV, reinforces the standard markers of indigenous resistance (ferocity, tenacity, and strength) so common in epic accounts of the Spanish New World conquest, Alonso de Ercilla y Zúñiga's *La Araucana* being the best known.[38] The Acoma are represented as formidable opponents, a trope that is of course intended to exalt the Spanish, as the Amerindians ultimately succumb to Spanish imperial authority. As an eyewitness to the battle of Acoma Rock, Villagrá relates how

> *Looking upon us all, they said to us:*
> *soldiers, take note that hanging here*
> *from these strong tree trunks we leave you*
> *Our miserable bodies as spoils*
> *Of the illustrious victory you won.*
> *Over those wretched ones who are*
> *Rotting amid their weltering blood,*
> *The sepulcher they chose since infamous*
> *Fortune chose so to pursue us*
> *With powerful hand and end our days.*
> *You will remain joyful for we now close*
> *The doors of life and take our leave,*
> *And freely leave you our lands.* (301–2)

The Acoma, about to commit suicide lest they have to deal with the shame of the Spaniards' "illustrious victory" or—worse—live subjugated under Spanish rule, speak in unison ("they said") of the mass suicide that will be a public spectacle of Spanish authority, military victory, and superiority. The textual erasure of the Amerindian body from the landscape is posited as part and parcel of conquest and colonization. The Acoma dead bodies hanging from the tree—perhaps America's first "bitter fruit"—will serve as a visual referent of Spanish might. In the process, the Amerindians' dead bodies become a text in which the discourse of subjection to Spanish power is inscribed into the poetic medium, a medium that makes the "truth value" of the event secondary to the possibilities it affords the Spanish subject to display power.

In relating how violence is the attendant quality of conquest, the poetic persona partakes in what Rabasa has called "the aesthetics of colonial violence" (*Writing Violence,* 138). Completing the circle he began with his prologue, Villagrá closes the final canto (XXXIV) with an allusion to both sword and pen as the accompaniment of empire:

> *And if your famous Majesty*
> *Should wish to see the end of this story*
> *I beg upon my knees that you will wait*
> *and pardon me, also, if I delay,*
> *For 'tis a thing difficult for the pen*
> *To lose all shyness instantly,*
> *having to serve you with the lance.* (302)

The pen is fashioned as the phallic embodiment of power, working in unison with the lance to promulgate the prerogatives of empire. These metonyms of power threaten to dissolve into each other and become indistinguishable as they serve a single imperial purpose. Villagrá succeeds, lack of literary originality notwithstanding, in establishing a correspondence between language as a symbolic power and as a tool of empire. His stock tropes fuse with historical reportage in his *History of New Mexico,* creating an effect of verisimilitude in his palimpsest of literary artifice and historical detail that exalts Spanish power.

The force and symbolic power of Villagrá's exaltation of Oñate's expedition cannot be underestimated. Cabeza de Vaca's topological errancy facilitated the establishment of the first Spanish stronghold in New Mexico, as well as an intercultural conflict with the Amerindian populations that continues to spur controversy to this day. The year 1998 marked the anniversary of Oñate's ascent to power in New Mexico after declaring war on the Acoma and the commemoration of the slaughter of Acoma warriors who threatened to destabilize Spanish authority over the area.[39] In the highly symbolic turn of events with which I began this chapter, 1998 also marked the metaphorical "amputation" of Oñate's right foot in a highly charged battle over the politics of American cultural memory in a counter "aesthetics of colonial violence."

The scene of dismemberment that opened this chapter was an occasion to remember both a past colonial violence and a very present amnesia about "the facts" of the consolidation of the American Southwest. By attempting to forestall the celebratory cultural narratives of closure regarding Oñate's role in the colonization of the Southwest, the commandos were calling attention to both the literal and symbolic costs of Spanish violence. A press release indicated the obvious with aplomb: "We took the liberty of removing Oñate's right foot on behalf of our brothers and sister [sic] of Acoma Pueblo. . . . We see no glory in celebrating Oñate's fourth centennial, and we do not want our faces rubbed in it" (Brooke, "Conquistador Statue," A10). With the statue's dismemberment, the Acoma commandos write the memory of their shared history on Oñate's metaphorical body; the process in turn reinvests American cultural memory with more nuanced meanings about national belonging, the role of memory in the nation's social conscience, and the importance of ethnic remembrance.

The Word in the Flesh, or How Cabeza de Vaca's Body Became a Book

"In the beginning was the Word, and the Word was with God, and the Word was God"; so begins the oft-cited first verse of the first chapter of the Gospel According to John (John 1:1). Like the assertion about the Word, Cabeza de Vaca's signs perform so that an audience might come to believe in his words. In *Castaways,* incorporation becomes one of the central metaphors through which Cabeza de Vaca's literal hunger for food eventually collapses under the metaphorical weight of the food for thought that he offers his audience; forsaken in the New World, he must consume (eat) so that he can eventually relate what others must believe (his words) about his experiences and competencies over the American environment. His New World quest is, fundamentally, a search for the restoration of subject integrity for which his body serves as a central trope. Cabeza de Vaca's survival becomes dependent on his ability to keep his body from being literally dismembered or, worse, cannibalized like the bodies of some of his compatriots. Once his words are in the hands of his explicit reader, the king, his nearly dismembered body will be remembered as a reconstituted and resilient entity.

Such a rendering of his urbody serves as an epistemological model for colonial situations insofar as his survival is predicated upon the simultaneous differentiation and identification between his body and the American environment he wishes to act upon. This insistence on an inside/outside dichotomy, so central to Christian transubstantiation, involves the total identification of opposites as the Christian archetypal resolution to conflict. So it is that St. John relates Jesus's assertion that "unless you eat the flesh of the Son of Man and drink his blood, you have no life in you" (John 6:53) and "As the living Father sent Me, and I live because of the Father, so he who feeds on Me will live because of Me" (John 6:57). Ingestion, digestion, and identification are the fundamentals of incorporation (literally, taking into the body) for God's son, who himself is at once God and man through transubstantiation.

However, the type of assimilative and complete identification Bruce-Novoa wishes to read into *Castaways* is an overt literalization of the events related by Cabeza de Vaca. These events must be understood in relation to a series of identity negotiations that were fashioned discursively and—it is important to restate the obvious—retrospectively in and through *Castaways*. No matter how successful he was in fashioning his urbody through *ingenio*, as Villagrá's "historical" reading so aptly demonstrates, Cabeza de Vaca did so discursively, and his success should be measured in relation to the "effects of verisimilitude" he creates, not a transcendental truth outside his text. As a model for proto-Chicano or Latino subjectivity, the myth of total identification supported by what I have here called Latino literature's "genealogical critics" positions *Castaways* dangerously close to a unidirectional cultural capitulation that reifies assimilation, even if unwittingly.

It is precisely this colonial model of assimilation, by and through identification, that Oswald de Andrade sought to denounce when he mocked New World imperialist European gluttony in his ludic "Cannibalist Manifesto":

> I am only interested in what does not belong to me. Law of Man. Law of the Cannibal. . . .
> The spirit refuses to conceive a spirit without a body. Anthropomorphism. Needs for the cannibalistic vaccine. To maintain our equilibrium, against meridian religions. And against outside inquisitions.[40]

The image of the consuming cannibal on the loose and in need of incorporating all that "does not belong to me" was Andrade's way of inverting the roles of the "civilized" European colonizer and the "savage" Amerindian. For Andrade, if Europe constitutes itself through the gluttonous incorporation of the Other, then the Other must offer "food for thought" in deed and action. He posits becoming "human" as an alternative to assimilation (total identification) with the colonizer by refusing to "conceive of a spirit without a body," that is, by asserting the primacy of corporeality over the Word of man ("the Law of Man"), of asserting corporeal difference over cultural identification and assimilation. Andrade's reversal of roles is instructive to the extent that it confronts the myth of assimilation by offering the gluttonous European "cannibal" unassimilable flesh, the ultimate "cannibalistic vaccine" against those anxious to devour Amerindian culture for imperial gain. I would suggest that Andrade's anthropophagous model can also shed light on critical practices that consume Amerindian culture, even if unwittingly, by attempting to establish genealogies of cultural co-existence and understanding where none exist outside of our desire to be seduced by a benevolent "forefather." Understanding *Castaways* as a text that consumes Amerindian culture for the accouterments of empire is a beginning.

This process of substitution, from word to flesh, is precisely the type of maneuver readings like Bruce-Novoa's perform when they assert that Cabeza de Vaca is a Chicano or Latino forefather, without considering the ethical costs associated with the strategic assimilation that makes Cabeza de Vaca such a competent reader of the Amerindian body politic. Spaniard or proto-Chicano, Cabeza de Vaca's success was ultimately contingent on a series of strategic identity performances that assured his survival. This move toward the celebration of multicultural difference, without a sustained analysis of the material conditions that brought about Cabeza de Vaca's retrospective recounting of his travails in and through discourse, should alert us to the limits and costs associated with uncritical multicultural inclusion.

Cabeza de Vaca's usable past must be read in dialectical relation to the end of his quest: the accouterments of monarchical favors, favors sustainable only under the discursive conditions that posit "going native" and strategic assimilation as the answer to cultural conflict instead of engaging the exacting, taxing, but necessary task of forging a democratic cross-cultural model of understanding. The possibility that each generation has to "write its own books . . . for the next succeeding," as Emerson declared in "The American Scholar," should not be understood as genealogical license, lest we believe Cabeza de Vaca when he stated, "hunger never gave me a chance to choose," as if to say, hunger never gave me chance but to assimilate, ergo I became human.

Coterminous with the interdisciplinary legitimation crisis that beset

Chicano and Latino studies and literature programs—and the endangered-knowledge projects they were entrusted to document and represent in the academy—was the absence of the very people these representative texts spoke of and for, and whose limited possibilities for access into academia these critical enterprises mourned. Read together, the crisis of legitimation in Latino literary studies and *Castaways* as its foundational conceit, these narratives point to our need to believe (to be seduced, as Rabasa would have it) in a benevolent (fore)father that would in turn allow us to restore our belief in the benevolence of state power. Refusing such a gesture, the belief in the benevolence of the (fore)father, like the belief in benevolence of the state, allows us to awaken from the elusive embrace of a national fantasy incapable of reciprocating our love of difference. Such are the limits and responsibilities of becoming historical, forsaking the patronym in order to awaken from the elusive—albeit seductive—dream of inclusion.

Practices of Freedom

The Body Re-membered in Contemporary Latino Writing

"That Difficult Remembering"

> It is through the terrain of national culture that the individual subject
> is politically formed as the American citizen: a terrain introduced by the
> Statue of Liberty, discovered by the immigrant, dreamed in a common
> language, and defended in battle by the independent, self-made man.
> . . . Culture is the medium of the *present*—the imagined equivalences
> and identifications through which the individual invents lived relation-
> ship with the national collective—but it is simultaneously the site that
> mediates the *past,* through which history is grasped as difference, as
> fragments, shocks, and flashes of disjunction. It is through culture that
> the subject becomes, acts, and speaks itself as "American." It is likewise
> in culture that individuals and collectivities struggle and remember
> and, in that difficult remembering, imagine and practice both subject
> and community differently.
>
> —Lisa Lowe, *Immigrant Acts*

Contemporary constructions of Latino subjectivity are taking part in that
"difficult remembering" Lisa Lowe alludes to and in the process are re-
configuring the national community "differently" through the symbolic

contestation and subversion of dominant conceptions of Americanness.[1] Central to Lowe's conception of ethnic community making is the role of memory in refashioning national narratives of Americanness: how the ethnic subject engages with majority culture and inflects the National Symbolic with ever more dynamic renditions of what it means to voice oneself into the cordoned representational circuits of power through acts of will and imagination. Imagining the "national culture" differently is the imperative and ever-regenerative promise of democratic institutions. In the texts I study in this chapter, the promise of democratic participation in the national culture entails the recognition that Latino identitarian strategies are dynamic and relational. The texts posit that it is in the intersections of identities, not in their compartmentalization, that communities grow in loving measure with their respect for "difference," and that sexuality is the necessary ground from which to conjoin ethnic and racialized identities with the possibility of sexual fulfillment. The process entails restructuring the dominant forms of sexual subjection that have left queer desire and love outside the calls to equality enacted in the public sphere by the Chicano and Latino identity projects of the late 1960s and onward.

The crisis moment in question—coterminous with the need to legitimate Chicano and Latino studies in the academy—saw a veritable explosion in the way that not only majority culture but Latino culture as well was critiqued from within the Latino community by some of the most important voices to emerge out of the Chicano and Latino equality-rights struggle. Works by Chicana authors such as Cherríe Moraga and Gloria Anzaldúa's *This Bridge Called My Back: Writings by Radical Women of Color* (1983) and Anzaldúa's *Borderlands/La frontera: The New Mestiza* (1987),[2] reclaiming the role of the committed public intellectual, changed the terms of engagement with both the majority culture and the heteronormative assumptions underpinning the master narratives of a Latino politics that could envision equality of opportunity for Latinos but could not recognize the need with regard to the Latinas in their own homes and communities. This gendered intracommunity critique was also intermeshed with the public-sphere realignment of what it meant to be an American, since— for these writers—the question of sexuality and citizenship were inseparable. This was, indeed, one of Cherríe Moraga's principled assertions in *The Last Generation*: "I hold a vision requiring a radical transformation of consciousness in this country, that as the people-of-color population increases . . . we will emerge as a mass movement of people to redefine what an 'American' is."[3]

In the history of Chicano and Latino literary and cultural studies the importance of both Anzaldúa and Moraga is incontrovertible. It is unnecessary for me to rehearse their importance to Chicano, Latino, and American cultural studies in their reconfiguration of citizenship as a gendered, racialized, and desiring mobile imaginary written on the body. A "1,950 mile-long open wound," is how Anzaldúa referred to the Mexico-U.S. border in decidedly corporeal terms, "running down the length of my body / staking fence rods in my flesh" (*Borderlands*, 2). Their work continues to invigorate third-world feminisms or what Emma Pérez and Chela Sandoval have termed "the third space," a type of intellectual mobility that can conceptualize the lived reality of subaltern life outside the strictures of two-dimensional, binary knowledge systems.[4] Yet it is important to also register that other writers from often neglected Latino Atlantic communities have also been engaged in a similar critique of gender orthodoxy, heteronormativity, and citizenship. Though they are not as well known, they speak "differently" about the role of nationalism and sexuality as regards their respective communities of origin by historicizing their relationship to U.S. colonialisms. Not having as defined a cultural genealogy in the United States as Chicanos have had, the authors I discuss in this chapter represent "immigrant acts" against marginalization through narrative renderings of the historical colonial circuits of power that have bound their respective national histories to the United States. The texts in question imbricate their generative local histories associated with the United States' 1898 military intervention in Cuba and Puerto Rico with American cultural and literary history in order to signal the elusive and bitter memories of Cuban and Puerto Rican diasporas occasioned by military force. In so doing, these texts offer immigrant acts that demand historical accounting by calling attention to the cultural amnesia surrounding the military interventions in Cuba and Puerto Rico that for over a century have led to Cuban and Puerto Rican (im)migration to the United States. It remembers the "why we are here" as a proposition inexorably linked to political, military, and historical entanglements with Cuba and Puerto Rico. Beyond the most obvious military presence in either "Gitmo" or Vieques that could be gleaned from contemporary news media, these texts position broader macrostructures in the context of personal narratives proffered for national rememory.

I am also interested in the texts I include in this chapter for far more than what they could tell us about U.S. imperial designs in the Americas. In the process of their becoming historical, these texts also posit the need to render queer desire visible at the intersections of American nationalism and its possessive investment in a monological and monolingual American cultural identity.

Luz María Umpierre's *Margarita Poems* (1987), Elías Miguel Muñoz's *The Greatest Performance* (1991), and Rafael Campo's *What the Body Told* (1996) focus on the politics of confrontational Latina and Latino sexualities and its relation to the construction of national culture.[5] These texts tell a moving story about the importance of political engagement. They also point to the growing importance of Atlantic Latino cultures in the politicization of questions of citizenship and national belonging that are necessarily historically distinct from the Chicano-specific concerns I discuss in the previous chapters. Their cultural interventions engage issues of nationalism, language, and sexual identity (Umpierre), the construction of "ethnic" subjectivities and antiessentialism (Muñoz), and the subversion of American modernist aesthetic agencies in the age of AIDS (Campo). They partake in "that difficult remembering" by politicizing Latino writing as an antidote to American cultural exscription, the cultural erasures of the very specificities these texts will not forget. I offer Umpierre's, Muñoz's, and Campo's readings of our cultural milieu as three distinct interventions from an emerging "tradition" of antihegemonic American writing that cuts through the frontiers of nation, philosophy, poetry, political critique, and sexuality. Their collective "re-memberings" offer up stories that return to their respective cultural histories and relationship to the United States not to establish their present as an inescapable heritage born of imperial colonizations and aggression but to ask how colonial legacies might be turned to different purposes.

"Una Isla Amazónica Libre": Luz María Umpierre and the Critique of Transnational Boricua Subjectivity

In his significant 1995 essay "Toward an Art of Transvestism: Colonialism and Homosexuality in Puerto Rican Literature," Arnaldo Cruz-Malavé established the connection between compulsory heteronationalism and the near absence of lesbians and gays as agents in Puerto Rican literary history: "prior to the 1970s [there is] no poetic persona or writing subject for whom homosexuality is seen as the key factor that determines his or her being, as the source (or one of the sources) of his or her identity. There is no lesbian or gay writing subject."[6] This absence, seen as the historical erasure of the queer Boricua[7] body from Puerto Rican literary history, has led Luz María Umpierre to the critical practice she terms "homocriticism."[8] Homocriticism entails the signaling and teasing "out" of homo-identifications and subtexts in Boricua writing.

I would like to extend Umpierre's homocriticism to undoing cultural histories of exclusion by analyzing how "Immanence" and "The Mar/Garita Poem," the principal poems of *The Margarita Poems*, form a dialogue with its implicit subtext, Antonio S. Pedreira's *Insularismo*.[9] More specifically, I address the strategic importance of a geographically and linguistically unfixed subject of enunciation in *The Margarita Poems* as a creative response to Pedreira's compulsory heteronationalism and subjectivity in rewriting Boricua literary history. Umpierre begins to deface "American" and Boricua/ Puerto Rican disciplinary boundaries in an attempt to reconfigure what Efraín Barradas has called "el pésimo caso de los que se atreven a incursionar en el estudio de las letras de los latinos en los Estados Unidos" (the sad situation that besets those who venture to study the literature of Latinos in the United States).[10]

The Margarita Poems comprises nine prose poems prefaced with three references to actual and metaphorical "Margaritas": Jimmy Buffet's popular song "Margaritaville" ("wasting away at Margaritaville"); a popular danza puertorriqueña ("Margarita, my más bella ilusión"); and Julia de Burgos ("Cuando ya no te acunen margaritas / porque me van siguiendo, . . . / ¿Con qué amor, amor mío, cuidarás de mis versos?"). The first two are geographically fixed, in the United States and Puerto Rico, respectively; the last is interstitial between Puerto Rico and New York. Umpierre also notes that calling "Julia forth" is invoking the muse Julia de Burgos, whose presence permeates the collection and whose identity extends from the island of her birth to the concrete streets of New York, where she died anonymously and unclaimed (*The Margarita Poems*, 3).

Umpierre summarizes the importance of the names Margarita and Julia: "I met two women poets who have these names and who have had an impact on me over the years: Margret Randall and Julia Álvarez. This book is for them. . . . And yet it is also for a place between New Jersey and Massachusetts; in other words, Margarita. And it is addressed to another place between New Jersey and Kansas called Julia. I have to add that it is also from Puerto Rico. Most of these poems were written in movement" (2). The prepositions for, to, and from point to the difficulty of situating a movable subject of enunciation—the poetic voice of *The Margarita Poems* is at once in Puerto Rico, the U.S. heartland, and the eastern seacoast. I focus on the geopolitics of subject location and positionality because the text symbolically thematizes the Boricua transnational migrant *cuerpo en sexilo*, a body in sexile, that resists intra- as well as extranational identity scripts.

For Donald Pease, these "postnational" markers of dislocation partake in the questioning of national narratives that have produced "national identities by way of a social symbolic order that systematically separated an abstract, disembodied subject from resistant materialities, such as race, class, and gender."[11] Umpierre's symbolic rendering of Boricua identity as transnational is significant because it displaces the nation as a geographical construct, suggesting that Puerto Rico is more than mere geography—it is body, that is, lived experience, and also (s)exile. I read Umpierre's deterritorialization of Puerto Rican cultural history, on and through her poetic persona's aestheticized body, as a symbolic rewriting of Antonio Pedreira's version of that history. Pedreira's *Insularismo,* read brilliantly by Cruz-Malavé as a failed bildungsroman ("Art of Transvestism," 149), performed a narrative of Puerto Rican national identity as a *nación* in a state of *confusión.*[12] Umpierre symbolically writes off Pedreira's stagist and heteronormative conception of Puerto Rican identity through the aesthetic play of the corporeal.

In the first poem of *The Margarita Poems,* "Immanence" (16), the body emerges as a forgotten site of knowledge resurrected like a "new lady lazarus" (18) in the figuration of the Amazon. The figuration of the Amazon coincides with the colonial period thematized by Pedreira. For Pedreira, during this period, from 1493 to the early nineteenth century, Puerto Rican cultural identity did not exist. Umpierre's figure of the colonial Amazon further problematizes Puerto Rico's cultural dependence on empire with the critique of the absence of women in *Insularismo,* the erasure of women from Puerto Rico's cultural milieu, signaling "insularity," not only from the realm of the cultural, as Pedreira would have it, but also from the realm of the sexual. The Amazon motif runs counter to the colonial representations of New World women that circulated in the European imagination.

European representations of the ready, willing, and able heterosexual Amerindian woman obtained de facto status in the early modern imagination. Americo Vespucci's widely circulated "Letter to Lorenzo Pietro de Medici" (1503) puts in relief the mythical status of the Amerindian women and the issue of sexual desire:

> their women, being very lustful, cause the penis of their partners to swell up to such an enormous size as to appear deformed and grotesque. This is accomplished through a certain trick, namely the bite of a poisonous lizard. By reason of this, many lose their virile organ, which burst through a lack of attention, and they remain eunuchs.[13]

Vespucci's anecdote provided for the collective imagination of his readers a cautionary tale of heterosexual desire, sexual anticipation, panic, and titil-

lation. The sexed and unruly Amerindian woman's body is to be subjected
to heteromasculinist scrutiny and control, lest all men within a lizard's
throw of her lose their virile signifiers of power.
Constructing a locus of enunciation for female agency necessarily entails
reinscription of the image of an/other unruly woman in the colonial imaginary. In "Immanence," the Amerindian nymphomaniac is displaced by
the Amazon. This unruly Amazon differs from the nymphomaniac in both
sexual-object choice and geographic placement. The Amazons, written into
mythic existence by Columbus, in their own "isla Amazónica libre" ("The
Mar/Garita Poem," 39) were geographically separate from both Amerindian men and Christians desirous of copulating with native women. The
ironic linguistic play of the signifier "Amazon" in Spanish is worth noting:
la(s) Amazona(s) are zonas de amor (Ama[r]zona), "love zones."[14] The play of
words and the Amazon as a motif offer a decidedly different take on colonial situations in Umpierre's heterotopia. The poetic voice crosses the river
MAD in Ohio with "armies of Amazons" ("Immanence," 16) that are in-
voked to bring forth a sexual union with Julia. "Julia" serves as a symbol
for Boricua culture (Julia de Burgos), as well as an object of lesbian desire
and transnational Boricua identity, a symbol that fuses with the poetic
voice's search for a locus of subjectivity:

> I am traversing
> this river MAD,
> crossing myself
> against the evil eye,
> hectic, in movement,
> my narrow body
> covered with pictures
> of women I adore or desire,
> armies of Amazons
> that I invoke
> in this transubstantiation
> or arousal
> that will bring my Julia forth. (Ibid.)

The poetic voice's search for a place from which to speak desire is facilitated by the presence not only of "armies of Amazons" but also of "pictures / of women I adore or desire." These pictures point to an enduring
absence in the poetic voice's personal and collective history that must be
articulated and recovered through a representation of desire that goes

against the heteronormative grain. The invocation of a Boricua figuration of Julia de Burgos is meant to suggest the forgotten foundational mother in Puerto Rican literary history. Julia de Burgos's absence from Pedreira's period of "transition" is important insofar as the absence bespeaks unfulfilled lesbian desire (the desire to touch "the fall under our skirts") and the absence of women from the symbolic cultural milieu of Boricua writing by "incestuous writers . . . who fucked your head and mine." The critique posits personal *herstory* as an antidote to the erasure of the Boricua lesbian body from the discourses of cultural participation and national belonging.

> *I am traversing*
> *This body full of water,*
>   *MAD,*
> *cursing all Hopkinses*
> *incestuous writers,*
> *who fucked your head and mine*
> *in spring and summer*
> *with images of death and sin*
> *when all we wanted*
> *was to touch the yellow leaves,*
>   *the fall under our skirts.* (16–17)

The foundational fictions of nation building are laid bare as writing is conceived not as a national romance but as a series of "incestuous" romps, the reproduction of values that degenerate generation after generation. Not surprisingly, Julia (like the figure of the Amazon) appears as a literary-historical counteragent, rewritten and reborn through the poetic voice's transformation and sexual awakening after crossing the river MAD at the poem's conclusion:

> *I am Julia,*
> *I have crossed the river*
>   *MAD,*
> *I have come forth,*
> *new lady lazarus*
> *to unfold my margarita,*
> *my carnal daisy*
> *that buds between*

my spread out legs.
I touch my petals:
"I love me,
I love me not,
I love me,
I love me not,
I love me!" (18)

After crossing the river MAD, the verb "to be" affirms a newly formed identity: "I am Julia."

Umpierre's recourse to Julia (de Burgos) is also meant to represent the unacknowledged participation of Boricua women from Puerto Rican cultural and literary history. This multiple Julia, "a new lady lazarus," also establishes a thematic affinity with Sylvia Plath's "Lady Lazarus."[15] In Plath's poem, Saint Lazarus, patron saint of lepers and beggars, rises reconstituted and gendered. Plath's poetic voice is likened to that of an Amazon by virtue of the ability to incorporate phallic power, literally, through the mouth, by ingesting "men" and the notions of power the signifier "men" embodies:

Out of the ash
I rise with my red hair
And I eat men like air. (9)

Umpierre's poetic voice obtains her tenuous freedom through knowing her body, writing the body, if you will, not by incorporating the body of "men" as a generic signifier for power as in Plath's cannibalistic metaphor. The masculinist images of "death" and "sin," imposed by writers who "fucked the head," become displaced by the "carnal daisy between" the poetic voice's spread legs by marking identity on and through the migrant body that is Julia, Margarita, "Lady Lazarus," and Puerto Rico at once.

I would suggest that the reference to Plath's "Lady Lazarus" is not coincidental. Like Plath's, Umpierre's biography has been the subject of rumor and speculation. She has publicly noted how the spectacle and rumors about her mental state were akin to a witch hunt that attempted to silence her because of her open lesbianism and her constant confrontations with sexual and ethnic prejudices. In "Manifesto: Whose Taboos? Theirs, Yours or Ours," she notes how she has been considered " 'mentally ill,' for having trespassed the delicacy of a stereotypical Latina woman and the passivity of a 'closeted' Latina lesbian."[16] This question of mental health and

"MADness" informs both Pedreira's reading of Puerto Rico's dysfunctional identity and the Boricua identity Umpierre rewrites through her "difficult remembering" of the Boricua body politic. The function of madness as heir to nineteenth-century conceptions of the nation and the national subject's health was a recurrent motif in Pedreira's *Insularismo*. His analysis of Puerto Rico's "adolescence," the period roughly beginning with an emerging sense of *criollo* identity in the nineteenth century, has been characterized as "paternalistic" by Juan G. Gelpí, who notes that "*Insularismo* puede leerse como un relato sobre un país-niño enfermo. Insisten en el texto las metáforas mediante las cuales se presenta al país como un cuerpo enfermo. En las páginas del libro, Puerto Rico es un país raquítico, anémico, agotado, abúlico, paralítico, invertebrado" (*Insularismo* could be read as a story about a sickly child-country. The text abounds with metaphors through which the country is presented as an infirm body. In the book's pages, Puerto Rico is a rachitic, anemic, exhausted, apathetic, paralytic, invertebrate).[17] Indeed, Pedreira's stock repertoire of images is obsessively corporeal. As Gelpí has noted, the rhetoric of pathology in Pedreira's *Insularismo* "viene acompañada de la presentación de la historia nacional a partir de metáforas que remiten a la circulación sanguínea. Así, el Grito de Lares se ve como 'una inyección de glóbulos rojos,' un prócer es una 'célula' y la adaptación de elementos de otras culturas figura como una especie de 'metabolismo'" (comes accompanied with the presentation of a national history through which metaphors refer to the circulation of blood. This way, the Cry of Lares is seen as an 'injection of red globules,' a patriot is a 'cell' and the adoption of elements from other cultures figures as a type of 'metabolism') (*Literatura y paternalismo*, 25). This sickly body is also related to what Cruz-Malavé has called Pedreira's *patología* (*pato*, "faggot," and pathology, *pato-logía*) ("Art of Transvestism," 150). Puerto Rico, read in Pedreira's cultural history as both "sick body" and effeminate, is symbolically rewritten by Umpierre on her poetic persona's body in "The Mar/Garita Poem," the final and longest poem of the collection.

Here the poetic voice, obsessed with corporeal metaphors, wishes "to dismember the patriarch" (34) by inventing a new language to coincide with a newfound subjectivity. The poetic voice symbolically attacks two of Puerto Rico's most visible national symbols, the El Morro fortress and the sea:

> *Hay que salvar el mar/la musa*
> *y demoler las garitas del Diablo Morro*

de my mente.

. . . .

Si vamos a crear nuestra historia,
nuestra lengua,
debemos liberar el mar
de la garita

[*The sea / the muse has to be saved / and demolish the gatekeeper's box of*
the Devilish Morro / of my mind. . . . If we are to create our history, / our
language, / we should free the sea / from the gatekeeper]

The patriarch, who keeps vigil in the Morro and whose proxies stand
guard in their *garitas* (gatekeepers' boxes) must be demolished before the
sea can be liberated from the gatekeeper's panoptical watch over the Morro.
Otherwise, there could only be "an island without a sea," a national identity without a point of reference:

hay una isla sin mar;
porque entre el mar y la isla
han construído una pared,
un muro extenso,
una muralla.
Y para que entre el mar
a tocar la tierra de esa isla
se necesitan
tus palabras
. . . . .
Llena tu boca mujer
mujer sabia
llena tu boca
con todas las palabras
que has guardado
en el estómago
en el esófago
en el recto,
en la matriz,
en las bilis,
en la columna vertebral,
en los riñones

en el vaso sanguíneo,
en los ovarios,
en los tubos de falopio,
en la vagina

[*there is an island without a sea; / because between the sea and the island / they've constructed a wall, / an extensive rampart, / a rampart. / And for the sea to come / to touch that island's land / one needs / your words.* . . . *Fill your mouth woman / wise woman / fill your mouth / with all the words / that you put away / in the stomach / in the esophagus / in the rectum / in the womb / in the bile / in the kidneys / in the blood stream / in the ovaries / in the fallopian tubes / in the vagina*]

The words ("las palabras") the poetic persona invokes as a precondition of freedom from the patriarch's Morro are to surge literally from the body, from the stomach, kidneys, blood system, vagina. This corporeal understanding of Boricua subjectivity is Umpierre's direct assault on Pedreira's remedy for Puerto Rican national malaise, when he calls on Puerto Rico's youth to "inject health" and "new blood" as a remedy for the wasted social body (*Insularismo*, 170), precisely the prescription for health the poetic persona delivers corporeally.

It is this corporeal construction of a deterritorialized subjectivity that Umpierre offers through her poetic persona. The poetic voice can reclaim all her erased selves (Margarita, Julia, the Muse, Umpierre herself) and finally assert that

Hay un pueblo isleño
esclavo en el Caribe
pero una isla amazónica libre
en el exilio:
aquí en mi cuerpo
que hoy se llena de libertad y luz
y la desplamación de nuestro idioma inventado. (39)

[*There is an island nation / slave in the Caribbean / but a free amazon island / in exile / here in my body / that today is filled with liberty and light / and the displacement of our invented language*]

This newly invented language ("idioma inventado") of liberation is posited as the manifestation of the care of the self,[18] a strategy of difficult remembering as an antidote to the exscription of female and lesbian experience from Boricua cultural history. Umpierre's preface to *The Margarita Poems* states her trepidation about writing poems that might turn her life into a battleground: "I have been warned that these words may be hurled against me by those seeking biographical data in my poems" (1). Her response to Pedreira suggests that she has entered the battleground. Her courageous posture notwithstanding, critics still ignore her gendered and queer identity negotiations. That Umpierre does this in a collection that alternates effortlessly between the diasporic English and the island Spanish further allows her to defamiliarize the assumed monolingual logic of national languages and borders. Her "bilingual aesthetics," as Doris Sommer has recently called the deadly serious play of bilingual games' assault on English-only calls for national unity, proffers the added value of multiple linguistic registers, not its remediation.[19]

Cruz-Malavé's deconstruction of Pedreira's *Insularismo* notes that "Pedreira finds in the island's abundant number of effeminates a visible sign of the geographical, historical, and political limitations that hamper Puerto Ricans' ability to create and thus to constitute the nation. It is against this background of Puerto Rico's 'transitional' state of adolescence, conceived of as effeminacy and impotence . . . that he calls on Puerto Ricans to transcend their youth" ("Art of Transvestism," 150). Cruz-Malavé goes on to say that this challenge is already being met, that "Puerto Rican Writers have decided to speak not from the space of a stable, 'virile' . . . identity but from [the] 'patological milieu' " (150–51). He concludes by stating that these writers, all of whom happen to be male (Luis Rafael Sánchez, René Marqués, Manuel Ramos Otero), "restore for us a patology, or a *mariconería* . . . in Puerto Rico's future and in Puerto Rico's past" (151).

But if we are to speak of *mariconería* (faggotry) as a counterdiscourse to the legacy of *insularismo,* are we not reinstating the masculinist subject (queer or not) as the measure and source of Boricua identity negotiations? Are we not reproducing the very hegemony Umpierre so adamantly displaces through her own figurations of the transnational Boricua body? Would we be so willing to replace the art of *mariconería* with the practice of *tortillería* (literally "omeletry," figuratively lesbianism), at least the practice of being Julias or Margaritas, as a response to Puerto Rico's foundational fictions? Umpierre's poetic persona offers another possibility, one where self-preservation means problematizing difference to engage sexual difference, ethnic identity, and the possibilities for becoming historical both in and "out" of Puerto Rico. In engaging these issues, *The Margarita Poems* perform as an Amazonic counternarrative to Pedreira's myopic paternalism.

If for Umpierre the difficult remembering means recalling the transnational and gendered absence of Boricua women into the realm of the national, Elías Miguel Muñoz's *The Greatest Performance* will remember another absence from the realm of the National Symbolic, the haunting specter of AIDS on the Latino body. It is to this memory of invisible loss that I now turn.

"I Shall Inscribe My Name on It with My Teeth": The Subject Dis-membered and the Body Re-membered in the Greatest Performance

> And now he sees me. The boy I used to be. And he cries, and he tries to break away. His body convulses, shrivels up. I shall make it burn. . . . I shall inscribe my name on it with my teeth: Marito.
>
> —Elías Miguel Muñoz, *The Greatest Performance*

Inscribing a name on "it" refers to a cock, not just any cock but a child abuser's cock that will bear the inscriptural marks of the abused child's name: Marito. Marito wishes to mark and inflict pain upon the abuser's body, as his body was pained, filled, and emptied by his abuser's intrusive phallus. But this time the orifice has a bite: the very mouth that bore witness and eventually related the terror of his rape is now a writing instrument with teeth, in both deed and action. Even more curious is the fact that the one who writes Marito's revenge in Elías Miguel Muñoz's *The Greatest Performance* is Rosita: two voices from two different material bodies converge on one textual body. Like an inverted (pink) triangle, Marito and Rosita's story is funneled into one textual unity. In *The Greatest Performance* Muñoz suggests that in Latino culture the body is a battleground of meaning. The survival of the body as a historical and material entity is directly related to its gender, ethnicity, and class, and although it follows that almost every "body" has a story to tell, not all bodies matter equally to everyone. AIDS is perhaps our generation's most blatant example of the tenuous connection between material existence and the legacy or oblivion of a loved (or any) body. In *The Greatest Performance*, Marito's queer body is literally rewritten by Rosita in a "transgressive"[20] act against oblivion and the ravages AIDS enacts against the body's ability to prolong or transcend its material existence, even if only as a textual entity; it is a reconstituted textual body, what Moraga would call a "body against oblivion."[21] Through Rosita, Marito's ethnically marked body underlines the public significance of dying as a queer Latino and, most important, the significance of being remembered.

I propose Rosita's rewriting of Marito's body as a textual strategy of resistance to forms of social closure that demand that queer bodies and queer pursuits of pleasure be subjected to the orders of discipline, punishment, and shame. Rosita's "difficult remembering" reconceptualizes the issue of identity politics and its relation to alterity by raising the question of corporeal difference in ways that traditional notions of subjectivity, and the concomitant appeal to agency and the privileging of consciousness over matter, cannot. We are reminded that bodily contours and appendages, like queer pursuits of pleasure or ethnic and class markers, readily demonstrate, problematize, and force us to confront the neutralizing and neutering category of the masculinist humanist subject that is presumed to be the stand-in for philosophical ruminations.

Rosita Rodríguez and Marito are Cuban émigrés negotiating the slippery terrain between ethnic and sexual identities. Their history of exile, as Cuban transnationals who—even as children—are embraced by the United States as Cuban political "defectors," suggests that they are situational political exiles and queer s/exiles at once. Whereas the country of origin would presumably not embrace them for political reasons, their adopted country shuns them for their sexual alterity. The first six divisions of the text situate, in alternating fashion, Rosita's and Marito's experiences in Cuba, Spain, and the United States. The seventh division, a dialogue between Rosita and Marito, ends with Rosita's account of the ethnic and sexual identity conflicts that arise from her confrontations with her Anglo-American girlfriend, Joan. The eighth division is a poetic revindication and retelling of Marito's revenge against Hernando, the *bugarrón*[22] who abused Marito's body. The last two divisions revolve around Rosita's recounting of meeting Marito and the subsequent "difficult re-membering" of Marito's socially dismembered body. Rosita's narrative presence is the structuring point and axis of the text's dialogue with itself, the issue of writing as a contestatory and transgressive practice in the age of AIDS, and the forms of cultural amnesia it attempts to deconstruct.

Michel Foucault's critique of subjectivity "has argued that the production of modern subjects has involved a certain disciplining of the body, an attempt by institutions such as the church, the military, and the school to render the body 'docile,' cooperative, useful for, among other things, a continued investment of the body by power."[23] The subjugated body of the Other nevertheless offers possibilities for contesting the complicitous relations between power and oppression by offering a corporeal site of resistance. For Foucault, sexual desire offers possibilities for transgressing the orders of institutional domination.

In ethnically marked narratives, the issue of sexuality is complicated by the role of desire in the construction of subjectivities, because not all bodies have equal access to desire's expression—agency, the ability to act on desire. Insofar as agency is the enabling possibility for subjects to dissent, to desire against the grain and act upon that desire, it behooves us to justify not the "why" but the "how" behind desire. Exploring the "how" offers possibilities for determining how dissent can be deployed in the aesthetic sphere of writing and be ethically and politically useful.

Writing, like love, sexual or otherwise, is as much a performance of desire (as lack) as it as of our failed attempts to possess what we evoke, of our very real failure at adequately re-membering or knowing an Other. Like Rosita's fictional evocation of Marito's life, prompted by her love for him, both love and writing turn out to be "performances of loss, [an] ongoing and virtual discrepancy with the thing, the person, or text being sought, *read*. To perform any text or love any person is to perceive and participate in their virtuality, their evanescence."[24] In *The Greatest Performance* Rosita partakes of the desire to perform Marito's life by vesting his material absence with a textual presence. What is curious about her particular use of writing and love, however, is her disavowing her personal history for an account of a shared childhood history with Marito that never happened. This strategy functions as both a critique and a reconfiguration of love's heteronormative function. If this function is the reproduction of bodies that will reproduce class ideologies, what are we to make of the fusion of Marito's re-membered body onto Rosita's textual body as an instance of a nonreproductive corporeal love-union? What implications does this transsubstitutive[25] union offer for a configuration of subjectivities that counters the sexless subject of humanism? Before engaging these questions, I would like to turn my attention to the critical (mis)readings and missed opportunities for reading agency to which *The Greatest Performance* has been subjected.

In a review of *The Greatest Performance* in the journal *Chasqui*, Jorge Marbán states that Rosita and Marito's friendship "extends back to their childhood" and is "a powerful bond because they both share homosexual inclinations and are in the middle of the sexual spectrum."[26] The text, however, does not support this interpretation. The events narrated by Rosita reconstruct not a friendship that "extends back to their childhood" but the desire to reconstruct the shared experiences of ethnic, cultural, and sexual marginalization. Rosita clearly articulates meeting Marito for the first time in a gay bar: "We finally meet today, 1978, we actually meet for the first time at The Laguna" (*The Greatest Performance*, 149).[27] Perhaps Marbán's misreading signals a disjuncture that is a function less of Muñoz's dexterous interplay of polyphonic voices than of readerly practices that resist oppositional subjectivities that are both gendered and capable of agential transformations. Far from an unproblematical humanist subject that is assumed to be male, Muñoz's Rosita constructs Marito's subjectivity through rewriting his body and their shared history. When Marito seeks revenge against Hernando for having subjected his "baby" body to domination by fear, shame, and coercion, it is Rosita who recounts it by simulating if not altogether appropriating his voice, all the while rewriting the outcome of Marito's greatest fear: corporeal dismemberment.

> I lived in terror thinking of Hernando, imagining myself butchered by the machete he used to cut off the plantain bunches. My little bloody pieces spread over the floor of his hut, over his cot and over his prick. (121)

Elaine Scarry has noted, "What assists the conversion of absolute pain into the fiction of absolute power is an obsessive, self-conscious display of agency. On the simplest level, the agent displayed is the weapon."[28] Marito's fear of dismemberment by the literal as well as the figurative machete (Hernando's menacing phallus) serves as an interesting analogue to Rosita's weapon: the bite behind Marito's teeth and their writerly agency. The machete, as the terror-inducing metonym for phallic power, will be replaced by Marito's vaginal mouth, a vagina with a bite, which he shares as an extension of Rosita by virtue of being rewritten by her. The terror of child abuse experienced by Marito is retraced and retold by Rosita. The body's submission to the orders of shame and terror is reconfigured in Rosita's recounting of Marito's revenge through Marito's voice:

> Shouldn't he suspect that I have a plan . . . that in a matter of minutes I will drag his body to the bed and tie it up? . . . There he is sprawled on my bed, naked. For real. . . . And now he sees me. The boy I used to be. And he cries, and he tries to break away. His body convulses, shrivels up. I shall make it burn. . . . I shall inscribe my name on it with my teeth: *Marito*. (123, emphasis in original)

The force of this account resides precisely in the telling of the revenge as well as in the teller's accounting. Whether Marito related this to Rosita before his death we do not know, and it is secondary to her telling it in his voice through her narrative rememory. What we do know is that what Hernando sees before him is the "boy [Marito] used to be." The balance of power, the ability to incite terror and inflict pain, is reconfigured: the torturer is now the tortured.

I focus on this issue because I find it curious that Marbán, for all his good intentions, apparently cannot conceive of a Cuban American lesbian who loves a deceased Cuban American "homosexual" (Marbán's term) enough to provide an account of his revindication, "real" or "fictionalized" by her, while impersonating his voice. The presumption that it is Marito who recounts the events cannot be seen as an innocent lapsus mentalis. Marbán's misreading can be useful, however, to point to a wider field of heteronormalizing readerly and critical practices that subsume the subject's possibility for agency as a function of the subject's (presumed) phallus. This is further reinforced by Marbán's belief that Rosita and Marito "share homosexual inclinations and are in the middle of the sexual spectrum" (review of *The Greatest Performance*, 131). The need to characterize their queer sensibilities and expressions of pleasure as in "the middle of the sexual spectrum" dichotomizes the possibilities for thinking about sexual expression into two polarized binary pairs, the exclusively homosexual and the exclusively heterosexual. The subordinated extreme (the exclusively homosexual) is posited as the Other of the primary extreme (the exclusively heterosexual), while Rosita and Marito are citizens of neither. Far from recognizing that such extremes are possible or even desirable, Marbán's insistence on characterizing a "middle" ground for sexual pleasure and identity formation implicitly defines queer bodies as nonhistorical intrusions onto "the sexual spectrum."

Marbán further asserts that "Muñoz leaves his readers somewhat confused about Marito's psychological identity. . . . we don't really know if we should consider him a pitiful and pathetic victim or the willing participant in many sexual acts" (132). Following Marbán's grammar, it would appear that Marito is "a willing participant in many sexual acts," ergo his "pitiful and pathetic" victimization, as if to suggest that, any way you read Marito, the proverbial "you asked for it" is called for. The adjective "many" qualifies, as well as quantifies and moralizes, the number of sexual acts that purportedly result in Marito's "pitiful and pathetic" existence. It apparently never occurs to Marbán that "we" need not consider Marito "a pitiful and pathetic victim" any more than "we" might be a "willing participant" in

Marbán's readerly tastes or his critical omissions, not to mention his readerly competence. Marbán's misreading signals the heteronormative presumption of (phallic) subjectivity as a precondition for agency. It interpolates homosexuality and AIDS by positing the "foreign" virus that infects the body as anti-American: Marito is literally a "foreigner" whose "pitiful and pathetic" queer existence signals his very demise, his apparent inability to accommodate himself to the protocols of heteronormative forms of belonging and desiring.

Marbán's critically missed reading of Muñoz's rhetorical maneuver of having Marito speak through Rosita is cautionary for understanding oppositional narratives that refuse to take the presumptive power of the phallic subject seriously. Doris Sommer, commenting on resistance in oppositional writing and readerly incompetence, states that if a text "seems easy, if it allows possession without a struggle and cancels the promise of self-flattery for an expert reading, our hands may go limp at the covers. . . . We take up an unyielding book to conquer it and to feel enriched by the appropriation and confident that our cunning is equal to the textual tease that had, after all, planned its own capitulation."[29] Marbán's reading attempts to decenter the text's authority by imposing his mastery. His assertion that "Muñoz leaves his readers somewhat confused about Marito's psychological identity" sidesteps his ethico-aesthetic responsibility to the text and the act of reading.

Sommer refers to texts that resist critical readings that attempt to possess a text by calling into question the reader's presumption of competence over the text; Marbán provides an example of a resistant critic whose reading derails understanding by misreading the signposts or, worse, ignoring them altogether through heteronormalizing complacency. By erasing Rosita's presence he misses one of the most crucial concerns that the text attempts to come to terms with: that performing a life and constructing a locus of enunciation for it is a political intervention. The poststructuralist maxim that every representation enacts a price could not be clearer here, and Marbán's is not cost-effective. Evidently the confusion to which he refers lies elsewhere. For professional readers who presume to be on top of the text, Muñoz's strategic positioning of Rosita as the addresser offers a gendered actant that desires to know and tell of a life (Marito) so loved that it becomes difficult, but not impossible, to distinguish the dancer from the dance.

This literal re-membering of Marito's body by Rosita offers some insights into the construction of gendered subjectivities that eschew the very category of the purportedly sexless subject of humanism as the enabling condition for agency. At the same time, the text tackles the postmodern interventions currently being staged in cultural theory about the performativity of gender positions. In order to situate my argument, it will be useful to briefly review the variety of interventions being staged in the charged arena of gender studies and their functionality in relation to ethnically marked oppositional narratives.

Thinking through the Body

The body is difference. Its orifices and protrusions designate sites of pleasure that cannot be accounted for by the post-Cartesian subject's believed supremacy of the mind over the body, because subjects are orgasmic and sexuality binds us to the senses. The simplest maxim holds true—every body is different in differing ways. Even the conscious decision to be celibate is, after all, a sexed decision. Just how is it, then, that the body has been posited as the mind's (read: subjectivity's) Other?

Since Plato, the materiality of the body has been conceived as a denigrated and imperfect version of the Idea. Elizabeth Grosz has noted that "Aristotle, in continuing a tradition possibly initiated by Plato in his account of chora in *Timaeus* where maternity is regarded as mere housing, . . . distinguished matter or body from form, and in the case of reproduction, he believed that the mother provided the formless, passive, shapeless matter which, through the father, was given form." Grosz further contends that "[t]he binarization of sexes, the dichotomization of the world and of knowledge has been effected already at the threshold of Western reason."[30] In Christian doctrine, the tradition was cemented through the teachings of St. Paul, in his first letter to the Corinthians, 12:12–27: "For just as the body is one and has many members, and all the members of the body, though many, are one body, so it is with Christ. For by one Spirit we were all baptized into one body—Jews or Greeks, slaves or free. . . . Now you are the body of Christ and individually members of it."

In more recent Western history, Kant made the idea of thinking through the body philosophically untenable. Juliet Flower MacCannell points out that Kant's universalizing reason "had to be made independent of the sensations and sensitivities, of suffering and pleasure," since for "Kant (in *The Critique of Pure Judgment*), bodying forth ideas of pure reason through sensible representation is impossible." Recovering from this legacy "may take us back to materialism, if not Epicurus, but it is a detour made necessary by the loss of the Kantian body of rational feeling."[31] This "detour" is being undertaken in various disciplines to contest the supposedly empirical science biology as the determiner of sex and the male and female binaries. Martine Rothblatt, in her/his *The Apartheid of Sex: A Manifesto on the Freedom of Gender,* offers a populist "manifesto" for a new sexual paradigm that accommodates varieties of gender identity positions:

> I learned how one's genitals are not the same as one's sex. And I experienced sex as a vast continuum of personality possibilities, a frontier still scarcely explored after thousands of years of human development. Yet the apartheid of sex has denied us these possibilities, forcing men and woman alike into narrow role models that leave us frustrated, angry, and ultimately cheated from experiencing fully the only life we have.[32]

Rothblatt's account, however, belies her/his antiapartheid stance insofar as it says that these "personality possibilities" can be instrumented by "men and woman," as opposed to, say, human beings. S/he cannot escape the very duality s/he wishes to nuance because men, women, and their personalities are not interchangeable cultural terms. I mention her/his important contribution to the debate because it is symptomatic of our current epistemic impasse on thinking through the body, or in spite of it.[33]

In academic discourse on queer theory and institutional discipline and control, few have been more polemical, more cited, or more revered than Judith Butler. Butler has challenged the idea that anatomical difference is a material fact, as her repeatedly cited formula makes clear: "Gender is not to culture as sex is to nature; gender is also the discursive/cultural means by which 'sexed nature' or a 'natural sex' is produced and established as 'prediscursive,' prior to culture."[34] Her idea of gender as performance proposes that agency is not predicated on a subject ("doer" in her analysis) prior to the initiation and "transformation of relations of domination within society"; rather, subject effects can be simulated by "doers" (*Gender Trouble,* 25).

In deference to viable political action a crucial question emerges: can transformation take place through the deployment of performances of power? And if so, can a performance of power produce such a transformation? John Champagne addresses this in his critique of Butler's famous assertion that "[t]here is no gender identity behind expressions of gender; that identity is performatively constituted by the very 'expressions' that are said to be its results" (ibid.). Champagne warns that

> [t]here is no guarantee that mischief in the register of gender will necessarily alter the production of, for example, the classed subject. I am not

147

maintaining that class or the economic is the sole or determining element of politics. But I mistrust the historical tendency in gay and lesbian studies to make class disappear from discussions of the political. Even if, as Butler suggests, we rewrite the definition of politics from "a set of practices derived from the alleged interests that belong to a set of ready made subjects" to one that acknowledges subjects as always (already) in production, the vexing category of interest still remains, its role largely unelaborated by Butler. Perhaps the problem is that we have no clear sense from Butler of what she means by politics. . . . My fear is that the new configuration of politics that might emerge from the subversively gendered subject would leave too much the same. (*Ethics of Marginality*, 127)

In addition to Champagne's "classed subject," we would do well to include Butler's ethnically inflected "doer." The importance of Champagne's cautionary stance cannot be overemphasized, for how can a performance of power be subversive (truly transformative) when it depends on successful performance of reference to an "original" ("real") power? Simply put, this type of ludic postmodern subversion reinstates the primacy of the original by evoking its simulacra. Butler's "performativity" is reminiscent of postmodernism's agent provocateur Jean Baudrillard and his "simulations" from the book of the same title: "The very definition of the real has become: that of which it is possible to give an equivalent reproduction. . . . The real is not only what can be reproduced, but that which is always already reproduced: that is, the hyperreal . . . which is entirely simulation."[35] If we replace "simulation" with Butler's "performance," we have another version of Butler's dictum: "gender is a kind of imitation for which there is no original."[36]

Butler, like Baudrillard, partakes of a postmodern resurgence toward idealism without problematizing, as Champagne attempts to do, the importance of a materially grounded conception of the subject for gendered and ethnically inflected subjectivities.[37] Materialism's emphasis on the structure of conflicts, coupled with a Foucauldian[38] understanding of the care of the self as a practice of freedom, can provide a more differentiated and nuanced approach to the study of subject-identity negotiations and possibilities for agential transformations in liberationist Latino cultural projects.

One might ask whether it is ethical to propose that the subaltern Latino body can emancipate itself, even if only provisionally, by performing the simulacra of subversion in oppositional narratives without problematizing difference to the extent that it problematizes ethnicity in a national context. I believe this question is important because it does not take for granted that all or even most bodies "perform" in quite the same ways. In what follows I explore these tensions in *The Greatest Performance*.

Most of the first division of the text is structured around Rosita's second-person-singular address to Marito, where she begins to mesh her history of young Marito's body onto her textual body. This dialogue between Rosita and Marito makes her address not only a re-membering of Marito's life but also a virtual reconstruction of her own as she grafts his apocryphal presence onto her childhood history. "Look at this picture," she tells Marito, "See the cute guy there, in the back, behind Maritza? He's the one. My buddy. In my childhood story *you have become that kid, Marito. Or rather, he has become you*" (16, my emphasis). Directly in front of Marito in the picture is Rosita's childhood love, Maritza. Her sexual longing for Maritza is mirrored by her writerly evocation of Marito: as absent in death as Maritza is now in distance and geography, he takes the place behind Rosita's love of another boy whose name Rosita cannot remember. Rosita re-members what never was and aligns Maritza (her love) directly in front of Marito (her Other love). His fictive presence in her real photograph fashions history out of need. As in Baudrillard's account of the hyperreal, Marito functions as the simulacrum of the real, a necessary effect of the real. However, by the aesthetic performance of Marito's life, Rosita casts more than just an effect. The material presence of her reverie is the representation of both a somatic and a textual entity by virtue of the very materiality we are reading, the body re-membered through representation and the textual body, the book itself.

It is also at this instance of direct address that Rosita's account of Marito's queer body gains gravity as a material entity. The orders of discipline and shame as corporeal subjugation mount on Marito's young queer body as Rosita recounts:

> You didn't go to the restroom at school because the prospect of exposing yourself in front of the other boys horrified you. . . . Was it because the ogre you had for a father punished you by making you take off all your clothes and then had you sit in the living room, stark naked? . . . Did you associate your nudity with punishment and shame?
>
> I saw you there once, on the floor, in the middle of the living room, covering your parts and begging me with your eyes to end your torture, to leave perhaps, or bring you a blanket.
>
> I'm sure I saw you naked once. (20)

Marito's nude body, tortured into shame and humiliated into submission, becomes the spectacle of the oppressor's power. It bestows the visible phallic rule of his "ogre" of a father with a material referent of submission. This visible display of agency on the part of the torturer makes patent the extent to which power must always have a tangible referent. Marito's punishment, the result of his inability to control his body's need to defecate (19), is amplified by the specularity of the event as witnessed by a passerby, Rosita. Constructing herself as an eyewitness to an event she really did not witness but merely heard from Marito when he was alive, Rosita circumvents this display of the "ogre's" agency by putting the tenuous nature of that power into relief. Her testimony acts to neutralize the event first by simply recounting it and making it "public," as she interpolates herself as "witness" to an event she never saw, and then by demonstrating that the subjugated subject can act in fact, not just in effect, even if subjected to silence ("begging me with your eyes to end your torture") and death.

As an adult, Marito learns to regulate his (social) body with regard to what Georges Bataille has called "nonproductive expenditure," which includes "loss, waste, and often violent pleasure" and is in opposition to so-called productive society (Champagne, *Ethics of Marginality*, 28). Marito's nonreproductive sexual activity for a fee structures an exchange between his body's use for monetary gain and its antiheterosocial use value against reproduction, against Bataille's "homogeneous society." Marito's role as a male prostitute in the text's fourth division counters the heteronormative logic that sex for pay is woman's work. At a time when queer men recognize that their bodies are a political battlefield, this portion of Marito's history centers the discussion on an ethnically marked Latino body that must sell pleasure to survive, even if giving pleasure could equal the body's very demise:

I should yank him off the floor, turn him on his back after I come. I should then smack him . . . and hit his face. . . . The next morning I will comb my hair . . . repulsed by the smell emanating from my clothes and my skin. Tired of performing. (70)

If the "performance" is tiring, the excess violence against the john's body politicizes the varieties of possible queer pleasure as well as its cost on the "performer's" body. Politicizing the body to this extent lays bare the socially scripted narratives of blame that inform public discourse about AIDS, as Marbán's finger-pointing so disturbingly attests. It makes manifest the degree to which sexuality must be explicit in privileged spheres like writing, especially Latino writing, as long as silence and value judgments reproduce harm and delimit privilege. That Marito's body is imbricated in this economic web of power relations signals the representational participation of an absent and strongly affected body in the public discourse about AIDS: the Latino body.

The imbrication of Marito's life evoked by Rosita's writing creates a participatory narrative of queer allegiances between two queer characters who negotiate agency through united subjectivities. Rosita's narrative locates Marito's body as a site of queer gender negotiations that demonstrate the politicizing effects of the Latino body and its relation to the body of criticism that posits "effects" as an agential force without recognizing that agency is a function of subjectivity, since not all subjected bodies have equal access to political agency, or "effects" that produce the simulacra of agency. As soon as knowledge is conceived in relation to the culturally inflected body (with attendant markers of difference), the corporeality of both knowers and texts becomes historically grounded. In *The Greatest Performance,* the subject is dis-membered insofar as it is effectively queered, assigned a multisexed site of enunciation, by Marito's re-membered body in Rosita's text of "difficult remembering."

Marito's re-membered queer Latino body is a transgressive act against oblivion and the ravages AIDS enacts against the body. His is a body that will not go away. Rosita's tapestry of love for Marito before, during, and after his death points to the importance of queer intimacy as necessary political action. Like a quilt made for a friend dead of AIDS, there is a poignant significance to the narrative tapestry that recounts Marito's life after his death which makes his passing both public and significant. Rosita's and Marito's passion offers a reconfiguration of the familial; fleeing from their essentializing families they construct ties that are loving, contestatory, queer.

The Greatest Performance is Rosita's re-membering of a life, Marito's life, with all its contours and bare appendages. Self-exposure is the sole courageous act that, through Rosita's writing, can situate his contestatory body at the center of her textual body. In her difficult re-membering, AIDS becomes the catalyst for her tapestry of care and compassion. If he could not act in life in his body, Marito will live re-membered as a body that matters.

The *Corpus Delicti*: *What the Body Told* and Wallace Stevens's Body (of Modernism)

Like Muñoz's text, Cuban American Rafael Campo's *What the Body Told* also addresses AIDS and memory. In Campo's case, however, the inability of language to adequately account for and remember loss generates a dialogue with language itself and the literary institutions that privilege poetry as a representational medium. For Campo, *What the Body Told* offers a reading of modernism as the *corpus delicti*,[39] the body of the crime, crime conceived as the insufficiency of modernist aesthetic agencies to give evidence of the "truth" about the body. Campo's implicit dialogue is with modernism in general and Wallace Stevens in particular. Campo attempts to confront the inadequacy of the modernist literary theory of aesthetic autonomy by establishing an intertextual dialogue with Stevens. My reference to Stevens as Campo's "intertext" signals Campo's own provocative deauthorization of the modernist notion of "genius" as a trope, a fiction of authority.

Wallace Stevens has been considered an exemplary American modernist. As Andrew Larkin has noted, Stevens, along with other masters of the "constellation of modernist American verse" like Eliot, Frost, Pound, Williams, and Crane, attempts to answer the quintessential modernist question: "how does one remake a poetry, and a culture, on the grounds of an exhausted tradition?"[40] For Stevens, this was a daunting question indeed, but one he attempted to answer within the constraints of Anglo-American New Criticism's emphasis on "aesthetic autonomy." The call for aesthetic autonomy registered an important metaphor in its desire for "a close reading," a practice that simultaneously created and reinforced the cult of genius, the belief that the poet's intention was tantamount to his artistic truth.[41] A close reading demanded above all else a hermeneutics of engagement within the text's formal boundaries, an analysis of and for meaning that considered the text to be an autonomous cultural artifact produced by a great mind. Crudely speaking, this posited the poet as the purveyor of "truth" and the critic as the purveyor of meaning.

Frank Lentricchia reminds us that this critic-centered monopoly on meaning had "the ideological effect in the United States of sustaining, under conditions of higher education, the romantic cult of genius by dispossessing middle-class readers of their active participation in the shaping of a culture and a society 'of and for the people.' The New Criticism strip[ped] those readers of their right to think of themselves as culturally central storytellers."[42] Lentricchia is too generous, of course, in his critique of modernist aesthetic agencies. His concern for the middle-class reader leaves too many "culturally central storytellers" outside New Criticism's prison-house of meaning.

If Lentricchia is right about New Criticism's ideological hegemony on American culture, and the weight of his critical authority should indemnify me (an irony he might not appreciate given his antiauthoritarian material-ist critique of modernism), then what is it precisely that interests Campo in this modernist Stevens? As a Cuban American poet, should he not write of things Cuban, at least of the experience of being Latino? Wallace Stevens's literal and metaphorical ties to Cuba and Cuba's premier organ of modern-ism, *Orígenes: Revista de arte y literatura*, provides a telling answer.

Wallace Stevens and José Rodríguez Feo, founder and one of the editors of Cuba's influential *Orígenes*, shared an epistolary interest that resulted in an enduring friendship, as evidenced by the ninety-eight extant letters be-tween 1944 and Stevens's death in 1955.[43] Rodríguez Feo was only twenty-four when he began his correspondence with Stevens, but they had much in common. Both had graduated from Harvard and had an interest in George Santayana and an appreciation for Cuban things (*Secretaries of the Moon*, 2). Stevens's affinities with the younger man suggest as much, as in a letter dated 20 June 1945: "Even though there appears to be a vast differ-ence between us in respect to our age, I am most interested in finding out how alike we are" (60). Rodríguez Feo admired Stevens and translated his poetry into Spanish for *Orígenes*, allowing his Cuban readership to be the first Spanish-speaking audience to appreciate the American modernist (6). During the almost eleven-year friendship, Stevens had occasion to send Rodríguez Feo some "lovely ties" (3) that the young man no doubt appreci-ated as a symbol of the literary ties between the two.

The literal and metaphorical ties with Cuba were evident in Stevens's concern for the nature of "Cuban things" in *Orígenes*. Stevens chides Rodrí-guez Feo for including too many things un-Cuban in *Orígenes*:

Assuming that you have a passion for Cuba, you cannot have, or at least you cannot indulge in, a passion for Brinnin and Levin. . . . it is a question of expressing the genius of your country, disengaging it from the mere mass of things, and doing this by every poem, every essay, every short story which you publish—and every drawing by Mariano, or anyone else. . . . *Cuba should be full of Cuban things and not essays on Chaucer*. (57, my emphasis)[44]

The advice to the young man manifested itself in a poem Stevens wrote for him, "A Word with José Rodríguez Feo," which appeared in Stevens's collection *Transport to Summer*.[45] Stevens's advice is summarized in the last lines of the first stanza, when the poetic persona asks, "Night is the nature of man's interior world? / Is lunar Habana the Cuba of the self?" (333). Ste-vens's use of "Habana" in his last rhetorical question is important in that

Cuba's "self" is linguistically marked, implying that "night" (the unknown) is not the nature of man's true self, his "interior world." The essence of things Cuban resides in language, performed in the poem by the signifier "Habana," that is, Habana as a Cuban thing.

Stevens's concern for things Cuban in a Cuban journal edited by Cubans reflected his anxieties about things American, which made him note that "[n]othing could be more inappropriate to American literature than its English source since the Americans are not British in sensibility."[46] Robert Rehder has noted that for Stevens, "Being an American poet . . . was the inevitable consequence of living in America" (*Poetry of Wallace Stevens*, 97). Rehder adds that Stevens "needed Europe in order to define America" and that the poem "Academic Discourse at Havana" was precisely about defining America in contradistinction to Europe. Stevens's conceptualizing America, that is, the United States, meant defamiliarizing it and re-creating it in another place, Cuba. I cite the first two stanzas from Stevens's decidedly hermetic "Academic Discourse at Havana":

I

Canaries in the morning, orchestras
In the afternoon, balloons at night. That is
A difference, at least, from nightingales,
Jehovah and the great sea-worm. The air
is not so elemental nor the earth
So near.
      But the sustenance of the wilderness
Does not sustain us in the metropoles.

II

Life is an old casino in a park.
The bills of the swans are flat upon the ground.
A desolate wind has chilled Rouge-Fatima
And a grand decadence settles down like cold.[47]

The modernist question ("how does one remake a poetry, and a culture, on the grounds of an exhausted tradition?") finds a tentative resolution in this poem. Within the internal logic of the poem, the locus amoenus is America, broadly conceived. The topos of the locus amoenus is reconceptualized in the figuration of the "casino in a park," which also serves as a metaphor for life: "Life is an old casino in a park." That is, life is seen as a gamble (the casino) in a place (park/locus amoenus) where "the sustenance of the wilderness / Does not sustain us in the metropoles." This place of "wilderness" may be taken to refer to the new American locus amoenus. The medieval cultural topos of the locus amoenus is literally transported to a place away from the "metropoles." Stevens's poetic voice, the "us," creates a subject of enunciation that identifies with the "old casino" (the old life/the old continent) brought to the "wilderness" (America)—Europe in America, if you like. Life in the "wilderness," however, cannot sustain the needs of those in "the metropoles," the "us" in the poem. Conversely, this new place requires a new language if it is to flourish. The distinction between competing forms of identity, Europe (the old) and America (the new), is further reinforced by the "grand decadence" that "settles down like cold." This is meant to suggest the northern imposition of form, literally climatological in this instance, in a new place that cannot accommodate an old form, figuratively an old aesthetic. The "cold" from the north (Europe) settles on the park (America) and chills "Rouge-Fatima."[48] Even Rouge-Fatima, red-warm María, is cold, the red suggesting the warmth of the south subjected to the north's cold imposition of form.

The significance of "swans" and "decadence" in the second stanza is perhaps the most important in situating the thematic axis of the poem in relation to its form. It reinforces how the imposition of an old form in a new environment is culturally inappropriate. The swan is suggestive both of Latin American Modernismo's "swan" par excellence, Ruben Darío, and his modernist attempt at aesthetic rupture with the old, with the heavy weight of Spain bearing on América, through "decadence" understood as an attempt to make one aesthetic supersede another. Stevens conjures Darío's modernist recourse to aesthetic decadence as a response to América's cultural dependence on Europe: Darío's attempt at revitalizing modernist aesthetic agencies under the aegis of something "new," Modernismo americano proper, in another place, América. I would like to suggest that Stevens's "Academic Discourse at Havana" attempts to define America by virtue of what (to him) it is not. He accomplishes this by defamiliarizing America and recreating it as América, à la Darío. Stevens then twice removes himself from the American identity problem he attempts to work out in the poem by displacing it geographically and culturally: a Cuban locale (the ostensible discourse at Havana) and a Latin American aesthetic movement (Modernismo).

By deferring the problem of American cultural identity by way of the swan, the poetic voice can summarize the issues of cultural dependency that inform the poem's thematic axis thus: "The world is not / The bauble of the sleepless nor a word / That should import a universal pith / To Cuba" (144). That is, reality (and I would suggest, ideology) is neither a dream

155

("The bauble of the sleepless") nor dependent on form for verification (the modernist last "word," as it were); it is coterminous with language ("the word") but not subservient to it. The poetic voice's "incantation" ends the poem by making the displacement of aesthetic agencies, from America to *América,* clear:

> *And the old casino likewise may define*
> *An infinite incantation of ourselves*
> *In the grand decadence of the perished swans* (145)

The "old casino" is conceived as a mere modernist conceit: the belief in language's ability to account for reality, to "define" (impose form over reality) an identity ("incantation of ourselves"; incantation, of course, suggests words that are to produce magical results) infinitely—in and through language—but that will not change the fact that swans perish. The symbolic death of the swan is also the death of language, crudely embodied in the figure of the genius, that poet as purveyor of meaning and truth. Stevens's body of evidence seems to suggest his tone of resignation before the "word," his lack of "rage against the dying of the light."

Stevens's resignation is related to the recognition that an attempt to replace one aesthetic with another merely replaces one hegemony with another, another way of replacing one master by another. If Rehder is right that " 'Academic Discourse at Havana' shows Stevens' relation to British literature . . . in the warm south of the imagination" (*Poetry of Wallace Stevens,* 97), and I believe he is partly right,[49] then the pith of America for this quintessential American modernist is up for grabs. As a privileged New Critical "voice of genius," Stevens speaks softly and goes quietly into the night. Responding to the question "how does one remake a poetry?" he seems to be saying that no poetic or cultural identity can be fully comprehended or adequately articulated by language; even the privileged practitioners of language, like the swan, ultimately perish. What remains is the utterance, the trace of the essence, but not "the" essence.

Rafael Campo takes Stevens's critical legacy to task, wishing, it would seem, to do what the Mexican poet Enrique González Martínez was purported to have wanted to do to Darío when he commanded, "Tuércele el cuello al cisne de engañoso plumaje" (Wring the neck of the swan with suspect plumage) in his aptly named sonnet, "Tuércele el cuello al cisne."[50] The similarities with Stevens notwithstanding (for example, the use of iambic pentameter and correlative verse), Campo ultimately differs in important respects from Stevens with regard to his relationship with language. Where words are ultimately bound to their insufficiency in Stevens's universe of meaning, Campo offers the materiality of the body as evidence of another type of writing, another type of meaning: the body as a greater sort of writing, the body semanticized.

Campo, a practicing physician and AIDS-treatment specialist at Harvard Medical School, is the author of four collections of poetry, *The Other Man Was Me: A Voyage to the New World* (1994), *What the Body Told* (1996), *Diva* (1999), and more recently, *Landscape with Human Figure* (2002).[51] Like Stevens and Rodríguez Feo, Campo graduated from Harvard and has an interest in "Cuban things" that ethnically marks much of his poetry. *What the Body Told* extends the concerns in his previous collection: identity and corporeality, positing that words may be the most vital of the body's parts. The collection is divided into five sections: "Defining Us," "Canciones de la vida," "For You All Beauty," "Canciones de la muerte," and the titular section, "What the Body Told." My specific concern is with Campo's rewriting of Stevens's legacy as it pertains to "things Cuban" and his implicit critique of modernism. I focus on one of Campo's most important intertextual rewrites: the thematic rewriting of Stevens's "The Cuban Doctor," from Stevens's important collection *Harmonium.*[52] The poem is emblematic of Campo's engagement and dialogue with Stevens's version of modernist aesthetic agencies, performing a reverse narrative of authority by rewriting Stevens's thematics (signifiers) by altering Stevens's connotative language (signified).

Campo's intervention in Latino poetry is significant because it marks a discernible turn away from emphasis on social protest[53] toward poetry as the subversion of a privileged and reified language. Both contestation and subversion can be said to be forms of protest; the important distinction is in subversion's parody of authority. Parody—in Campo's case the ostensible parody of New Criticism's cult of poetic genius—implies that the object of protest itself (modernism and its poetic conceits) has been mastered to the point where the performance of mastery supersedes its referent by putting into question its presumptuous cultural authority, its hegemony in the cultural sphere.

Campo's "The Good Doctor" is a rewriting of Stevens's well-known "The Cuban Doctor." Campo's good doctor is literally a Cuban doctor insofar as the poetic persona draws a parallel between the doctor in the poem and the explicit poet who is also a doctor, Campo himself. Biography, the proverbial "no-no" of New Criticism's reification of the meaning within the poem, combines with poesy as an aesthetic dimension in the construction of meaning in Campo's rendition of Stevens's classic poem:

"THE GOOD DOCTOR"

A doctor lived in a city
Full of dying men and women.
He ministered to them
A medicine admittedly
Not curative, and only
Slightly toxic. The medicine
Was known as empathy. It worked
Until the doctor grew more lonely—
His patients only died less quickly—
And in a fit of rage
He burned its formula.
Word spread to the sickly
As the virus had: precise
And red, omitting nothing.
The doctor's reputation changed.
No longer was he viewed as wise;
Instead, when patients came
To him they brought suspicion;
They held their breath when he would try
To hear their songs. His names,
Once various and musical,
were soon forgotten.
When he died of the disease,
They left him where he fell. (*What the Body Told,* 60)

The theme of the poem is of course death, literally and metaphorically conceived. The doctor's loss of faith in his words equals his literal death. "Once various and musical," the doctor's words, like the poet's truth and belief in language and the word, signal an ontological crisis in meaning. The literal crisis in meaning results in the doctor's inability to care for his patients' bodies with his usual dosage of "empathy," understood as his words' ability to soothe, which had once allowed the patients to die "less quickly," even if this medicine was "admittedly / Not curative, and only / Slightly toxic." Figuratively, the medicine that fails is his own faith in both the discourse about medicine's ability to save the bodies he treats and, more important, the inability of language to comprehend that loss.

The figuration of the doctor must be understood on two different connotative planes. On the literal plane, the poetic persona's limitations brought on by the unnamed disease—the specter of AIDS—are the cause of his death in that the disease leaves him incompetent to treat, to read, if you will, his patients' signs of illness appropriately and cure them. This crisis in meaning, understood as his inability to perform his role as a doctor adequately and competently, occasions another crisis in meaning, a metaphorical one. The metaphorical crisis is the result of his loss of faith in language, as the doctor is also a practitioner of a language that no longer provides meaning but becomes subservient to it in its inability to account for loss. "His patients only died less quickly," even when he had "ministered to them."

The powerful figuration of language as a virus is introduced in the fourth stanza when, after the doctor burns his formula (his doses of empathetic words as a poultice, a deferral of death), "Word spread to the sickly / As the virus had: precise / And red, omitting nothing." "Word" here refers to language and is associated with "virus": Word spread . . . / As the virus had" spread. Once the doctor loses his literal faith (in his ability to perform his duties) and his metaphorical faith (in his ability to account for the "city / Full of dying men and women") his patients bring "suspicion." Suspicion is brought both literally, to the doctor's office, and metaphorically, to the poet's house of meaning. Yet this very suspicion is not for want of evidence, as it were. The doctor's own body becomes evidence of the epistemic inability to cure or provide solace, but all is not in vain. The doctor/poet's body is the cultural *corpus delicti,* the body of the viral crime for which the doctor/poet's body serves as evidence. Though "His names" "Were soon forgotten," the body remains as evidence "where he fell." Like Muñoz's construction of an anesthetized body of loss, Marito's body remembered in and through narrative, the doctor/poet's body here is evidence of loss. The body left where it "fell" is devoid of language and identity; it cannot speak and its identity is stripped of its use value (the body "identified" as both a practitioner of language and of medicine). Then there is the body's haunting of language and the spaces of memory.

Avery F. Gordon, in *Ghostly Matters: Haunting and the Sociological Imagination,* conjures "haunting" in the following manner:

> Haunting is a constituent element of modern social life. It is neither premodern superstition nor individual psychosis; it is a generalizable social phenomenon of great import. To study social life one must confront the ghostly aspects of it. This confrontation requires (or produces)

a fundamental change in the way we know and make knowledge, in our mode of production.[54]

For Gordon, this entails a "thoroughgoing epistemological critique of modernity as what is contemporaneously ours with an insurgent sociological critique of its forms of domination" (*Ghostly Matters*, 10–11). Following Max Horkheimer and Theodor Adorno's critique of modernity, Gordon engages their "On the Theory of Ghosts" (from *The Dialectic of Enlightenment*) in order to designate a space of meaning that recognizes an "Other-knowledge," the weight of memory, the contours of feeling, and the shape of desire's willingness and need to know a lost sense of being through the legacy of beings. The "dead" speak to the living through memory: hauntology.

It is in this sense that Campo's *corpus delicti*, the poet/doctor's body of the crime as it were, haunts and is haunted by Stevens's fetishization of things Cuban by performing a reverse reading of modernism from the subject position of a Cuban doctor in Stevens's America. Where Stevens's teleology posits the end of the word as the end of meaning, Campo's dialogue with the ghost of modernism is meant to suggest an aesthetic rage against the dying of the light, the body understood as meaning by virtue of what it "told" when it was alive, the incomplete but necessary memory of the body. In Stevens's "Cuban Doctor," the poem proper, this is an impossibility, something Stevens's Cuban doctor cannot apprehend:

"THE CUBAN DOCTOR"

I went to Egypt to escape
The Indian, but the Indian struck
Out of his cloud and from his sky.
This was no worm bred in the moon,
Wriggling far down the phantom air,
And on a comfortable sofa dreamed.
The Indian struck and disappeared.
I knew my enemy was near—I,
Drowsing in summer's sleepiest horn. (*Harmonium*, 64–65)

The poem's theme is death and, like Campo's rendition, a literal and metaphorical death. In Stevens's poem the Cuban doctor's enemy is the Indian who brings death, like the virus that brought death (AIDS) in Campo's poem. Stevens once again defamiliarizes the theme's form from its execution. The poetic persona, the speaking subject, is a Cuban doctor who attempts to elude death by "escaping" to Egypt. But death's figuration, "the Indian," strikes all the same. The Indian functions here like Campo's "virus" in that he is a vector of death that the doctor attempts to elude without success. In the second stanza, the doctor's fear of death is clearly not unfounded. Death is no "worm bred in the moon," not something created in the imagination, not a ghost in the "phantom air" dreamed "on a comfortable sofa." Its presence is the opposite: complete discomfort for the living doctor. Resignation before the dying of the light manifests itself in the third stanza, when the doctor receives death's final call: "The Indian struck and disappeared." This prompts the speaking subject to recognize that his "enemy was near." His enemy is both the Indian's curse, death, and the poetic "I's" inability to counter the finality of the Indian's visitation. As in Campo's version, the Cuban doctor dies, "Drowsing" suggesting permanent sleep as the poetic persona succumbs to death. The end of summer, "summer's sleepiest horn," marks the literal fall (the season) as well as the metaphorical fall, death.

As a Cuban doctor in Stevens's America, Campo's dialogue with Stevens's "Cuban doctor" performs a haunting, a conversation with the specter of modernism and with the emblematic American modern whose fascination with things Cuban occasions his own query into that which is distinctly "American." Campo's questioning of modernism's principal fiction, read as absolution from an ethic of care of the self in the face of linguistic insufficiency—the lack of rage against the dying of the light—forces him to pursue a corporeally grounded recourse to meaning—a conceit of meaning, but nonetheless one of ethical action. As when Odysseus visits Hades and realizes that he must listen to the dead before he can leave—since all dead souls crave an audience with the living—Campo's dialogue with modernism performs a haunting of "The Cuban Doctor" that offers the literal *corpus delicti,* the dead "Good Doctor," as evidence of the need to write as well as re-member the body in theory and in deed. Neither in denial of death or in terror of it, Campo effectively renders America's spaces of death livable through memory, the spaces of images and words.

The Latino Body, in Theory

The versions of the national body posited by the writers I study in this chapter refute the social symbolic ideals of citizenship and national belonging that govern bodies and mark them as legible and legitimate within the confines of the National Symbolic. They confront the fact that, at century's opening, American national identity still requires a conception of citizenship that entails the rejection of the very difference that paradoxically defines "America."

Umpierre's need to deterritorialize the Boricua experience from geography onto the body suggests that the exscription of lesbian Latina identity is as much a function of Puerto Rican discourses of paternalism and exclusion as it is of dominant American conceptions of subjectivity. For Umpierre, compulsive nationalism, like compulsive heteronormalization, is an index of state oppression.

Inflecting American cultural memory with representations of difference, Muñoz and Campo engage the popular medical discourses that describe the AIDS virus as an invasion of parasites that need to occupy host bodies to survive. Current medical discourse continues to metaphorize host and parasite relations on the level of the National Symbolic by blurring boundaries, borders, and thresholds of meanings. Like the "illegal" immigrant in the Chicano context explored in the previous chapters, the metaphor of illegality in this juncture is the AIDS body, a process that allows AIDS to be read as anti-American. That queer Latinos and African American males are the hardest hit in this epidemic is no coincidence.[55] Both Muñoz and Campo graft Latino-specific cultural memories onto the National Symbolic by tapping into collective fears surrounding the finitude of life, the vulnerability of body and state, and the possibility of ethical community building through commemoration as a form of cultural continuity and survival.

The *corpus delicti,* then, as the texts I have studied demonstrate, requires bringing evidence into the public sphere of signification, regardless of how difficult that re-membering may be. As collective practices of freedom, these texts are civic interventions that remind the dominant collectivity that the Latino body shapes the National Symbolic in practice, not just in theory. In the process, these bodies form Other national narratives, Other stories of cultural contribution and survival of the Latino body politic that tell of "Anatomy and physiology . . . / The tiny sensing organs of the tongue— / Each nameless cell contributing its needs. / It was fabulous what the body told" (Campo, *What the Body Told,* 122).

Democracy's Graveyard: Dead Citizenship and the
Latino Body

Body Parts

From its inauguration on January 1, 1994, the North American Free Trade Agreement (NAFTA) allowed for the development of "free trade contact zones" along the Mexican side of the U.S.-Mexico border and with it an expendable labor force: not just the poor but the destitute of Mexico's southern provinces, mostly women in search of work. The assembly plants and factories along the border found fertile ground and unprecedented growth in Ciudad Juárez, Mexico, across from El Paso, Texas. From its inception, the NAFTA experiment in North American "free trade" made Ciudad Juárez what Charles Bowden called the globalized "laboratory of our future."[1] In a disarming piece first published in 1996 by *Harper's* magazine, Bowden noted how the NAFTA boom had made Juárez not only the largest industrial zone in Mexico but also the killing field of the new world order.

This experiment in the flow of commodity capital and globalization had, and still has, an unrepresentable side. Bowden reported in words and, for the first time to an audience in the United States, photographs that documented the slaughter of Mexican border bodies that were being found in the Rio Grande, which separates the two countries, and in the desert surrounding Juárez. The killings have come to be known as "*los femicidios de Juárez*," the Juárez femicides, or simply the Juárez murders.

The "Juárez murders" refers to the killing and often ritualized dismemberment of mostly female workers from the interior of Mexico who come looking for work in the transnational *maquiladoras*. Though the estimates surrounding the deaths are not dependable (the law-enforcement agencies are said to be implicated in the killings), they range from more than four hundred documented cases of murdered women since 1993 (when the pattern of killings was first reported), a figure that does not include the women who have been "disappeared."[2]

Bowden writes of the underside of NAFTA that had not yet registered in the public sphere at the time of his initial report:

> The cities of Ciudad Juárez and El Paso, Texas, constitute the largest border community on earth, but hardly anyone seems to admit that the Mexican side exists. Within this forgotten urban maze stalk some of the boldest photographers still roaming the streets with 35-mm cameras. Over the past two years I have become a student of their work, because I think they are capturing something: the look of the future. . . . We have these models in our heads about growth, development, infrastructure. Juárez doesn't look like any of these images, and so our ability to see this city comes and goes, mainly goes. (44)

The stark contrast between the promise of globalization ("growth, development, infrastructure") and its lived realities make this laboratory of post-NAFTA "free-trade" a dystopian space where industrial growth generates poverty at a much faster pace than it distributes wealth (ibid.). It is the literal image of Juárez, however, as reproduced and printed by the photographer-stalkers, that allows this dystopian image to counter the theoretical storehouse of "models we have in our heads about growth, development, infrastructure," the belief in the benevolence of the United States' economic model as a sustainable reality anywhere in the world. If the *maquiladoras* had to comply with the same working conditions, job security, and pay in Juárez as across the border in El Paso, there would, of course, be no need to have these factories on the Mexican side of the divide.

Bowden's sharp critique of NAFTA's failed promise registers its counterpoint in the images that speak to another side of reality in Mexico's laboratory of the future, the darker side the neoliberal moment. Politicians and economists may speculate about a global economy fueled by free trade, but these speculations are not necessary because in Juárez the future has already arrived. And this dystopian future in our midst is making the subaltern body an expendable commodity in the new economic world order: "Most of the workers are women and most of the women are young. By the late twenties or early thirties the body slows and cannot keep up the pace of work. Then, like any used-up thing, the people are junked" (ibid., 48). What made Bowden's piece in *Harper's* so haunting was not the statistics surrounding the growth of trade and the benefits to the northernmost major NAFTA players, or the predictable loser in tripartite flow of capital— that is a familiar story—but rather the photographs of the dismembered and mutilated factory workers. The images reproduced in his *Harper's* piece could be said to be redundant in their ability to concretize human devaluation through their literal indexical relationship to corporeal disintegration and dismemberment. The photographs themselves all pointed to a set of prior actions and motivations. This is what Benjamin, as I mentioned in my discussion of *Earth* in chapter 2, noted as the essence of what photographs of crime scenes refuse to abjure: the onus of responsibility, the perpetrator or perpetrators of the crime, the questions surrounding motivation.

The images of the Juárez murders—burned skeletal remains, of body parts rotting in the desert heat like unclaimed or discarded perishable goods —registered long enough to make reader-viewers recoil in horror but ultimately defer action to those entrusted to represent the interests of the dead: their government representatives. Indeed, in the early phase of the massacre of Juárez the bodies were dumped in the Rio Grande, the ambiguous terrain of floating citizenship where, bloated and unclaimed, they remained in a state of *statelessness*. And who would claim them in an act of postmortem "naturalization," much less investigate the nature of their deaths, when these stateless bodies have not had anyone to represent their interests? Such are the limits of democracy and the promise of representation through democratic proxy. The images of the dead forced an accounting, but inaction on the part of the state, both Mexico and the United States, relegated their referents—the very materiality of the dead—to democracy's graveyard on the Mexican side of the border. It is against this backdrop, this gross literalization of the *corpus delicti*, that I now turn to the Latino body's latest crisis of representation.

Desert Blood and Narrative Agency

Alicia Gaspar de Alba's *Desert Blood: The Juárez Murders* (2005) offers a narrative accounting of the national *corpus delicti's* most recent crime *across* the

165

U.S. border in Juárez.[3] It is significant that this accounting is undertaken within the narrative demands and genre constraints of "detective fiction,"[4] where solving the crime is central to the restoration of reason in the narrative logic of the world enacted on the page. That the crimes as well as the characters who populate Gaspar de Alba's novel have real-life referents extends the concerns of speculative fiction and positions this whodunit as a testimonial-like accounting of a place in time in need of what I have called, following Toni Morrison, narrative rememory: a counterhistorical re-presentation of past events in need of national reevaluation. Gaspar de Alba's *Desert Blood* attempts to offer a narrative recapitulation of deadly serious events that refuses to capitulate to the demands of the historical elision, the official story, as it were, of the Juárez murders.

Set in the late 1990s, the novel tells the story of a circumstantial sleuth, Ivon Villa. Ivon is a young scholar teaching at a small college in Los Angeles while trying to finish her dissertation, "Marx Meets the Women's Room: The Representation of Class and Gender in Bathroom Graffiti (Three Case Studies)." The dean at the college "hadn't thought much of the topic . . . finding it too frivolous for a Ph.D. candidate, until she explained that public bathrooms are a type of exhibition space in which bodies of women and the graffiti they write and draw on walls . . . can be read semiotically to analyze the social construction of class and gender identity in what Marx called the 'community of women'" (*Desert Blood*, 18–19). Realizing that she cannot put her personal life on hold for the unremitting demands of the academy, she and her partner, Bridgit, decide to adopt a Mexican child. The child's mother, Cecilia, is a *maquiladora* worker in Juárez who agrees to the adoption through some shady legal wrangling that will allow the baby to be born across the border in El Paso. As Cecilia nears her due date, Ivon flies to her hometown of El Paso to make preparations for the delivery and the adoption.

On the plane Ivon picks up a magazine and begins to read about the Juárez murders, incredulous that the murders have received such scant media coverage. Upon her arrival, the murders affect her directly when she learns that Cecilia is the latest victim of the femicides. Soon her own sister, Irene, disappears after an evening in Juárez. Despair and horror turn to resolve, and with the help of her cousin, Ximena, and a social-activist priest, Father Francis, Ivon desperately searches for her sister amid the chaos and corruption of Juárez. Though the novel itself demands a fuller accounting of the *corpus delicti*, I will here limit myself to the pivotal moment for Ivon as she searches for the traces of her sister's body.

The moment in question interpolates Ivon into the shared histories and secrets between the sister cities of El Paso and Juárez and sets the stage for the critique of how the mutual dependence between the two cities foments the collusive veil of silence that allows the femicides to take place: the cities' entangled economies that have created comforts for the managerial classes who cross the border to safe, depoliticized homes in El Paso, and the possibility of literal dismemberment for Juárez *maquila* workers. What Bowden calls our ability—from this side of the border—to forget that the other side exists is put into relief when the porousness of citizenship is exposed literally through the border.

Irene's disappearance occurs after going to a carnival in Ciudad Juárez, directly over one of the bridges that connects the two cities. Left to the care of Ivon's former lover, Raquel, Irene is introduced to a group of youngsters who consider her a *pocha*, an assimilated Mexican. In an effort to fit in she drinks with her high-school-age peers in the carnivalesque atmosphere. Under the influence of the visual and ingested intoxicants she jumps into the Rio Grande and begins to taunt the Border Patrol on the other side of the river, "daring the Border Patrol vans cruising the bridge to take her in so she could laugh at them and tell them she was an American citizen" (111).

It is in this space of fluid citizenship that the purported permeability of the border is reduced to its arbitrary ability to signify. The space between appearing to be a "wetback" and the identity enacted by the state through citizenship makes patent the extent to which identity papers are indeed a convention, but a deadly serious convention.[5] When Ivon realizes that her sister has disappeared, she cannot depend on the state to help her: Irene, who she hopes is still alive, loses all ability to signify citizenship on either side of the border as Mexican and U.S. authorities alike defer involvement. Like the women dumped in the river after death, the river that delineates citizenship and delimits the body's ability to *mean* sets the narrative pretext from which to indict both Mexico and the United States for the Juárez murders.

Gaspar de Alba's novel suggests that the principles of publicity must be turned against the orders of silence and inaction. The novel itself includes newspaper editorials about the femicides, composites of actual abductions and murders, along with the flyer that Ivon creates and plasters all over Juárez. Indeed, it is Ivon's insistence on taking matters into her own hands that allows the events to unfold and shows how both the Border Patrol and the Mexican police, the *Judiciales,* are imbricated not only in her sister's disappearance but in the Juárez murders. The clues that lead her to the criminal infrastructure that is Juárez and El Paso are discreetly written on the wall:

> She took a quick look at the graffiti, thinking maybe someone was leaving clues on the walls of women's toilets. Amid a hodgepodge of sexual innuendoes, dirty drawings, and comments on food coupons and contraceptives, she spotted two remarks that could be useful. Over the screw holes where the toilet paper holder might have been fastened once, inside a box decorated with stars, was the statement: *Aquí no hay cholas ni maqui-locas* [there aren't any Mexican American women here or crazy *maquiladora* female workers]. And in tiny letters at the bottom edge of the door: *El Nuevo gobernador le chupa la verga a la migra* [the new governor sucks the Border Patrol's cock]. (211)

It is through the foreshadowing written outside the officiating discourse of the state that the countertext emerges on the hidden bathroom wall of reckoning and allows her to put into practice what her training permits her to read—the discarded language of the Other. Like the traces of her disappeared sister that she renders visible through the flyers she hands to strangers in desperation, Ivon's search for the "truth" is motivated by an ethical and loving call to action evincing the latest crisis moment for the Latino body in ostensibly transnational times.

The Ends of the Latino Body

> The ceremony always begins for me in the same way . . . always the hungry woman. Always the place of disquiet (*inquietud*) moves the writing to become a kind of excavation, an earth-dig of the spirit found through the body. The impulse to write may begin in the dream, the déjà-vu, a few words, which once uttered through my own mouth or the mouth of another, refuse to leave the body of the heart. Writing is an act prompted by intuition, a whispered voice, a tightening of the gut. It is an irrevocable promise to not forget.
> —Cherríe Moraga, *A Xicanadyke Codex of Changing Consciousness*[6]

The previous chapters have proposed that the racializations of Latinos and the presumptive grounds by with they have been constructed almost exclusively as extranationals in the public sphere—from the Mexican-American War to the present—have sustained and implicitly sanctioned a "tiered democracy of bodies" where certain national bodies matter more than others. The inherent contradiction, the incommensurability between the democratic imperative of equality and the lived experience of a national hierarchy of bodies marked by race, ethnicity, gender, sexuality, and language, suggests that the national culture cannot recognize difference as its own creation for its very sustainability requires adherence to a fiction of equality that the texts I study belie. This is the "irrevocable promise to not forget" that Cherríe Moraga so poignantly refers to, the contestation and reelaboration of a haunting that requires acts of continuous rememory. It is in the memory of *inquietud*, "disquiet," that prompts Moraga's excavation that mines, like a Benjaminian translator, the buried memory, the haunted national history, that the heart guards and the mouth utters.

The practice of freedom, the "impulse" to utter and to write from this place of *inquietud*, is the promise to construct a space in "the body of the heart" that publicly registers what the National Symbolic would seek to deny; it is tantamount, at the risk of sentimentality, to writing a heart onto the national body politic. The motivation to do so, to act against oblivion, is marked by what could be understood as the political agency and utopian longings of "brown affect." Lawrence Grossberg positions the importance of emotion as an enabling force in political struggles within our critical grasp when he names the difficulty of articulating affect in critical terms: "Emotion is itself a notoriously difficult topic for cultural critics who often try to explain it as if it were merely the aura of ideological effects." He continues, "Affect is perhaps the most difficult plane of human life to define and describe . . . because there is no critical vocabulary to describe its different forms and structures."[7] For Grossberg, "Affect identifies the strength of the investment which anchors people in particular experiences, practices, identities, meanings, and pleasures. . . . it is in their affective lives that people constantly struggle to care about something, and to find the energy to survive, to find the passion necessary to imagine and enact their own projects and possibilities" (*We Gotta Get Out,* 82–83). In this sense, in the difficulty of apprehending the elusive vocabulary of feeling, affect both marks and produces history, substantiating—as Frederic Jameson would have it—that "[h]istory is what hurts."[8]

The various and variegated narratives and cultural interventions staged in this book enact brown affect as the salvo from which to utter and enable an indexical Latino relationship to the United States by becoming historical. The "Latino" subject is constructed discursively in a series of disarming and—as we have seen—sometimes collusive identity practices that engage majority culture in order to enact and envision an inclusive space that attempts to position democracy's promise within its collective reach.

The Latino Body: Becoming Historical

Anthropologist Emily Martin points out how Claude Lévi-Strauss's description of the category of the "primitive" in *Tristes tropiques*[9] became the focus of attention in the academy at the moment when the phenomenon itself was ending. Martin suggests that the body is presently "ending," at least as we know it, much like Lévi-Strauss's "primitive," which was then in the process of disappearing for the last time.[10] Despite the literalist implications of Martin's "end of the body," I have attempted to demonstrate how the Latino body has been central to discussions regarding American citizenship, subjectivity, ethnoracial identity and nationalisms, and the subject of civil society in ways that make the body anything but an exhausted trope for subaltern subjects. The Latino body's role in the construction of ethnic identity in the national culture has been key to negotiations that have put the status of both the dominant and the ethnically marked body into question. It has negotiated the possibilities for national belonging during pivotal crisis moments in American cultural history, which have in turn generated crisis responses to the politics of cultural engagement with the dominant majority culture. From the American 1848 to the present, these subject modalities can be divided into a series of principal, and often overlapping, subject positions that posit *becoming historical* in response to cultural conflict and the ever-looming possibility of imminent erasure.

The subject of Latino cultural history emerges at a time of racial, ethnic cultural, and linguistic disjunctures after the consolidation of the United States in the nineteenth century, when the dominant discourses of national belonging attempted to relegate the Latino body to the national archives. The historical subject, the Latino body written into American history, emerges as a response to the limited possibilities for participating in the national culture. In Eulalia Pérez's *An Old Woman and Her Recollections* and María Amparo Ruiz de Burton's *The Squatter and the Don,* becoming historical entails interpolating themselves as representative Mexican citizens who are historically tied to the newly consolidated American republic as well as racially compatible with the hegemonic national ideations of "Americanness" and whiteness as its structuring principle. The recourse to the politics of "passing" signals the limited possibilities for participating in the National Symbolic. Passing and the discourse of racial accommodation ultimately become a strategy of unidirectional cultural, linguistic, and ethnoracial accommodation, placing the onus of belonging solely on the racially, ethnically, and linguistically inflected body of the Other. This is not to suggest that all Mexican public-sphere engagements attempted to align Mexicanness with Anglo-American racial notions of white supremacy. Other texts resist national incorporation and compulsive whiteness by haunting the national archive of meaning with memories of violence that recall and re-member the cost of national consolidation written on the bodies of those murdered at the heels of national territorial consolidation. Catarina Ávila de Ríos's *Memoirs* graphically detailed the human costs associated with frontier expansion and the ethnoracial composition that was already present and commonplace in the newly incorporated Alta California, Mexico's northernmost province, before Anglo-American encroachment and colonization. The limited, if not altogether absent, inclusion of such narratives from Bancroft's *History of California* tells us something about the limits of cultural *convivencia* and California living (and dying) after the American 1848.

A Latino counterpatriotic subject emerges when it is no longer possible to believe, much less rely on, the national constructions of citizenship perpetuated in the public sphere that purportedly protect all nationals. Patriotism is thus conceived as Chicano militancy in the first cultural-nationalist assault on majority culture by what today are understood to be "Chicanos." This counterpatriotic subject seeks to account for and reenact the scene of the cultural crime, the national *corpus delicti*. Tomás Rivera's *Earth* both evinces the crime and creates a narrative of counterpatriotism by calling attention to the national dead, the Chicano body as the *habeas corpus* of the national crime. The Chicano body is offered as proof of nationalism's oppressive grip gone awry in the National Symbolic order. As an heir to the previous cultural engagements that sought to racially refashion Latino relations with the majority culture in the public sphere, *Earth* dismisses the two most prevalent claims to cultural enfranchisement that were perpetuated well into the twentieth century: "passing for Spain," the spurious myth of the "Spanish Southwest," as well as the truncated image of Mexican Americans depicted in José Antonio Villareal's *Pocho* as immigrants attempting to assimilate through the broader largesse of the national culture.

Born of the Chicano equality-rights movements of the 1960s and early 1970s, the institutionalization of Chicano studies in the West and of Latino studies in the East faced a nativist and neoconservative assault by the late 1980s and 1990s. The crisis generated by the so-called Culture Wars of the

Reagan-Bush era created the need to legitimate the study of ethnic, racial, and sexual minorities in the U.S. academy through theoretical and methodological "rigor." Multiculturalism allowed for the theoretical inclusion of the Latino body in the academy, while at the same time Reaganomics and its emphasis on economic restructuring, as well as the professionalization and rise of the corporate model in the academy, delimited the entry of the very bodies these texts sought to represent as the various assaults on affirmative action make clear.

The genealogical subject emerges at the borderlands of Latino, Latin American, and American literary history when it becomes strategically expedient to create and situate a Latino subject of enunciation in the national past and *on* the national territory. This is the case with Alvar Núñez Cabeza de Vaca's *Castaways* and the critical readings that have attempted to imbue the body of the text and the text on the body with anachronistic meaning. Juan Bruce-Novoa's influential 1989 essay, "Naufragios en los mares de la significación: De *La Relación* de Cabeza de Vaca a la literatura chicana," and the English translation that appeared in 1993 as "Shipwrecked in the Seas of Signification: Cabeza de Vaca's *Relación* and Chicano Literature," conditioned the reception of Latino literary studies and its inclusion in the greater rubric of American literature. In justifying the greater legacy of "Chicanos" in the territories that were to compose the United States after the American 1848, Latino criticism resuscitated the "genealogical model" of origins in order to "prove" that the Latino was not an interloper on the national scene of culture or the geographic contours of the country. I have contended that such celebrations of difference—Cabeza de Vaca as the nation's first multicultural subject—have paradoxically reinstated the very cultural recourse to accommodation they have sought to denounce in theory: assimilation. This crisis of academic legitimation offered an anachronistically untenable Chicano forefather that could assuage liberal guilt through the theoretical inclusion of people of color, while unwittingly maintaining the very real and lived exclusion of the peoples it sought to represent outside the halls of the academy.

Coterminous with the crisis of legitimation in the academy, the desiring Latino subject emerged out of the civil rights movement and began to reveal the movement's blinders with regard to sexuality and gendered participation in the construction of national Chicano and Latino identity projects. Luz María Umpierre's *Margarita Poems* posited the Boricua body as a floating signifier and symbol for Puerto Rican subjectivity in an attempt to free the gendered body from socially scripted narratives of love, nation, paternalism, and desire. The desiring subject in Elías Miguel Muñoz's *The Greatest Performance* likewise engaged cutting-edge critical questions about the body, subjectivity, performativity, and the purportedly sexless subject of philosophy. Reacting against aesthetic agencies that duplicitously depoliticize the writing scene, the desiring subject in Rafael Campo's *What the Body Told* "translated" a modern's fascination with *cubanalia*, all things distinctly Cuban, in order to question modernism's legacy and the role of ethics in writing, Latino forms of mourning and remembrance, and representation in the age of AIDS. The literal death enacted on the Latino body politic through national neglect and cultural unintelligibility found a parallel on the Mexico-U.S. border.

Where Anzaldúa had politicized the border as a site of continuous racial, sexual, and cultural strife, the "1,950 mile-long open wound" written on the Chicana body through exclusion and homophobia, the flow of transnational capital after the creation of NAFTA ushered in the most recent and deadly crisis moment for the Latino body. As *maquiladoras* sprung up on the Mexican side of the U.S.-Mexico border, Mexico's poor were lured to the precipice of their nation's fringes to partake in the benefits associated with "free trade," without the labor protections required on the U.S. side of the border. So it is that the latest Latino crisis is again enacted on the border over a century after Bourke's emblematic piece with which I began this study. Gaspar de Alba's *Desert Blood* registers the life force that transforms the orders of subjection through the possibilities offered by narrative rememory. The text offers a critique of neither neoliberalism nor the states that sustain it as the new global order of commerce. It is a representation in the world, tooled with hope and the simplicity of brown affect as the structuring principle from which to account for love in one's immediate world. As such, it is a utopian move, the emancipatory potential of brown affect enacted. The accounting and re-memberings offered by the texts in this study, and the versions of the Latino body they leave in their wake, allow us to envision cultural transformations that might prove to be practices of freedom outside of the confines of democracy's graveyard.

Notes

Notes to the Introduction

1. I invoke the nationalistic popular meaning of the terms "America" and "American" as connotative shorthand for "democracy" and "equality," the presumed foundational markers for the United States as an "imagined community."

2. For a reading of Bourke's "The American Congo" as an exemplar of U.S. imperial designs, see José David Saldívar, *Border Matters: Remapping American Cultural Studies* (Berkeley: University of California Press, 1997), 161–68. Saldívar follows José E. Limón's important analysis of Bourke and "The American Congo" in Limón's *Dancing with the Devil: Society and Cultural Poetics in Mexican-American South Texas* (Madison: University of Wisconsin Press, 1994), 21–42. I am indebted to the important and pioneering work of these scholars even if the readings of the texts they have brought to critical attention differ from my own.

3. I am referring to publicly rendered forms of symbolic representation facilitated by print culture, as well as topological spaces that define a citizen's place in an emerging and expansive nineteenth-century America. As Benedict Anderson has noted, "print-capitalism" allows a seemingly disparate citizenry to think of themselves as a coherent nation (*Imagined Communities: Reflections on the Origins and Spread of Nationalism* [London: Verso, 1991], 67–82).

4. The title of this book registers the singular Latino body as an enabling fiction of identity for strategic political gain insofar as individuals in democratic systems are most influential in groups. This "enabling fiction" can therefore never encapsulate the diversity of class, ethnic, gender, linguistic, and racial realities lived in the United States by the people it seeks to render politically and culturally visible through rhetorical expediency. It can, however, help move debates surrounding the Latino body politic toward theorizations of the plural collectivity it should be understood to be if it were unconstrained by the limits imposed by national forms of subjection and the specter of ahistoricity that I engage in this book.

5. R. Philip Buckley offers a critique of the phenomenological notion of crisis in *Husserl, Heidegger, and the Crisis of Philosophical Responsibility* (Dordrecht: Kluwer Academic, 1992). He observes how Heidegger mediates the "messianic tone or oracular pronouncements" inherent in Husserl's notion of crises by asserting a crisis's relational *response to* what it invariably signals: forgetfulness and memory's concomitant, fragmented attempts at recovery (269).

6. I borrow the term "cultural citizenship" from Renato Rosaldo, who uses it to describe both the legal category of U.S. citizenship and the forms of engagement and cultural reciprocity sustained by subaltern subjects who are not citizens but

still live and work in the United States whether they are "documented" or "undocumented." See Renato Rosaldo, "Cultural Citizenship, Inequality, and Multiculturalism," in *Latino Cultural Citizenship: Claiming Identity, Space, and Rights,* ed. William V. Flores and Rina Benmayor (Boston: Beacon, 1997), 27–38.

7. Jürgen Habermas, *The Structural Transformation of the Public Sphere: An Inquiry into a Category of Bourgeois Society,* trans. Thomas Burger with Frederick Lawrence (Cambridge, Mass.: MIT Press, 1989).

8. Habermas's analysis of the public sphere, born of reiterations of the Enlightenment project's well-known ideals regarding justice, equity, and representation, has been subjected to considerable critical scrutiny. For a feminist critique, see Nancy Fraser, "Rethinking the Public Sphere: A Contribution to the Critique of Actually Existing Democracy," in *The Phantom Public Sphere,* ed. Bruce Robbins (Minneapolis: University of Minnesota Press, 1993), 1–32; for a critique of race and the public sphere, see the essays in Black Public Sphere Collective, *The Black Public Sphere: A Public Culture Book* (Chicago: University of Chicago Press, 1995).

9. See Gayatri Chakravorty Spivak, *Outside in the Teaching Machine* (New York: Routledge, 1993). In the opening interview with Ellen Rooney, Spivak states that "[i]n a personalist culture, even among people in the humanities, who are generally wordsmiths, it's the idea of a *strategy* that has been forgotten. The strategic has been taken as a point of self-differentiation," that is, an overdetermined generalization, rather than as a possible site of potentiated power for subaltern subjects (5).

10. Lauren Gail Berlant, in *The Queen of America Goes to Washington City: Essays on Sex and Citizenship* (Durham, N.C.: Duke University Press, 1997), notes how the "National Symbolic" is the archive of "official texts" (the flag, Uncle Sam, Mount Rushmore, the Pledge of Allegiance) that create "a national 'public' that constantly renounces political knowledge where it exceeds intimate mythic national codes" (103). In other words, through identifying with the national storehouse of images citizens renounce public agency by allowing affective affiliation to stand in for democratic participation. Berlant's "National Symbolic" encapsulates in critical and political short-hand what Lisa Lowe refers to as "the national collective" in her important book *Immigrant Acts: On Asian American Cultural Politics* (Durham, N.C.: Duke University Press, 1996). I mediate the highly useful tensions between Lowe's culturalist and Berlant's political critique of U.S. nationalism in this study.

11. Paul Gilroy, *Against Race: Imagining Political Culture beyond the Color Line* (Cambridge, Mass.: Harvard University Press, 2000), 12.

12. David R. Roediger, *Towards the Abolition of Whiteness: Essays on Race, Politics, and Working-Class History* (New York: Verso, 1994), 12.

13. Richard Dyer, *White* (London: Routledge, 1997), 1.

14. One of the first and most notable examples of the conflation of U.S. Latino literature with Latin American literatures is Frank N. Magill's *Masterpieces of Latino Literature* (New York: HarperCollins, 1994), in which Mexican José Joaquín Fernán-

dez de Lizardi (1776–1827) is anthologized along with Brazilian Joaquim María Machado de Assis (1839–1908) and Chicano Tomás Rivera (1935–1984). The implicit ideological association is, of course, delimiting rather than inclusive: any way you parse them, Latinos are not of the United States but foreign, and thereby —so this logic presumes—alienated from the national culture. This makes it possible for mainstream audiences and publishing houses to domesticate Latino literature by reading "Magical Realism" into the most improbable places. Karen Christian notes how reviewer Andrei Codrescu stated in the *New York Times Book Review* that U.S. Cuban Roberto Fernández's bilingually exquisite novel, *Raining Backwards*, could have been greatly improved if "the echoes of García Márquez . . . had been made conscious." Karen Christian, *Show and Tell: Identity as Performance in U.S. Latina/o Fiction* (Albuquerque: University of New Mexico Press, 1997), 126.

15. Andrés Bello, "Autonomía cultural de América," in *Conciencia intelectual de América: Antología del ensayo hispanoamericano, 1836–1959,* ed. Carlos Ripoll (New York: Eliseo Torres, 1974), 49. Ripoll reminds us in his introduction to the essay that the original title was "Modo de escribir la historia" ("Method for the Writing of History") (48).

16. Doris Sommer, *Foundational Fictions: The National Romances of Latin America* (Berkeley: University of California Press, 1991).

17. Juan E. De Castro, *Mestizo Nations: Culture, Race, and Conformity in Latin American Literature* (Tucson: University of Arizona Press, 2002), xii.

18. For a discussion of narration, nation building, and Latino literatures, see Christian, *Show and Tell.* In Latin American literatures, see Doris Sommer, *One Master for Another: Populism as Patriarchal Rhetoric in Dominican Novels* (Lanham, Md.: University Press of America, 1983), and *Foundational Fictions.* Other important texts in the field are Anderson, *Imagined Communities,* Homi K. Bhabha, *The Location of Culture* (London: Routledge, 1994), and Christopher Looby, *Voicing America: Language, Literary Form, and the Origins of the United States* (Chicago: University of Chicago Press, 1996).

19. For an important analysis of the expediency of the term "Latino," see Suzanne Oboler, *Ethnic Labels, Latino Lives: Identity and the Politics of (Re)Presentation in the United States* (Minneapolis: University of Minnesota Press, 1995), 171.

20. The literalization of this elusive embrace is to be found in the 108th Congress's dubiously named "DREAM ACT." The Development, Relief and Education for Alien Minors Act (DREAM ACT) has had several incarnations in the Senate and has been reintroduced by senators Orrin Hatch of Utah and Richard Durbin of Illinois. It states that those children of "illegal" immigrants who are willing to either serve in the U.S. armed forces, graduate from a two-year college, or perform 950 hours of community service may be granted temporary legal residency. In the guise of a patriotic embrace, the military-service option obviates the others by making military service the most "feasible" to the undocumented poor. A similar bill has been introduced in the House addressing the same issue and is commonly known as the Student Adjustment Act.

21. Anderson, *Imagined Communities*, 204.

22. I thank Cherríe Moraga for giving me a copy and allowing me to quote from her forthcoming collection of essays, *A Xicanadyke Codex of Changing Consciousness* (unpublished manuscript, 2005). The quotation comes from a chapter titled "An Irrevocable Promise: Staging the Story Xicana," part of which she presented as a public lecture at Bryn Mawr College on February 25, 2005, "Still Loving in the War Years: Portrait of a Chicana/Latina Consciousness." I will turn to this essay in the conclusion.

23. In Toni Morrison's *Beloved* (New York: Plume, 1987), Sethe's gnawing intrusions from her past require a black vernacular expression to give name to the heavy weight of personal and national history bearing down on her conscience. She says, "Some things go. Pass on. Some things stay. I used to think it was my *rememory*. You know. Some things you forget. Other things you never do. But it's not. Places, places are still there. If a house burns down, it's gone, but the place— the picture of it—stays, and not just in my rememory, but out there, in the world" (35–36, my emphasis).

24. In legal terms, the *corpus delicti* is the standard of evidence that must be met for trial. A trial cannot be held unless it is proved that a crime has been committed.

25. A 2005 article by Madeline Pelner Cosman in the *Journal of American Physicians and Surgeons* noted how "[i]llegal aliens' stealthy assaults on medicine now must rouse Americans to alert and alarm. Even President Bush describes illegal aliens only as they are seen: strong physical laborers who work hard in undesirable jobs with low wages, who care for families, and who pursue the American dream. . . . What is unseen is their free medical care that has degraded and closed some of America's finest emergency medical facilities, and caused hospital bankruptcies" (6). Here, as in the rest of the piece, the "illegal alien" is a priori assumed to be a vector of disease, ready to ravage the national body through economic assault, leading to the body politic's eventual "bankruptcy." See Madeline Pelner Cosman, "Illegal Aliens and American Medicine," *Journal of American Physicians and Surgeons* 10, no. 1 (spring 2005): 6–10.

26. See Jonathan Xavier Inda, "Foreign Bodies: Migrants, Parasites, and the Pathological Nation," *Discourse* 22, no. 3 (fall 2000): 46–62; quotation from 47.

27. See Rosaura Sánchez and Beatrice Pita's introduction to their edition of Ruiz de Burton's first novel, *Who Would Have Thought It?* which first appeared in 1872 (Houston: Arte Público, 1995), vii–lxv. Pérez's and Ávila de Ríos's testimonials and Ruiz de Burton's *The Squatter and the Don* are cited in full in chapter 1.

28. The Recovering the United States Hispanic Literary Heritage (RUSHLH) project has been responsible for much of the important archival and recovery work to unearth and rediscover texts otherwise destined to oblivion in archives and individual collections across the country. See chapter 2.

29. Tomás Rivera's . . . *y no se lo tragó la tierra/. . . And the Earth Did Not Devour Him*, is cited in full in chapter 2.

30. Manuel M. Martín-Rodríguez, *Life in Search of Readers: Reading (in) Chicano/a Literature* (Albuquerque: University of New Mexico Press, 2003), 3.
31. Alvar Núñez Cabeza de Vaca, *Los naufragios*, ed. Enrique Pupo-Walker (1992), cited in full in chapter 3. In what follows I use Frances M. López-Morilla's translation of Pupo-Walker's edition, *Castaways: The Narrative of Alvar Núñez Cabeza de Vaca* (Berkeley: University of California Press, 1993).
32. Luz María Umpierre's *Margarita Poems*, Elías Miguel Muñoz's *The Greatest Performance*, and Rafael Campo's *What the Body Told* are cited in full in chapter 4.
33. Through the genre conventions of the crime novel and detective fiction, Alicia Gaspar de Alba's *Desert Blood: The Juárez Murders* (Houston: Arte Público, 2005) poses an ethical accounting of the national *corpus delicti's* relation to art and the very real crimes the novel indexes.

Notes to Chapter 1

1. As noted in the introduction, I invoke the nationalistic popular meaning that the terms "America" and "American" embody. Likewise, "memory" refers to the discursive condition that puts "truth effects" over liminal accuracy by narrativizing the past to presentist needs.
2. The testimonials I analyze are housed at the University of California, Berkeley, Bancroft Library. The library was named after Hubert Howe Bancroft, a San Francisco book dealer who bequeathed his holdings to the university. The original holdings included thirty-nine volumes related to the history of the American Southwest that Bancroft wrote with the help of a staff of interviewers, transcribers, translators, and writers. His *History of California* alone consisted of seven volumes (*History of California*, 7 vols., San Francisco: History Company, 1884–89). Pérez's 1877 testimonial was published partially with a translation by Vivian C. Fisher et al. in *Three Memoirs of Mexican California* (Berkeley: Friends of the Bancroft Library, 1988). In this study I use the Bancroft Library's complete translation of the original manuscript by Ruth Rodríguez, *An Old Woman and Her Recollections* (1957), as well the complete translation of Ávila de Ríos's 1877 manuscript by Earl R. Hewitt, *Memoirs of Doña Catarina Ávila de Ríos* (1935) (BANC MSS C-D 35 Translation). My references follow the library system: the letters following the abbreviations BANC and MSS refer to the specific manuscript. For example, Pérez's *Una vieja y sus recuerdos* is cited as BANC MSS C-D 139, Rodríguez's translation as BANC MSS C-D 139 Translation. María Amparo Ruiz de Burton's *The Squatter and the Don: A Novel Descriptive of Contemporary Occurrences in California* was first published in 1885. I use the edition edited by Rosaura Sánchez and Beatrice Pita (Houston: Arte Público, 1992).
3. Genaro Padilla, *My History, Not Yours: The Formation of Mexican American Autobiography* (Madison: University of Wisconsin Press, 1993); and Rosaura Sánchez, *Telling Identities: The Californio Testimonios* (Minneapolis: University of Minnesota Press, 1995).

4. The image of Eulalia Pérez found its way into contemporary Latino narrative in Alejandro Morales, *The Brick People* (Houston: Arte Público, 1988). In this version of Eulalia Pérez, a character from the novel relates how she dies a tragic death in a sinkhole after her home is sacked and her family dies, only to be resurrected as revenge incarnate. Neighbors who reluctantly exhume her body after her mysterious death find hundreds of "indescribably large brown insects" that cause paralysis and make their way through the town of El Rincón de San Pascual as symbolic avengers of her dispossession as well as that of the Mexican peoples she is made to represent (11).

5. In his influential *Border Matters: Remapping American Cultural Studies* (Berkeley: University of California Press, 1997), José David Saldívar sees Ruiz de Burton's novel as "an interpreter's guide to the late nineteenth century's emergence into what social theorists call monopoly capitalism" (182). In what follows I will critically engage Saldívar's important reading of Ruiz de Burton. As will become evident, I am interested in foregrounding the primacy of race over his emphasis on American imperialism, as I see the former as the constitutive enabler of the latter.

6. María Amparo Ruiz de Burton's first known novel, *Who Would Have Thought It?* ed. Rosaura Sánchez and Beatrice Pita (1872; Houston: Arte Público, 1992), is to date considered the first Latina novel published in English.

7. Shelly Streeby, *American Sensations: Class, Empire, and the Production of Popular Culture* (Berkeley: University of California Press, 2002), 6.

8. Homi K. Bhabha, "Introduction: Narrating the Nation," in *Nation and Narration,* ed. Homi K. Bhabha (London: Routledge, 1990), 2.

9. *Congressional Globe,* U.S. Congress, Senate, 30th Cong., 1st sess., 1848, 98–99. David Weber gives an abridged version of Calhoun's speech in *Foreigners in Their Native Land: Historical Roots of the Mexican Americans* (Albuquerque: University of New Mexico Press, 1973), 135–36. Weber's collection of documents relating to the Mexican-American War and its aftermath still provides one of the most comprehensive accounts of the crisis through documents relegated to near oblivion. It is through Weber's work that I became acquainted with the tremendous lacunae regarding the Mexican question in the United States. In his introduction he notes how ironic it is that "the descendants of Spaniards and Indians received almost no scholarly attention until the 1960s. Up to that time, no historian had written a book about the Mexicans and their descendants, and just a handful of popularizers and sociologists had taken note of them" (vii). The situation has improved only marginally, this in part thanks to the Chicano movement's reclamation of history from the 1960s onward. The institutional elision of the Mexican question in the academic field of history begs a logical enough question: What has made this elision possible in the field entrusted with documenting and remembering the past?

10. Mexico's territorial vastness made a centralized government difficult to consolidate, a fact that greatly enhanced the United States' ability to destabilize its sense of nation. As Rosaura Sánchez noted in *Telling Identities,*

Mexican independence in 1821 would bring the formation of a territorial state but not the formation of a nation. As the historian Ruiz has indicated, national identity during the first half of the nineteenth century was not particularly strong in Mexico. This lack of nationalism became evident during the U.S.-Mexico war, when Mexico faced an invasion that took U.S. troops all the way to its capital. (228) Sánchez rightly distinguishes between protonationalism and nationalism, the former designating a developing sense of national values and the latter the consolidation of those values en masse, however provisional they might be. This (proto)national identity crisis was further augmented at the onset of the Mexican-American War as Alta California was neglected "by an impoverished Mexican government" (234).

11. Padilla refers to these texts as "autobiographies"; Sánchez makes a compelling case for understanding them as testimonials. For Sánchez, the texts are a type of "dependent production" that create a "collective identity" mediated by the interviewers themselves: "Narrating agency in texts of this nature is thus not simply of the speaking subject but also that of the editing and writing subject" (*Telling Identities,* 8).

12. According to Padilla, "There are, by my count, nearly one hundred Californio personal narratives of lengths varying from ten pages to some that are hundreds of pages" in Bancroft's *History of California* (*My History,* 22). Sánchez notes that there are "about sixty-two" (*Telling Identities,* iv). Further archival research is needed to determine a more accurate number. Part of the problem, of course, revolves around a central question not yet elaborated in any study: What counts as a Mexican American "testimonial" or a Mexican American "autobiography"?

13. *Frank Leslie's Illustrated Newspaper,* distributed nationally, combined pictures and print to provide news and "picture news" events of the day and allowed literate, semiliterate, and illiterate citizens to "read" the news.

14. Jane M. Rabb, "Notes toward a History of Literature and Photography," in *Literature and Photography: Interactions 1840–1990,* ed. Jane M. Rabb (Albuquerque: University of New Mexico Press, 1995), xxxviii.

15. Betty Bergland has noted in her important essay "Reading Photographs and Narratives in Ethnic Autobiography: Memory and Subjectivity in Mary Antin's *The Promised Land,*" in *Memory, Narrative, and Identity: New Essays in Ethnic American Literatures,* ed. Amritjit Singh, Joseph T. Skerrett Jr., and Robert E. Hogan (Boston: Northeastern University Press, 1994), 48, that "studies emphasizing photography exist primarily in two arenas—photography as social documentation and photography as art." Pérez's image is an example of "social documentation" to the degree that it was a proxy for a people rendered outside Bancroft's historical present.

16. The photograph in Padilla's book is visually censored: the caption in the manuscript at the Bancroft Library, "eulalia perz, 139 years of age," is omitted altogether. I will address this omission later in my discussion.

17. BANC C-D 139 Translation, Savage's introduction, ii.

18. Benedict Anderson, *Imagined Communities: Reflections on the Origin and Spread of Nationalism* (London: Verso, 1991), 204.

19. Christian Metz, "Photography and Fetish," *October* 34 (fall 1985): 84, emphasis in original. French photographer Félix Nadar (Gaspard-Félix Tournachon) noted that Honoré de Balzac believed that "all physical bodies are made up entirely of layers of ghost-like images, an infinite number of leaflike skins laid one on top of the other. Since Balzac believed man was incapable of making something material from an apparition, from something impalpable—that is, creating something from nothing—he concluded that every time some-one had his photograph taken, one of the spectral layers was removed from the body and transferred to the photograph. Repeated exposures entailed the unavoidable loss of subsequent ghostly layers, that is, the very essence of life." "Balzac and the Daguerreotype," in *Literature and Photography: Interactions 1840–1990*, ed. Jane M. Rabb (Albuquerque: University of New Mexico Press, 1995), 8.

20. Bergland, "Reading Photographs," 46.

21. Upper-case letters often appear without the accent in Spanish, but the narrative effect in English is telling all the same as English cannot accommodate the accent mark. In the inscription under Pérez's image, she is "written in English."

22. Ellen McCracken's strategic notion of "the Other" in the context of Latino literatures is useful here, " 'the Other' represents anyone who has heretofore been understood only superficially, from the outside; it functions as a floating signifier . . . so that diverse elements of the audience fix its meanings differently, depending upon whom they are in a relation of alterity to." See Ellen McCracken, "Latina Narrative and the Politics of Signification: Articulation, Antagonism, and Populist Rupture," *Crítica: A Journal of Critical Essays* 2, no. 2 (fall 1990): 202–7.

23. Roland Barthes, *Camera Lucida: Reflections on Photography*, trans. Richard Howard (New York: Hill and Wang, 1981).

24. bell hooks, "In Our Glory: Photography and Black Life," in *Picturing Us: African American Identity in Photography*, ed. Deborah Willis (New York: New Press, 1994), 53.

25. In her formidable study of Hispanophone print culture in the United States, *Ambassadors of Culture: The Transamerican Origins of Latino Writing* (Princeton, N.J.: Princeton University Press, 2002), Kirsten Silva Gruesz has noted that *Leslie's Illustrated Newspaper* was "hugely popular" and "Leslie's family of periodicals was rivaled only by the house of Harper brothers" (186). Gruesz goes on to note how Mrs. Frank Leslie was actually Miriam Florence Follin, widow of publisher Frank Leslie. Follin had traveled extensively with her first husband, an archaeologist, to Central America and Mexico. She was fluent in Spanish and after the death of her second husband "moved . . . aggressively to enter the Spanish-language market, and thus one of the most significant Hispanophone papers of the time was born and funded," the illustrated biweekly *El Mundo Nuevo/La América Ilustrada*, which ran from 1871 to 1875 (187).

26. Mrs. Frank Leslie, "Eulalia Perrez, the Oldest Woman in the World," *Frank Leslie's Illustrated Newspaper,* January 12, 1878. The article is appended to Pérez's testimonial without reference to page number.

27. Pérez hints that the "contest" might have been arranged: "Fathers Sánchez and Zalvidea conferred," and "the gentlemen who were to decide on the merits of the three dinners were *warned ahead of time*" (BANC MSS C-D 139 Translation, 5– 6; my emphasis). The other two women, María Luisa Cota and María Ignacia Amador, were married and had work. Padilla ignores the implications of this advance warning and states that "Pérez does not gloat over her victory, saying that she proved herself so as to support her children and to gain self-sufficiency, not because she wished to supplant the other women" (*My History,* 134).

28. Rodríguez's translation is problematic. When Pérez said "colegio," a group united in a common cause, she most likely meant "mission." The last sentence in the manuscript reads, "Centinela alerta, y alerta está; pero ellos decían 'Centinela abierta!' Abierta está!" (BANC MSS C-D 139 Translation, 11). A more accurate translation would be, "Guards on alert! Alert we are!; but instead they said 'Guards on alert! We are now free!' " Since "centinela" refers to a group of guards, "sentinel" is inaccurate. The adjective "abierta," of course, modifies "centinela" and at the same time refers to the new status accorded the Amerindians as "free men" following Captain Barroso's announcement.

29. The original reads, "el dolor de cabeza no se le quitó," that is, "his headache did not end," as opposed to "his head never stopped paining him."

30. It is unlikely that Ávila de Ríos had none of her husband's papers, and it is probable that Savage also doubted this, since he sends Gómez to speak to her.

31. David Weber notes that "[t]he momentous discovery of gold at Sutter's Mill on January 24, 1848 (only a week before the signing of the Treaty of Guadalupe Hidalgo), had attracted adventurers from around the world" (*Foreigners in Their Native Land,* 148).

32. It should be noted, as Noel Ignatiev does in his study *How the Irish Became White* (New York: Routledge, 1995), that the Irish were not racialized as white in nineteenth-century America. Yet, curiously enough, it is Irish migration to the West that allows for the patent corporeal markers of difference to position the Irish within the acceptable limits of whiteness in contradistinction to Mexicans, who were racialized as Black, Indigenous, or both.

33. Geoffrey C. Ward, *The West: An Illustrated History* (New York: Little, Brown, 1996), 148.

34. Ibid., 149. Ward also notes how those who did pay their tax "and continued to stay on in the gold fields" had to contend with "whites [who] resorted to intimidation to drive them out." He mentions that "Mexicans" feared the "Americans' wrath" during the Gold Rush, apparently with good reason:

At Downieville, a Mexican woman—remembered only as Josepha—awoke to find a drunken American in her bedroom. She reached for a knife and stabbed him to death. A mob immediately seized her and, when she failed to express regret for what she had done, watched as she was hanged. "Had this woman been American instead of Mexican," one newspaper wrote, "instead of being hung for the deed, she would have been lauded for it. It was not her guilt which condemned this unfortunate woman, but her Mexican blood." (Ibid., 149–52)

35. "Californios" refers to the names Mexicans identified with as inhabitants of California and often appears as a class marker for the landed aristocracy.

36. Michel de Certeau, *Heterologies: Discourse on the Other*, trans. Brian Massumi (Minneapolis: University of Minnesota Press, 1986), 226–27, original emphasis.

37. José F. Aranda, *When We Arrive: A New Literary History of Mexican America* (Tucson: University of Arizona Press, 2003), 98.

38. Cited in José Saldívar, *Border Matters: Remapping American Cultural Studies* (Berkeley: University of California Press, 1997), 168–69.

39. For a brief biography of María Amparo Ruiz de Burton, see Rosaura Sánchez and Beatrice Pita, introduction to *The Squatter and the Don*, 8–14. They also mention Davidson's article (10–12).

40. Before her husband's death, concern over his rank and perhaps over her pension made her request a meeting with President Abraham Lincoln. See José F. Aranda, "Breaking All the Rules: María Amparo Ruiz de Burton Writes a Civil War Novel," in *Recovering the U.S. Hispanic Literary Heritage*, vol. 3, ed. María Herrera-Sobek and Virginia Sánchez Korrol (Houston: Arte Público, 2000), 64. After several attempts she secured a meeting with Lincoln in 1861, a meeting she fictionally reconstructed in her first known novel, *Who Would Have Thought It?* ed. Rosaura Sánchez and Beatrice Pita (Houston: Arte Público, 1995). In her meeting with Lincoln she discussed her husband's service to the Union and requested his promotion to colonel. This request did not fall on deaf ears. Lincoln wrote to Secretary of War Simon Cameron and asked him to promote her husband "if it could be done without injustice to other officers"; six months later the Senate formally approved the promotion of Henry S. Burton (cited in Aranda, "Breaking All the Rules," 64). Also see Aranda's *When We Arrive*, 114.

41. María Amparo Ruiz de Burton, *Don Quijote de la Mancha: A Comedy in Five Acts, Taken from Cervantes' Novel of That Name* (San Francisco: J. H. Carmany, 1876).

42. Miguel Hidalgo was executed in 1811 and ten years dead by 1821. His famous "Grito de Dolores" took place in 1810. Saldívar seems to be confusing Hidalgo with Agustín de Iturbide, who succeeded in expelling the Spanish in 1821.

43. Manuel M. Martín Rodríguez also makes this point in a seminal essay, "Textual and Land Reclamations: The Critical Reception of Early Chicana/o Literature," in *Recovering the U.S. Hispanic Literary Heritage*, vol. 2, ed. Erlinda Gonzáles-Berry and Charles M. Tatum (Houston: Arte Público, 1996), 40–58 (especially see 55n. 14). In this early essay Martín Rodríguez offers a measured and important (if not altogether overlooked) antiessentialist reading of *The Squatter and the Don* and the issue of "land," especially with regard to Aztlán.

44. One of the "laws" to which Don Alamar likely refers was the Federal Land Act of 1851, which placed the burden of proof on Californios to provide evidence of actual title on the lands they laid claim to.

45. For a historical account of Anglo-American perceptions and stereotypes of Mexicans during the nineteenth century, see Arnoldo De León, *They Called Them Greasers: Anglo Attitudes toward Mexicans in Texas, 1821–1900* (Austin: University of Texas Press, 1983). David Weber provides a useful catalog of these stereotypes in *Myth and History of the Hispanic Southwest* (Albuquerque: University of New Mexico Press, 1988), 153–67.

46. John M. González, "Romancing Hegemony: Constructing Racialized Citizenship in María Amparo Ruiz de Burton's *The Squatter and the Don*," in *Recovering the U.S. Hispanic Literary Heritage*, vol. 2, ed. Erlinda Gonzáles-Berry and Chuck Tatum (Houston: Arte Público, 1996), 23–39.

47. Michel Foucault, *Foucault Live: Collected Interviews, 1961–1984*, ed. Sylvère Lotringer, trans. Lysa Hochroth and John Johnston (New York: Semiotext(e), 1996), 124.

Notes to Chapter 2

1. José Antonio Villareal, *Pocho: A Novel about a Young Mexican American Coming of Age in California* (Garden City, N.Y.: Doubleday, 1959). The citations that follow are from the most recent edition (New York: Anchor Books, 1994). "Pocho" is a derogatory term most often used by Mexican nationals to refer to Mexican immigrants in the United States who are deemed too assimilated or "Americanized."

2. As noted earlier, Sánchez and Pita's important archival work enabled the recovery of what they consider to be the first Latina novel written in English, María Amparo Ruiz de Burton's *Who Would Have Thought It?* Sánchez and Pita's important contributions are part of the Recovering the United States Hispanic Literary Heritage (RUSHLH) project, originally funded by the Rockefeller Foundation. Directed by Nicolás Kanellos, the project seeks to "locate, identify, preserve and make accessible the literary contributions of U.S. Hispanics from colonial times through 1960 in what today comprises the fifty states of the Union."

3. Rosa Linda Fregoso, *MeXicana Encounters: The Making of Social Identities on the Borderlands* (Berkeley: University of California Press, 2003), 103.

4. Neil Foley is one of the few historians to study the uncomfortable terrain I have here called "passing for Spain." In his analysis of the early-twentieth-century history of Mexican Americans in the United States, he notes, for example, how the creation of the League of United Latin American Citizens (LULAC) in 1929 by predominantly middle-class Mexican Americans in Texas was an attempt at civic engagement that sought to align Mexicans with whiteness by asserting an essential commonality with Spain among all Latin Americans. That the group erased the almost exclusive Mexican presence in their ranks by referring to themselves as "Latin American Citizens" also signaled the race panic that led them to disassoci-

NOTES TO CHAPTER 2

ate themselves from predominantly poorer, darker indigenous Mexicans, on the one hand, and Blacks, on the other. See Neil Foley, "Becoming Hispanic: Mexican Americans and the Faustian Pact with Whiteness," in *Reflexiones 1997: New Directions in Mexican American Studies,* ed. Neil Foley (Austin, Tex.: Publications of the Center for Mexican American Studies, 1997), 53–70. Also see Foley's more recent "Partly Colored of Other White: Mexican Americans and Their Problem with the Color Line," in *Beyond Black and White: Race, Ethnicity, and Gender in the U.S. South and Southwest,* ed. Stephanie Cole and Alison M. Parker (College Station: Texas A&M University Press, 2004), 123–44.

5. Nicolás Kanellos, "A Socio-Historic Study of Hispanic Newspapers in the United States," in *Recovering the U.S. Hispanic Literary Heritage,* vol. 1, ed. Ramón A. Gutiérrez and Genaro M. Padilla (Houston: Arte Público, 1993), 110.

6. Raymund A. Paredes, "Mexican-American Literature: An Overview," in *Recovering the U.S. Hispanic Literary Heritage,* vol. 1, ed. Ramón A. Gutiérrez and Genaro M. Padilla (Houston: Arte Público, 1993), 31–51; quotation from 37.

7. See Héctor Calderón, *Narratives of Greater Mexico: Essays on Chicano Literary History, Genre, and Borders* (Austin: University of Texas Press, 2004), 85.

8. Jovita González's decidedly historical evocation of the Mexican-American War in *Caballero* and her folkloric *Dew on the Thorn* were published posthumously by Texas A&M University Press and Arte Público Press in 1996 and 1997, respectively. For a discussion of González's work, collaborations, and "feminist" engagement, see María E. Cotera's important study "Native Speakers: Locating Early Expressions of United States Third World Feminist Discourse: A Comparative Analysis of the Ethnographic and Literary Writing of Ella Cara Deloria and Jovita González," Ph.D. diss., Stanford University, 2001.

9. Even Richard's surname, Rubio (Spanish for "blond"), is meant to recall the whitening involved in becoming American within the narrative logic of the novel. Though in the novel Richard and his father are much darker than his mother and sisters, the patronymic drive toward "blondness" is about becoming racialized as "white."

10. This was also the case with Puerto Ricans. Though the island had been under U.S. occupation since 1898, Puerto Ricans were encouraged to join the armed forces in order to speed up their citizenship, as U.S. involvement in World War I seemed inevitable. As the United States entered the war in 1917, Puerto Ricans were granted citizenship through an act of Congress with the passing of the Jones Act, which also made Puerto Rico an "unincorporated" territory of the United States. Laura Briggs, in *Reproducing Empire: Race, Sex Science, and U.S. Imperialism in Puerto Rico* (Berkeley: University of California Press, 2002), writes, "In 1917, with little discussion and less consultation with the island's inhabitants, Congress made Puerto Ricans U.S. citizens"; she notes that "[t]he cynical view held that the Jones Act granting citizenship was passed in order to provide fresh cannon fodder for the coming World War I" (46). Since Puerto Rican citizenship was enacted through Congress, it was not guaranteed by the Constitution, a fact that has kept

Puerto Ricans from attaining the constitutional protections associated with due process on the island.

11. See Arturo Madrid, "In Search of the Authentic Pachuco," in *Velvet Barrios: Popular Culture and Chicana/o Sexualities,* ed. Alicia Gaspar de Alba, foreword by Tomás Ybarra Frausto (New York: Palgrave Macmillan, 2003), 17–40; quotation from 19. Briefly, the Sleepy Lagoon case began on August 2, 1942, when the body of José Díaz was found at a reservoir ("lagoon") in Los Angeles the morning after a gang fight among Mexican American youths. The press hysteria surrounding the incident declared a "crime wave," which resulted in the mass arrest of Mexican American youths, who were indicted because of "the color of their skin" (ibid.). The Zoot Suit Riots erupted on June 3, 1943, when several sailors claimed they were robbed by Mexican Americans. The following day over three hundred servicemen hired cabs and went into the barrios of Los Angeles to beat up young Mexican American men and strip them naked of their zoot suits. The city of Los Angeles responded by creating a "Foreign Relations Bureau" [*sic*] to investigate the Mexican American crime. That these "foreigners" were U.S. citizens was immaterial to a majority culture that was ready to vilify yet another group after the passage of Executive Order 9066, which jailed Japanese Americans in internment camps. Indeed, the appointed director of the bureau, E. Durand Ayres, concluded that because Mexicans were "Indians," they were therefore Oriental or Asian.

12. See George Mariscal, ed., *Aztlán and Viet Nam: Chicano and Chicana Experiences of the War* (Berkeley: University of California Press, 1999), 26–46.

13. My subsequent references to the novel are from . . . *y no se lo tragó la tierra/. . . And the Earth Did Not Devour Him,* bilingual edition, trans. Evangelina Vigil-Pinón (Houston: Arte Público, 1992). *Earth* has usually been read, along with Luis Valdez's well-known pieces (or *Actos*) of social protest, as the beginning of contemporary Chicano writing in its documentation of Chicano "reality." In what follows, I seek to read *Earth* in the context of the critique it enacted on a national scale by virtue of the "America" the text contextualized as evidence of nationalism gone awry. For a collection of important early essays about *Earth,* see Vernon E. Lattin, ed., *Contemporary Chicano Fiction: A Critical Survey* (Binghamton, N.Y.: Bilingual Press/Editorial Bilingüe, 1984), 113–48.

14. Walter Benjamin, "The Work of Art in the Age of Mechanical Reproduction," in *Illuminations: Essays and Reflections,* ed. Hannah Arendt, trans. Harry Zohn (New York: Schocken Books, 1968), 217–51.

15. I borrow the term from Josefina Ludmer, who employs the juridical concept of *corpus delicti,* the legal evidence of the crime, as a narrative trope of engagement and foundational marker for Argentine literature. For Ludmer, " 'Crime' is a particular conceptual instrument; it is not abstract but rather visible, representable, quantifiable, personalizable, subjectivizable; it does not submit to binary regimes; it has historicity and opens onto a constellation of relations and series. . . . As Marx and Freud well knew, it is an ideal critical instrument because it is at once historical, cultural, political, economic, legal, social, and literary: it is one of

those articulating notions which is in or between all fields." See *The Corpus Delicti: A Manual of Argentine Fictions*, trans. Glen S. Close (Pittsburgh: University of Pittsburgh Press, 2004), 4–5.

16. The term comes from the Spanish word for arm, *brazo*. Braceros are hired hands.

17. Quinto Sol Publications was founded in 1967 by University of California, Berkeley, anthropologist Octavio Ignacio Romano. Now Tonatiuh-Quinto Sol Publications, it was the pioneer publisher of Mexican American authors and nurtured the careers of important Chicano writers, including Rudolfo Anaya and Rolando Hinojosa-Smith. Under Romano's guidance, the press also published journals of Mexican American culture and social thought such as *El Grito* and one of the first anthologies of Chicano literature, *El Espejo—The Mirror: Selected Mexican-American Literature*, ed. Octavio Ignacio Romano (Berkeley, Calif.: Quinto Sol, 1969). Many authors associated with Quinto Sol included Aztec symbology and philosophy and appropriated the concept of Aztlán, the mythical ancestral home of the Aztecs believed to be located in the southwestern United States. As I noted in the introduction, Aztlán became the enabling conceit from which these authors could coalesce an identity grounded in logic of geography that made them heirs—*in* the United States—to traditions that associated them with one of the world's greatest civilizations.

18. For this and a list of the novel's translators and translations, see Ralph F. Grajeda, "Tomás Rivera's Appropriation of the Chicano Past," in *Modern Chicano Writers: A Collection of Critical Essays*, ed. Joseph Sommers and Tomás Ybarra-Frausto (Englewood Cliffs, N.J.: Prentice Hall, 1979), 74–85.

19. These underanalyzed novels and short stories by well-known writers deal with the bracero immigration and migration experience and span over half a century. For example, in Agustín Yañez's 1947 *Al filo del agua* (translated as *The Edge of the Storm*) one of the principal characters, Damían, returns to Mexico after working in the United States, only to confront prejudice for having abandoned his country as well as for criticizing the injustices he sees in Mexico. In Carlos Fuentes's 1958 *La región más transparente* (*Where the Air Is Clear*), Gabriel's return signals a similar plight. In Juan Rulfo's 1967 "Paso del Norte," from *El llano en llamas*, the nameless protagonist leaves his family to work as a bracero, only to return wounded and find that his wife has left him for another man. More recently, Carlos Fuentes's "Malintzin de las maquilas," from his *La frontera de cristal: Una novela en nueve cuentos* (México, D.F.: Alfaguara, 1995), and Alicia Gaspar de Alba's *Desert Blood: The Juárez Murders* (Houston: Arte Público, 2005) both deal with the current bracero crisis, transnational exploitation on the Mexican border, and the newest industrial "hired hands," the predominantly female workers in border *maquilas* (factories and assembly plants), albeit from decidedly differing perspectives.

20. Fred W. Friendly, *Harvest of Shame* (1960), docudrama, New Video Group, 2005.

21. Chicano Tino Villanueva's American Book Award winner, *Scene from the Movie Giant,* a poetry collection inspired by the movie, autobiographically relates how a fourteen-year-old boy is marked by the movie's anti-Mexican racism and the specter of that racism on his life (Willimantic, Conn.: Curbstone, 1993). Like Villanueva, José E. Limón offers an evocative interweaving of *Giant* with his own history in *American Encounters: Greater Mexico, the United States, and the Erotics of Culture* (Boston: Beacon, 1998), 119–24.

22. Edna Ferber, *Giant* (New York: Doubleday, 1952).

23. Julie Goldsmith Gilbert, *Ferber: A Biography* (Garden City, N.Y.: Doubleday, 1978), 174.

24. Charles Ramírez Berg, "Bordertown, the Assimilation Narrative, and the Chicano Social Problem Film," in *Chicanos and Film: Representation and Resistance,* ed. Chon Noriega (Minneapolis: University of Minnesota Press, 1992), 43.

25. Russ Castronovo, *Necro Citizenship: Death, Eroticism, and the Public Sphere in the Nineteenth-Century United States* (Durham, N.C.: Duke University Press, 2001), 4.

26. See George N. Green, "The Felix Longoria Affair," *Journal of Ethnic Studies* 19 (1991): 23–49. The Longoria affair also inspired community activism and rememory through corridos and song. See Manuel Peña, "Folksong and Social Change: Two Corridos as Interpretive Sources," *Aztlán* 13 (1982): 13–42.

27. In 1948 Dr. Hector P. Garcia and seven hundred other Mexican American veterans met in Corpus Christi and organized the American G.I. Forum. It evolved as a civil rights organization devoted to securing equal rights for Mexican Americans as guaranteed by the 1944 G.I. Bill of Rights. For a comprehensive history of the group, see Carl Allsup, *The American G.I. Forum: Origins and Evolution,* Mexican American Monographs 6 (Austin: Center for Mexican American Studies, University of Texas at Austin, 1982).

28. Francisco A. Lomelí and Donaldo Urioste, *Chicano Perspectives in Literature: A Critical and Annotated Bibliography* (Albuquerque: Pajarito Publications, 1976), 12.

29. Michael Kammen, *Mystic Chords of Memory: The Transformation of Tradition in American Culture* (New York: Vintage, 1991).

30. See the introduction, note 10.

31. Kammen, *Mystic Chords,* 577. U.S. marines provided security for the 127 documents, which had never before been removed from their permanent exhibits at the Library of Congress, State Department, National Archives, and War, Navy, and Treasury Departments.

32. Langston Hughes, "Freedom Train," in *The Collected Poems of Langston Hughes,* ed. Arnold Rampersad and David Roessel (New York: Knopf, 1994), 134.

33. Ellen Schrecker, *Many Are the Crimes: McCarthyism in America* (Princeton, N.J.: Princeton University Press, 1998), xii.

34. For a discussion of the legacy of McCarthyism in relation to the civil rights movement, see Schrecker, *Many Are the Crimes,* chap. 10, " 'A Good Deal of

Trauma': The Impact of McCarthyism," 359–415. The similarities between McCarthyism and the post-9/11 climate of fear surrounding "Homeland Security," levels of threat, patriotism, and race are too striking to ignore.

35. The historical magazine *American Heritage*, founded in 1947, was by the 1950s promising its readers "a good deal of nostalgia." The magazine enjoyed wide readership and focused on the "heritage" of the American nation, patriotism, and the spirit of the people (Kammen, *Mystic Chords*, 539).

36. Robert Littell (*Newsweek*'s general editor), Kent Biffle, and Nolan Davis, "Tío Taco Is Dead," *Newsweek*, June 29, 1970, 22–28. I am unaware of any other feature article during this period that dealt specifically with the Chicano civil rights movement in a magazine with *Newsweek*'s scope and influence. For an important historicist reading of this article, see Suzanne Oboler, *Ethnic Labels, Latino Lives: Identity and Politics of (Re)Presentation in the United States* (Minneapolis: University of Minnesota Press, 1995), 80–81.

37. Graffiti signed with the imprimatur "con safos" served to protect the message: the message could not be effaced without fear of the writer's revenge.

38. Matt S. Meier and Feliciano Ribera, *Mexican Americans, American Mexicans: From Conquistadores to Chicanos* (New York: Hill and Wang, 1995), 172–73.

39. In Reies López Tijerina's memoir, *They Called Me "King Tiger": My Struggle for the Land and Our Rights*, trans. and ed. José Angel Gutiérrez (Houston: Arte Público, 2000), he states how his involvement with the Mexican American civil rights movement was under surveillance from the FBI and the CIA: "The people must stay informed . . . and maintain vigilance on the criminal activity of these agencies" (230).

40. It is an often overlooked fact that the Spiritual Plan of Aztlán was based on the Ten-Point Platform for Black empowerment, developed by Huey Newton and Bobby Seale, that resulted in the creation of the Black Panther Party for Self-Defense. For a collection of documents and speeches of and from the Black Panthers, see Philip S. Foner, ed., *The Black Panthers Speak* (New York: Da Capo, 1995).

41. *Earth* is, however, reminiscent of Nellie Campobello's 1931 work *Cartucho*. In a series of vignettes Campobello reconstructs the banalization of death during the Mexican Revolution in strikingly elliptical interventions from a series of voices and characters, unified through the narrative voice of a young girl who is witness to the slaughter occurring literally in front of her. See Jorge Aguilar Mora's edition of Nellie Campobello, *Cartucho: Relatos de la lucha en el norte de México* (1931; repr., México, D.F.: Ediciones Era, 2000).

42. For example, Ramón Saldívar's illuminating *Chicano Narrative: The Dialectics of Difference* (Madison: University of Wisconsin Press, 1990) notes that Rivera documents "the life of the farmworker in the immediate post-WWII era," 75. Salvador Rodríguez del Pino in *La novela chicana escrita en español: Cinco autores comprometidos* (Ypsilanti, Mich.: Bilingual Press/Editorial Bilingüe, 1982) situates the novel's action in "La década de los cincuenta o de la posguerra" (the decade of the fifties or after the war) (24). Though Rodríguez del Pino is right to note that it

NOTES TO CHAPTER 3

takes place in the 1950s, his notion of "posguerra" implies that it was after the *Korean* War.

43. Rivera has been criticized by feminists for his masculinist recourse to agency. For one of the earliest critiques, see Judy Salinas, "The Image of Woman in Chicano Literature," *Revista Chicano-Riqueña* 4, no. 4 (fall 1976): 139–48. Angie Chabram-Dernersesian develops this in "I Throw Punches for My Race, but I Don't Want to Be a Man: Writing Us—Chica-nos (Girl, Us)/Chicanas—into the Movement Script," in *Cultural Studies*, ed. Lawrence Grossberg, Cary Nelson, and Paula A. Treichler (New York: Routledge, 1992): 81–95.

44. Saldívar, *Chicano Narrative*, 81. Rivera seems to be echoing a similar scene in *Pocho* where Richard Rubio fears he will be swallowed up by the earth for his defiance of "God": "I knew that the earth would open and it would swallow me up because I dared to demand explanations from Him" (65).

Notes to Chapter 3

1. James Brooke, "Conquistador Statue Stirs Hispanic Pride and Indian Rage," *New York Times*, January 9, 1998, A10.

2. In what follows I use Frances M. López-Morilla's translation, *Castaways: The Narrative of Alvar Núñez Cabeza de Vaca* (Berkeley: University of California Press, 1993), which follows Enrique Pupo-Walker's critical edition of *Los naufragios* (Madrid: Castalia, 1992). Pupo-Walker's edition is based on Alvar Núñez Cabeza de Vaca's corrected 1555 edition and not the Valladollid *editio princeps* of 1542, since the latter is "plagued with errors" (Pupo-Walker, preface to *Castaways*, xi).

3. Arte Público Press published Cabeza de Vaca's text as part of their Recovering the United States Hispanic Literary Heritage project (RUSHLH). See *The Account: Álvar Núñez Cabeza de Vaca's Relación*, ed. José B. Fernández and Martin Favata (Houston: Arte Público, 1993).

4. Luis Leal, "Mexican American Literature: A Historical Perspective," in *Modern Chicano Writers: A Collection of Essays*, ed. Joseph Sommers and Tomás Ybarra-Frausto (Englewood Cliffs, N.J.: Prentice Hall, 1979), 18–30; quotations from 19 and 21. The essay originally appeared in *Revista Chicano-Riqueña* 1, no. 1 (1973): 32–44.

5. Ralph Waldo Emerson, *Selected Essays* (New York: Penguin, 1985), 87–88. Emerson and Henry David Thoreau would eventually denounce the war against Mexico. Thoreau's essay "Civil Disobedience" (1849) was in part motivated by what he considered his country's uncritical and immoral zeal for "Manifest Destiny" politics, especially as related to slavery.

6. Ray Padilla, "Apuntes para la documentación de la cultura chicana," *El Grito*, 5, no. 2 (winter 1971–72): 3–36; quotation from 19. Leal credits Padilla for deploying this type of historiographical literary genealogy ("Mexican American Literature," 23).

7. It could be argued that Leal's academic prominence made "Aztlanese" a

tenable precondition for the institutionalization of Latin American literatures. As Rolando Hinojosa reminds us, not until the 1960s did scholars interested in Latin American literatures "beg[i]n to carve out their own territory in Romance languages departments." "Foreword: Redefining American Literature," in *Criticism in the Borderlands: Studies in Chicano Literature, Culture, and Ideology,* ed. Héctor Calderón and José David Saldívar (Durham, N.C.: Duke University Press, 1991), xii. Hinojosa goes on to say that "[t]he newness of Hispanic-American literature offerings in departments of Spanish and Portuguese may be appreciated when one learns that Luis Leal . . . produced over fifty Ph.D. theses while at the University of Illinois . . . and that the first thesis on Carlos Fuentes was not published until the sixties under his guidance" (ibid.).

8. Philip Ortego, "The Chicano Renaissance," *Social Casework* 52, no. 5 (May 1971): 294–307. For a recent appraisal, see David R. Maciel, Isidro D. Ortiz, and María Herrera-Sobek, eds., *Chicano Renaissance: Contemporary Cultural Trends* (Tucson: University of Arizona Press, 2000).

9. An important contribution to the rise and flowering of Chicano protest poetry from the late 1960s to the early 1980s is Juan Bruce-Novoa, *Chicano Poetry: A Response to Chaos* (Austin: University of Texas Press, 1982).

10. Luis R. Burrola and José A. Rivera, "Chicano Studies Programs at the Crossroads: Alternative Futures for the 1980s," Working Paper 103 (Albuquerque: Southwest Hispanic Research Institute, University of New Mexico, 1983), 13.

11. Lisa Lowe, *Immigrant Acts: On Asian American Cultural Politics* (Durham, N.C.: Duke University Press, 1996), 42.

12. See Carlos Muñoz, "The Quest for Paradigm: The Development of Chicano Studies and Intellectuals," in *Latinos and Education: A Critical Reader,* ed. Antonia Darder, Rodolfo D. Torres, and Henry Gutiérrez (New York: Routledge, 1997).

13. Juan Bruce-Novoa, "Naufragios en los mares de la significación: De *La Relación* de Cabeza de Vaca a la literatura chicana," *Plural* 19, no. 5, 221 (February 1990): 12–21, reprinted in *Notas y comentarios sobre Álvar Núñez Cabeza de Vaca,* ed. Margo Glantz (México, D.F.: Grijalbo, 1993); and translated as "Shipwrecked in the Seas of Signification: Cabeza de Vaca's *Relación* and Chicano Literature," in *Reconstructing a Chicano/a Literary Heritage: Hispanic Colonial Literature of the Southwest,* ed. María Herrera-Sobek (Tucson: University of Arizona Press, 1993), 3–23. The citations that follow are from the translated version.

14. Héctor Calderón and José David Saldívar, "Editors' Introduction: Criticism in the Borderlands," in *Criticism in the Borderlands: Studies in Chicano Literature, Culture, and Ideology,* ed. Héctor Calderón and José David Saldívar (Durham, N.C.: Duke University Press, 1991), 1–7; quotation from 2.

15. A. Francisco Lomelí, "Po(l)etics of Reconstructing and/or Appropriating a Literary Past: The Regional Case Model," in *Recovering the U.S. Hispanic Literary Heritage,* vol. 1, ed. Ramón A. Gutiérrez and Genaro M. Padilla (Houston: Arte Público, 1993), 221–40; quotation from 227.

16. Lomelí argues that "[f]ew would quibble today about the classification of

NOTES TO CHAPTER 3

Alonso de Ercilla's *La araucana* (1569) as a foundational work of Chile—and by extension Latin America—, although it was always claimed by Spain until modern times" (ibid., 230).

17. Harold Augenbaum and Margarite Fernández Olmos, eds., *The Latino Reader: From 1542 to the Present* (New York: Houghton Mifflin, 1997).

18. More recently Nicolás Kanellos's influential and RUSHLH-supported *Herencia: The Anthology of Hispanic Literature of the United States* (Oxford: Oxford University Press, 2002), co-edited with Kenya Dworkin y Méndez, José B. Fernández, Erlinda González-Berry, Agnes Lugo Ortiz, and Charles Tatum, begins precisely with Alvar Núñez Cabeza de Vaca's text.

19. See Guadalupe San Miguel, "Actors Not Victims: Chicanas/os and the Struggle for Educational Equality," in *Chicanas/Chicanos at the Crossroads: Social, Economic, and Political Change,* ed. David R. Maciel and Isidro D. Ortiz (Tucson: University of Arizona Press, 1996), 159–80.

20. Beatriz Pastor Bodmer, *The Armature of Conquest: Spanish Accounts of the Discovery of America, 1492–1589,* trans. Lydia Longstreth Hunt (Stanford, Calif.: Stanford University Press, 1992), 141–42; translation of *Discursos narrativos de la conquista: Mitificacción y emergencia* (Hanover, N.H.: Ediciones del Norte, 1988).

21. Rolena Adorno, "The Discursive Encounter of Spain and America: The Authority of Eyewitness Testimony in Writing History," *William and Mary Quarterly* 49 (1992): 210–28.

22. José Rabasa, *Writing Violence on the Northern Frontier: The Historiography of Sixteenth-Century New Mexico and Florida and the Legacy of Conquest* (Durham, N.C.: Duke University Press, 2000).

23. Tzvetan Todorov, *The Conquest of America: The Question of the Other* (New York: Harper and Row, 1984), 197; originally published as *La conquête de l'Amérique* (Paris: Editions du Seuil, 1982).

24. There is some confusion regarding the publication date of Gonzalo Fernández de Oviedo y Valdés's *Sumario de la natural historia de las Indias* (1562; repr., Madrid: Historia 16, 1986). Walter Mignolo makes a compelling case for more accurately placing the publication of Oviedo's complete *Historia* between 1551 and 1555. See Walter Mignolo, "Cartas, crónicas y relaciones del descubrimiento y la conquista," in *Historia de la literatura hispanoamericana,* vol. 1, *Época Colonial,* ed. Luis Iñigo Madrigal (Madrid: Cátedra, 1982), 103.

25. Juan Francisco Maura, "Escalvas españolas en el Nuevo Mundo: Una nota histórica," *Colonial Latin American Literary Review* 2 (1993): 188–89 (my translation).

26. Cabeza de Vaca profited from the appointment in numerous ways, including "rent" from territories he would "discover" in the Río de Plata area (Maura, "Escalvas españolas," 189).

27. According to Maura, *Castaways* is one of a series of shipwreck narratives in Spain and Portugal during the sixteenth century. See his provocative essay "Veracidad en los *Naufragios*: La técnica narrativa de Alvar Núñez Cabeza de Vaca," *Revista*

Iberoamericana 61, nos. 170–71 (January–June 1995): 187–95. Luis Fernando Restrepo notes that *Castaways* is also part of a tradition of travel writing, the *peregrinato vitae*, that allows these narratives to inscribe themselves within Christian teleology by mapping the cartographic unknown for the European subject. Luis Fernando Restrepo, "Las elegias de varones ilustres de Indias de Juan de Castellanos y la construcción del Nuevo Reino de Granada," Ph.D. diss., University of Maryland, 1996, 306–59.

28. See Jonathan Goldberg, *Sodometries: Renaissance Texts, Modern Sexualities* (Stanford, Calif.: Stanford University Press, 1992), for a speculative analysis about the function of Cabeza de Vaca's nudity. Goldberg claims that "[t]he desire to remain naked, which could be read as some zero degree of nature or even as a sign that despite himself Cabeza de Vaca has come to identify fully with those among whom he lived, is itself a differential sign of gendered identity" (213). Since nudity for Cabeza de Vaca is never posited as a question of choice, much less desire, it might be best to understand his naked state not as a "sign" but as another example of the material conditions of his predicament.

29. See Ann M. Ortíz, "The Prophetic Structure of the *Naufragios* of Alvar Núñez Cabeza de Vaca," *Journal of the Southeast Council on Latin American Studies* 27 (March 1996): 17–26.

30. By the time Cabeza de Vaca is reunited with his countrymen, there are only four other survivors of the six hundred who set sail in 1527: Andrés Dorantes, Estebancio "the black" (Dorante's slave), Alonso de Castillo Maldonado, and Juan Ortíz. Ortíz was rescued by the De Soto expedition; the remaining four reached the Spanish settlement of Culiacán on the west coast of modern-day Mexico.

31. By his own account, his coloring was affected by the weather: "we shed our skin like snakes twice a year, and with the sun and wind developed great sores on our backs" (*Castaways*, 75).

32. Maggie Kilgour, *From Communion to Cannibalism: An Anatomy of Metaphors of Incorporation* (Princeton, N.J.: Princeton University Press, 1990), 48.

33. Cabeza de Vaca refers to them more than any other foodstuff (pp. 56, 62, 64–66, 70–71, 75, 93).

34. Peter Hulme, *Colonial Encounters: Europe and the Native Caribbean, 1492–1797* (New York: Routledge, 1987), 3.

35. Philip III (r. 1598–1621) was monarch when Oñate began his expedition.

36. Gilberto Espinosa in his translation of Gaspar Pérez de Villagrá's *A History of New Mexico* (Los Angeles: Quivira Society, 1933) (hereafter cited as "Espinosa") notes that Villagrá's *History* was published a decade before the landing of the Pilgrims and fourteen years before John Smith's *Generall Historie of Virginia, New-England, and the Summer Isles* (17). I also use the translation of Villagrá's *Historia de la Nueva México* edited by Miguel Encinias, Alfred Rodríguez, and Joseph P. Sánchez, *History of New Mexico* (Albuquerque: University of New Mexico Press, 1992) (hereafter cited as "Encinias et al."), since, as a bilingual edition, it greatly facilitates

Spanish/English cross-referencing of the poem. Espinosa's 1933 translation is more literal and leaves less room for ambiguity since it does not try to make verse of Villagrá's twelve thousand eleven-syllable rhyming lines. Espinosa's translation has the advantage of including Villagrá's prologue and "Pindaric Verses in Honor of Captain Gaspar Pérez de Villagrá and Don Pedro de Oñate, Discoverer and Conqueror of New Mexico" (35, 37–39); Encinias does not include either.

37. Miguel Encinias, Alfred Rodríguez, and Joseph P. Sánchez, editors' introduction to Villagrá's *History of New Mexico*, xviii. Encinias et al. relate that Fray Marcos de Niza, author of *Las siete ciudades de Cibola*, was the first to follow Cabeza de Vaca's lead. This would suggest that by the time Villagrá published his *History* (1610), *Castaways* was already a well-diffused, if not altogether appropriated, text.

38. *La Araucana* was published in three parts, in 1569, 1578, and 1589.

39. For a detailed, uncritically celebratory treatment of Oñate's expedition, see Marc Simmons, *The Last Conquistador: Juan de Oñate and the Settling of the Far Southwest* (Norman: University of Oklahoma Press, 1991).

40. Oswald de Andrade, "Cannibalist Manifesto," trans. Leslie Barry, *Latin American Literary Review* 19, no. 38 (July-December 1991): 35–47, 38–39.

Notes to Chapter 4

1. Lowe Lisa, *Immigrant Acts: On Asian American Cultural Politics* (Durham, N.C.: Duke University Press, 1996), 2–3, emphasis in original.

2. Cherríe Moraga and Gloria Anzaldúa, *This Bridge Called My Back: Writings by Radical Women of Color* (New York: Kitchen Table Women of Color Press, 1983); Gloria Anzaldúa, *Borderlands/La frontera: The New Mestiza* (San Francisco: Aunt Lute Books, 1987).

3. Cherríe Moraga, *The Last Generation: Poetry and Prose* (Boston: South End, 1993), 61.

4. See Emma Pérez, *The Decolonial Imaginary: Writing Chicanas into History* (Bloomington: Indiana University Press, 1999), 31–54; and Chela Sandoval, *The Methodology of the Oppressed* (Minneapolis: University of Minnesota Press, 2000), 45–46.

5. Luz María Umpierre, *The Margarita Poems* (Bloomington, Ind.: Third Woman Press, 1987); Elías Miguel Muñoz, *The Greatest Performance* (Houston: Arte Público, 1991); and Rafael Campo, *What the Body Told* (Durham, N.C.: Duke University Press, 1996).

6. Arnaldo Cruz-Malavé, "Toward an Art of Transvestism: Colonialism and Homosexuality in Puerto Rican Literature," in *¿Entiendes? Queer Readings, Hispanic Contexts*, ed. Emilie L. Bergman and Paul Julian Smith (Durham, N.C.: Duke University Press, 1995), 137–67; quotation from 137–38. I am indebted to Cruz-Malavé for his brilliant sacking of the Boricua closet, and especially for this pioneering essay, from which I mine my own discussion of Boricua identity poetics,

the specter of Puerto Rican history, and its rememory as an inherently literary undertaking. As I modify the ends of his conclusions, and ultimately demand more from his literary sacking, I recognize that his work makes my own investment in Boricua queer writing possible.

7. Judith Butler contends that the term "queer" "will have to remain that which is, in the present, never fully owned, but always and only redeployed . . . in the direction of urgent and expanding political purposes. . . . it will doubtless have to be yielded in favor of terms that do that political work more effectively." *Bodies That Matter: On the Discursive Limits of "Sex"* (New York: Routledge, 1993), 228. Broadly speaking, "Boricua" refers to "Borinquen," the Arawak name for Puerto Rico, "the land of the brave lord." I use "Boricua" to invoke both the pre-Columbian name and the diasporic nature of Puerto Rican identity negotiations.

8. Luz María Umpierre, *Nuevas aproximaciones críticas a la literatura puertorriqueña contemporánea* (Río Piedras, P.R.: Editorial Cultural, 1983).

9. Antonio S. Pedreiro, *Insularismo* (1934), reprinted in *Obras*, vol. 1 (San Juan, P.R.: Instituto de la Cultura Puertorriqueña, 1970). Page numbers refer to the *Obras* edition.

10. Efraín Barradas, "1493 también es 1492," *Latin American Literary Review* 20, no. 40 (July-December 1992): 13–15; quotation from 14.

11. Donald E. Pease, "National Identities, Postmodern Artifacts and Postnational Narratives," in *National Identities and Post-Americanist Narratives*, ed. Donald E. Pease (Durham, N.C.: Duke University Press, 1994), 1–13; quotation from 3.

12. Pedreira's linear and stagist history of Puerto Rico was divided into three epochs: (1) from colonial conquest in 1493 to the nineteenth century; (2) from the nineteenth century to the war of 1898; and (3) from 1898 to Pedreira's present in the 1930s, a time of "transition" (*Insularismo*, 29).

13. Cited in Richard Zacks, *History Laid Bare: Love, Sex, and Perversity from the Ancient Etruscans to Warren G. Harding* (New York: HarperPerennial, 1994), 143.

14. For the Amazon in the early modern European imaginary, especially Columbus and Vespucci, see José Piedra, "Loving Columbus," in *Amerindian Images and the Legacy of Columbus*, ed. René Jara and Nicholas Spadaccini (Minneapolis: University of Minnesota Press, 1992), 230–65.

15. Sylvia Plath, "Lady Lazarus," in *Ariel* (New York: Perennial, 1965), 6–9.

16. Luz María Umpierre, "Manifesto: Whose Taboos? Theirs, Yours or Ours," *Letras Femeninas* 22, nos. 1–2 (spring-fall 1996): 263–68; quotation from 267.

17. Juan G. Gelpí, *Literatura y paternalismo en Puerto Rico* (Río Piedras: Universidad de Puerto Rico, 1993), 24; all translations from this book are my own.

18. In referring to his work in *The History of Sexuality*, vol. 3, *The Care of the Self* (New York: Vintage, 1988), Michel Foucault summarized the ethical cornerstone of his critique of normative forms of sexual subjection and the instrumentality of power by rhetorically positioning an answer within a question: "for what is morality, if not the practice of liberty, the deliberate practice of freedom? . . . Liberty is

the ontological condition of ethics. But ethics is the deliberate form assumed by liberty" (cited in James Bernauer and David Rasmussen, *The Final Foucault* [Cambridge, Mass.: MIT Press, 1994], 4). Foucault's "practice of freedom" as the principled ethic of the care of the self-cum-others was appropriated by Simon Watney in his important collection of essays, *Practices of Freedom: Selected Writings on HIV/AIDS* (Durham, N.C.: Duke University Press, 1994).

19. Doris Sommer, *Bilingual Aesthetics: A New Sentimental Education* (Durham, N.C.: Duke University Press, 2004), xiii–xxvii.

20. By "transgressive" I am referring, in broad terms, to Foucault's testing of institutional limits and the concomitant possibility of dismantling those limits.

21. See the introduction for a discussion of this.

22. *Bugarrón* is a curious term from the Cuban and, to a lesser extent, Caribbean sexual vernacular that refers to the active partner in homosexual anal sex. The active partner is understood to be heterosexual by virtue not of his sexual object choice but of his dominant intrusion and "taking" of the body of another male. Only the penetrated male is labeled *loca*. Within this cultural imaginary the *bugarrón* is able to maintain his (hetero)sexual subject integrity.

23. John Champagne, *The Ethics of Marginality: A New Approach to Gay Studies* (Minneapolis: University of Minnesota Press, 1995), xxvii.

24. Jefferson Humphries, *Losing the Text: Readings in Literary Desire* (Athens: University of Georgia Press, 1986), 299, emphasis in original.

25. That is, the eucharistic parody performed by Rosita's literal rewriting of Marito's life-body while intermeshing it with her own.

26. Jorge Marbán, review of Elías Miguel Muñoz's *The Greatest Performance*, *Chasqui* 23, no. 1 (May 1994): 131–32; quotation from 131.

27. Marbán's account is but one of many misreadings. The earliest review of the book that I am aware of, in *Kirkus Review*, September 1, 1991, stated that "[t]heir voices alternate in the book though Rosita is the more unusual narrator." Perhaps more surprisingly, the well-known Latino writer Virgil Suárez asserted in the *Miami Herald* that "[t]he friends separate when Rosa leaves for Spain. . . . Once they catch up in California, Marito and Rosa continue and intensify their friendship." Thomas Filbin, in his review of Elías Miguel Muñoz's *The Greatest Performance*, in *Review of Contemporary Fiction* (spring 1992), wrote, "Rosa (Rosita) and Mario (Marito) are childhood friends in Cuba who are reunited later in the United States. . . . In alternating chapters Rosa and Mario tell of their journey from childhood in a language of poignant revelation" (155–56).

28. Elaine Scarry, *The Body in Pain: The Making and Unmaking of the World* (New York: Oxford University Press, 1985), 27.

29. Doris Sommer, *Proceed with Caution, When Engaged by Minority Writing in the Americas* (Cambridge, Mass.: Harvard University Press, 1999), 11.

30. Elizabeth Grosz, *Volatile Bodies: Toward a Corporeal Feminism* (Bloomington: Indiana University Press, 1994), 5.

31. Juliet Flower MacCannell, introduction to *Thinking Bodies,* ed. Juliet Flower MacCannell and Laura Zakarin (Stanford, Calif.: Stanford University Press, 1994), 2, 6.

32. Martine Rothblatt, *The Apartheid of Sex: A Manifesto on the Freedom of Gender* (New York: Crown, 1995), 164.

33. Sharing this view is transgendered performance artist Kate Bornstein, in her/his suggestively titled *Gender Outlaw: On Men, Women, and the Rest of Us* (London: Routledge, 1994): "I keep trying to integrate my life. I keep trying to make all the pieces into one piece. As a result, my identity becomes my body which becomes my fashion which becomes my writing style" (1). The body is posited as transgressor, the body of an "outlaw." We might ask about the instrumentality or ambiguity of gender choice as it relates to bodies that do not have surgical or other access to "fashion" or "writing" (style).

34. Judith Butler, *Gender Trouble: Feminism and the Subversion of Identity* (New York: Routledge, 1990), 7.

35. Jean Baudrillard, *Simulations,* trans. Paul Foss, Paul Patton, and Philip Beitchman (New York: Semiotext(e), 1983), 146–47.

36. Judith Butler, *Bodies That Matter: On the Discursive Limits of "Sex"* (New York: Routledge, 1993), 313.

37. Butler is not the only thinker to "borrow" from her continental colleague Baudrillard. In a curious irony, Cuban-born Severo Sarduy (one of the Left Bank's least-known members of the journal *Tel Quel*) "borrowed" Baudrillard's title for his *La simulación* (Caracas: Monte Avila, 1982). Baudrillard's *Simulacres et simulation* was later partly published in English translation as *Simulations* (1983). I know of no study that engages the issues raised by this type of "borrowing"; they point—if nothing else—to a moment of postmodern saturation with regard to the Left Bank's literal figuration of the "Death of the Author."

38. I am well aware of the contradictions in a materialist approach combining Foucauldian discourse analysis. Their points of contact, however, can be viewed as antihegemonic alliances that provide a powerful critique of the ideologies of control over of the body.

39. See the introduction and chapter 2 for a discussion of the *corpus delicti.* In Campo's collection, the evidence of the "body of the cultural crime" manifests itself in the virulent onslaught of AIDS and its ability to "erase" Latinos.

40. Andrew M. Larkin, *Modernism and the Other in Stevens, Frost, and Moore* (Gainesville: University Press of Florida, 1996), 1.

41. I say "his" intentionally. Marianne Moore, loosely associated with the American modernists, was one of few women canonized in American letters as a modernist.

42. Frank Lentricchia, *Ariel and the Thought Police: Michel Foucault, William James, Wallace Stevens* (Madison: University of Wisconsin Press, 1988), 6.

43. The other principal members of the avant-garde *Grupo Origenes* were Eliseo Diego, Cintio Vitier, José Lezama Lima, Ángel Gaztelu, Fina García Marruz, Lo-

renzo García Vega, and the painter Mariano Rodríguez. The extant Stevens and Rodríguez Feo correspondence has been collected by Beverly Coyle and Alan Filreis in *Secretaries of the Moon: The Letters of Wallace Stevens and José Rodríguez Feo* (Durham, N.C.: Duke University Press, 1986). My page references refer to this compilation.

44. Stevens is referring to an essay by María Rosa Lida, an authority on medieval Spanish literature who edited the works of fourteenth-century Spanish poet Juan Ruiz.

45. Wallace Stevens, *Transport to Summer* (New York: Knopf, 1947).

46. Cited in Robert Rehder, *The Poetry of Wallace Stevens* (New York: St. Martin's, 1988), 95.

47. *The Collected Poems of Wallace Stevens* (New York: Vintage, 1982), 142. "Academic Discourse at Havana" originally appeared in *Ideas of Order* (New York: Knopf, 1936).

48. Fatima in Portugal is a major pilgrimage site to the Virgin Mary.

49. Rehder misses Stevens's allusions to *modernismo* symbology, not surprisingly, because for him the identity issue is an American (read: United States) and English problem.

50. Enrique Anderson Imbert and Eugenio Florit, eds., *Literatura hispanoamericana: Antología e introducción histórica,* vol. 1 (New York: Holt, Rinehart, and Winston, 1970), 139.

51. Rafael Campo, *The Other Man Was Me: A Voyage to the New World* (Houston: Arte Público, 1994); *What the Body Told* (Durham, N.C.: Duke University Press, 1996); *Diva* (Durham, N.C.: Duke University Press, 1999); *Landscape with Human Figure* (Durham, N.C.: Duke University Press, 2002).

52. Wallace Stevens, *Harmonium* (New York: Knopf, 1933).

53. Rafael Pérez-Torres's influential book *Movements in Chicano Poetry: Against Myths, against Margins* (Cambridge: Cambridge University Press, 1995) noted that Chicano and by extension Latino poetry's "significance" resides in its protest against established conventions and as such its status "as a resistant 'minority' critical practice is undeniable" (1).

54. Avery F. Gordon, *Ghostly Matters: Haunting and the Sociological Imagination* (Minneapolis: University of Minnesota Press, 1997), 7.

55. Marita Sturken, *Tangled Memories: The Vietnam War, the AIDS Epidemic, and the Politics of Remembering* (Berkeley: University of California Press, 1997), 145.

Notes to the Conclusion

1. Charles Bowden, "While You Were Sleeping: In Juárez, Mexico, Photographers Expose the Violent Realities of Free Trade," *Harper's* (December 1996): 44–52. His *Harper's* piece was expanded and later published as a book, *Juárez: The Laboratory of Our Future,* with a preface by Noam Chomsky and an afterword by Eduardo Galeano (New York: Aperture, 1998). I quote from the *Harper's* article.

2. Pheona Donohoe, "The City of Lost Girls," *Big Issue* 210 (August 2004): 18–19.

3. Alicia Gaspar de Alba, *Desert Blood: The Juárez Murders* (Houston: Arte Público, 2005).

4. In the acknowledgments to *Desert Blood* (342–43), Gaspar de Alba cites Stefano Tani's *The Doomed Detective: The Contribution of the Detective Novel to Postmodern American and Italian Fiction* and his analysis of the "antidetective" for elucidating her own project. In a recasting of the role of the traditional detective, the antidetective does not solve the crime but rather exposes and comments on it. The popularity of the genre itself allows social critique, the crime in question, to reach a broader audience than would be possible with the traditional novel.

5. José Limón has offered a reading of this transactional space of cultural citizenship which he calls "Greater Mexico" (following Américo Paredes's coinage) in an effort to move beyond the conventions of *identity papers,* into a space and a theoretical praxis that considers border crossings in this context to be the norm of lived experience despite the performance of impermeability enacted on the state stage that is the national border. See José E. Limón, *American Encounters: Greater Mexico, the United States, and the Erotics of Culture* (Boston: Beacon, 1998), 3, 9–14.

6. Cherríe Moraga, "An Irrevocable Promise: Staging the Story Xicana," in *A Xicanadyke Codex of Changing Consciousness* (unpublished manuscript, 2005).

7. Lawrence Grossberg, *We Gotta Get Out of This Place: Popular Conservatism and Postmodern Culture* (New York: Routledge, 1992), 79–80. Daniel T. Contreras also mines and renders visible Grossberg's well-known use of affect by making it a politically useful category of analysis in decidedly "Latino" terms in his beautifully written *Unrequited Love and Gay Latino Culture: What Have You Done to My Heart?* (New York: Palgrave Macmillan, 2005).

8. In situating the terms through which he understands historicity to be central to and constitutive of determining meaning, Jameson writes, "History is what hurts, it is what refuses desire and sets inexorable limits to individual as well as collective praxis, which its 'ruses' turn into grisly and ironic reversals of their overt intention." Fredric Jameson, *The Political Unconscious: Narrative as a Socially Symbolic Act* (Ithaca, N.Y.: Cornell University Press, 1981), 102.

9. Claude Lévi-Strauss, *Tristes tropiques,* trans. John Weightman and Doreen Weightman (New York: Atheneum, 1967).

10. Emily Martin, "The End of the Body," in *The Gender/Sexuality Reader: Culture, History, Political Economy,* ed. Roger N. Lancaster and Micaela di Leonardo (New York: Routledge, 1997), 543.

Works Cited

Adorno, Rolena. "The Discursive Encounter of Spain and America: The Authority of Eyewitness Testimony in Writing History." *William and Mary Quarterly* 49 (1992): 210–28.

Allsup, Carl. *The American G.I. Forum: Origins and Evolution.* Mexican American Monographs 6. Austin: Center for Mexican American Studies, University of Texas at Austin, 1982.

Anderson, Benedict. *Imagined Communities: Reflections on the Origin and Spread of Nationalism.* Rev. ed. London: Verso, 1991.

Anderson Imbert, Enrique, and Eugenio Florit, eds. *Literatura hispanoamericana: Antología e introducción histórica.* Vol. 1. New York: Holt, Rinehart, and Winston, 1970.

Andrade, Oswald de. "Cannibalist Manifesto." Trans. Leslie Barry. *Latin American Literary Review* 19, no. 38 (July-December 1991): 35–47.

Anzaldúa, Gloria. *Borderlands/La frontera: The New Mestiza.* San Francisco: Aunt Lute Books, 1987.

Aranda, José F. "Breaking All the Rules: María Amparo Ruiz de Burton Writes a Civil War Novel." In *Recovering the U.S. Hispanic Literary Heritage,* vol. 3, ed. María Herrera-Sobek and Virginia Sánchez Korrol. Houston: Arte Público, 2000.

———. *When We Arrive: A New Literary History of Mexican America.* Tucson: University of Arizona Press, 2003.

Augenbaum, Harold, and Margarite Fernández Olmos, eds. *The Latino Reader: From 1542 to the Present.* New York: Houghton Mifflin, 1997.

Ávila de Ríos, Catarina. *Memoirs of Doña Catarina Ávila de Ríos.* 1935. Trans. Earl R. Hewitt. BANC MSS C-D 35.

———. *Recuerdos históricos de California por la Señora Catarina Ávila de Ríos.* 1877. BANC MSS C-D 35.

Bancroft, Hubert Howe. *History of California.* 7 vols. San Francisco: History Company, 1884–89.

Barradas, Efraín. "1493 también es 1492." *Latin American Literary Review* 20, no. 40 (July-December 1992): 13–15.

Barthes, Roland. *Camera Lucida: Reflections on Photography.* Trans. Richard Howard. New York: Hill and Wang, 1981.

Baudrillard, Jean. *Seduction.* New York: St. Martin's, 1990.

———. *Simulacres et simulation.* Paris: Galilée, 1981.

———. *Simulations.* Trans. Paul Foss, Paul Patton, and Philip Beitchman. New York: Semiotext(e), 1983.

Bello, Andrés. "Autonomía cultural de América." In *Conciencia intelectual de América: Antología del ensayo hispanoamericano,* ed. Carlos Ripoll. New York: Eliseo Torres, 1974.

———. "Silva a la agricultura de la Zona Tórrida." In *Literatura hispanoamericana,* vol. 1, ed. Enrique Imbert Anderson and Eugenio Florit. New York: Holt, Rinehart, and Winston, 1970. 251–55.

Benjamin, Walter. "Theses on the Philosophy of History." In *Illuminations: Essays and Reflections,* ed. Hannah Arendt, trans. Harry Zohn. New York: Schocken Books, 1968. 253–64.

———. "The Work of Art in the Age of Mechanical Reproduction." In *Illuminations: Essays and Reflections,* ed. Hannah Arendt, trans. Harry Zohn. New York: Schocken Books, 1968. 217–51.

Berg, Charles Ramírez. "Bordertown, the Assimilation Narrative, and the Chicano Social Problem Film." In *Chicanos and Film: Representation and Resistance,* ed. Chon Noriega. Minneapolis: University of Minnesota Press, 1992.

Bergland, Betty. "Reading Photographs and Narratives in Ethnic Autobiography: Memory and Subjectivity in Mary Antin's *The Promised Land.*" In *Memory, Narrative, and Identity: New Essays in Ethnic American Literatures,* ed. Amritjit Singh, Joseph T. Skerrett Jr., and Robert E. Hogan. Boston: Northeastern University Press, 1994.

Berlant, Lauren Gail. *The Queen of America Goes to Washington City: Essays on Sex and Citizenship.* Durham, N.C.: Duke University Press, 1997.

Bernauer, James, and David Rasmussen. *The Final Foucault.* Cambridge, Mass.: MIT Press, 1994.

Bhabha, Homi K. *The Location of Culture.* New York: Routledge, 1994.

———, ed. *Nation and Narration.* London: Routledge, 1990.

Biffle, Kent, and Nolan Davis. "Tío Taco Is Dead." *Newsweek,* June 29, 1970.

Black Public Sphere Collective. *The Black Public Sphere: A Public Culture Book.* Chicago: University of Chicago Press, 1995.

Bornstein, Kate. *Gender Outlaw: On Men, Women, and the Rest of Us.* New York: Routledge, 1995.

Bourke, John Gregory. "The American Congo." *Scribner's Magazine* 15 (May 1884): 590–610.

Bowden, Charles. *Juárez: The Laboratory of Our Future.* Preface by Noam Chomsky and afterword by Eduardo Galeano. New York: Aperture, 1998.

———. "While You Were Sleeping: In Juárez, Mexico, Photographers Expose the Violent Realities of Free Trade." *Harper's* (December 1996): 44–52.

Briggs, Laura. *Reproducing Empire: Race, Sex Science, and U.S. Imperialism in Puerto Rico.* Berkeley: University of California Press, 2002.

Brooke, James. "Conquistador Statue Stirs Hispanic Pride and Indian Rage." *New York Times,* January 9, 1998, A10.

Bruce-Novoa, Juan. *Chicano Poetry: A Response to Chaos* (Austin: University of Texas Press, 1982.

———. "Naufragios en los mares de la significación: De *La Relación* de Cabeza de Vaca a la literatura chicana." In *Notas y comentarios sobre Álvar Núñez Cabeza de Vaca,* ed. Margo Glantz. México, D.F.: Grijalbo, 1993. An earlier version appeared in *Plural* 19, no. 5, 221 (February 1990): 12–21.

———. "Shipwrecked in the Seas of Signification: Cabeza de Vaca's *Relación* and Chicano Literature." In *Reconstructing a Chicano/a Literary Heritage: Hispanic Colonial Literature of the Southwest,* ed. María Herrera-Sobek. Tucson: University of Arizona Press, 1993. 3–23.

Buckley, R. Philip. *Husserl, Heidegger, and the Crisis of Philosophical Responsibility.* Dordrecht: Kluwer Academic, 1992.

Burrola, Luis R., and José A. Rivera, "Chicano Studies Programs at the Crossroads: Alternative Futures for the 1980s." Working Paper 103. Albuquerque: Southwest Hispanic Research Institute, University of New Mexico, 1983.

Butler, Judith. *Bodies That Matter: On the Discursive Limits of "Sex."* New York: Routledge, 1993.

———. *Gender Trouble: Feminism and the Subversion of Identity.* New York: Routledge, 1990.

———. "Imitation and Gender Insubordination." In *The Lesbian and Gay Studies Reader,* ed. Henry Abelove, Michèle Aina Barale, and David Halprin. New York: Routledge, 1993. 307–20.

Cabeza de Vaca, Alvar Núñez. *The Account: Álvar Núñez Cabeza de Vaca's Relación.* Ed. José B. Fernández and Martin Favata. Houston: Arte Público, 1993.

———. *Castaways: The Narrative of Alvar Núñez Cabeza de Vaca.* 1885. Ed. Enrique Pupo-Walker, trans. Frances M. López-Morilla. Berkeley: University of California Press, 1993.

———. *Los naufragios.* 1542. Ed. Enrique Pupo-Walker. Madrid: Castalia, 1992.

Calderón, Héctor. *Narratives of Greater Mexico: Essays on Chicano Literary History, Genre, and Borders.* Austin: University of Texas Press, 2004.

Calderón, Héctor, and José David Saldívar, eds. *Criticism in the Borderlands: Studies in Chicano Literature, Culture, and Ideology.* Durham, N.C.: Duke University Press, 1991.

———. "Editors' Introduction: Criticism in the Borderlands." In *Criticism in the Borderlands: Studies in Chicano Literature, Culture, and Ideology,* ed. Héctor Calderón and José David Saldívar. Durham, N.C.: Duke University Press, 1991. 1–7.

Campo, Rafael. *Diva.* Durham, N.C.: Duke University Press, 1999.

———. *Landscape with Human Figure.* Durham, N.C.: Duke University Press, 2002.

———. *The Other Man Was Me: A Voyage to the New World.* Houston: Arte Público, 1994.

———. *What the Body Told.* Durham, N.C.: Duke University Press, 1996.

Campobello, Nellie. *Cartucho: Relatos de la lucha en el norte de México.* 1931. Ed. Jorge Aguilar Mora. México, D.F.: Ediciones Era, 2000.

Castronovo, Russ. *Necro Citizenship: Death, Eroticism, and the Public Sphere in the Nineteenth-Century United States.* Durham, N.C.: Duke University Press, 2001.

Chabram-Dernersesian, Angie. "I Throw Punches for My Race, but I Don't Want to Be a Man: Writing Us—Chica-nos (Girl, Us)/Chican*as*—into the Movement Script." In *Cultural Studies,* ed. Lawrence Grossberg, Cary Nelson, and Paula A. Treichler. New York: Routledge, 1992. 81–95.

Champagne, John. *The Ethics of Marginality: A New Approach to Gay Studies.* Minneapolis: University of Minnesota Press, 1995.

Christian, Karen. *Show and Tell: Identity as Performance in U.S. Latina/o Fiction.* Albuquerque: University of New Mexico Press, 1997.

Contreras, Daniel T. *Unrequited Love and Gay Latino Culture: What Have You Done to My Heart?* New York: Palgrave Macmillan, 2005.

Cosman, Madeline Pelner. "Illegal Aliens and American Medicine." *Journal of American Physicians and Surgeons* 10, no. 1 (spring 2005): 6–10.

Cotera, Maria Eugenia. "Native Speakers: Locating Early Expressions of United States Third World Feminist Discourse: A Comparative Analysis of the Ethnographic and Literary Writing of Ella Cara Deloria and Jovita González." Ph.D. diss., Stanford University, 2001.

Cruz-Malavé, Arnaldo. "Toward an Art of Transvestism: Colonialism and Homosexuality in Puerto Rican Literature." In *¿Entiendes? Queer Readings, Hispanic Contexts,* ed. Emilie L. Bergman and Paul Julian Smith. Durham, N.C.: Duke University Press, 1995.

De Castro, Juan E. *Mestizo Nations: Culture, Race, and Conformity in Latin American Literature.* Tucson: University of Arizona Press, 2002.

de Certeau, Michel. *Heterologies: Discourse on the Other.* Trans. Brian Massumi. Minneapolis: University of Minnesota Press, 1986.

De León, Arnoldo. *They Called Them Greasers: Anglo Attitudes toward Mexicans in Texas, 1821–1900.* Austin: University of Texas Press, 1983.

Derrida, Jacques. *Spectres of Marx: The State of the Debt, the Work of Mourning, and the New International.* Trans. Peggy Kamuf. New York: Routledge, 1994.

Donohoe, Pheona. "The City of Lost Girls." *Big Issue* 210 (August 2004): 18–19.

Dyer, Richard. *White.* London: Routledge, 1997.

Eakin, Paul John. *Touching the World: Reference in Autobiography.* Princeton, N.J.: Princeton University Press, 1985.

Emerson, Ralph Waldo. *Selected Essays.* New York: Penguin, 1985.

Ferber, Edna. *Giant.* New York: Doubleday, 1952.

Fernández, Roberto G. *Raining Backwards.* Houston: Arte Público, 1988.

Ferriss, Susan, and Ricardo Sandoval, eds. *The Fight in the Fields: César Chávez and the Farmworkers Movement.* New York: Harcourt Brace, 1997.

Filbin, Thomas. Review of Elías Miguel Muñoz's *The Greatest Performance. Review of Contemporary Fiction* (spring 1992): 155–56.

Fisher, Vivian C., et al., trans. *Three Memoirs of Mexican California.* Berkeley, Calif.: Friends of the Bancroft Library, 1988.

Foley, Neil. "Becoming Hispanic: Mexican Americans and the Faustian Pact with Whiteness." In *Reflexiones 1997: New Directions in Mexican American Studies,* ed.

Neil Foley. Austin, Tex.: Publications of the Center for Mexican American Studies, 1997. 53–70.

———. "Partly Colored of Other White: Mexican Americans and Their Problem with the Color Line." In *Beyond Black and White: Race, Ethnicity, and Gender in the U.S. South and Southwest*, ed. Stephanie Cole and Alison M. Parker. College Station: Texas A&M University Press, 2004.

Foner, Philip S., ed. *The Black Panthers Speak*. New York: Da Capo, 1995.

Fornet-Betancourt, Raúl, with Helmut Beckner and Alfredo Gómez-Müller. "The Ethic of the Care of the Self as a Practice of Freedom: An Interview with Michel Foucault, January 20, 1984." Trans. J. D. Gautier. In *The Final Foucault*, ed. James Bernauer and David Rasmussen. Cambridge, Mass.: MIT Press, 1994.

Foucault, Michel. *Foucault Live: Collected Interviews, 1961–1984*. Ed. Sylvère Lotringer, trans. Lysa Hochroth and John Johnston. New York: Semiotext(e), 1996.

———. *The History of Sexuality*. Vol. 3, *The Care of the Self*. New York: Vintage, 1988.

Fraser, Nancy. "Rethinking the Public Sphere: A Contribution to the Critique of Actually Existing Democracy." In *The Phantom Public Sphere*, ed. Bruce Robbins. Minneapolis: University of Minnesota Press, 1993.

Fregoso, Rosa Linda. *MeXicana Encounters: The Making of Social Identities on the Borderlands*. Berkeley: University of California Press, 2003.

Friendly, Fred W. *Harvest of Shame* (1960). Docudrama. New Video Group, 2005.

Fuentes, Carlos. "Malintzin de las maquilas." In *La frontera de cristal: Una novela en nueve cuentes*. México, D.F.: Alfaguara, 1995.

———. *La región más transparente*. México, D.F.: Fondo de Cultura Económica, 1958.

———. *Where the Air Is Clear*. Trans. S. Hileman. New York: Ivan Obolensky, 1960.

Gaspar de Alba, Alicia. *Desert Blood: The Juárez Murders*. Houston: Arte Público, 2005.

Gelpí, Juan G. *Literatura y paternalismo en Puerto Rico*. Río Piedras: Universidad de Puerto Rico, 1993.

Gilbert, Julie Goldsmith. *Ferber: A Biography*. Garden City, N.Y.: Doubleday, 1978.

Gilbert, Sandra M., and Susan David Gubar. *The Madwoman in the Attic: The Woman Writer and the Nineteenth-Century Literary Imagination*. New Haven, Conn.: Yale University Press, 1979.

Gilroy, Paul. *Against Race: Imagining Political Culture beyond the Color Line*. Cambridge, Mass.: Harvard University Press, 2000.

———. *The Black Atlantic: Modernity and Double Consciousness*. Cambridge, Mass.: Harvard University Press, 1993.

Glantz, Margo, ed. *Notas y comentarios sobre Álvar Núñez Cabeza de Vaca*. México, D.F.: Grijalbo, 1993.

Goldberg, Jonathan. *Sodometries: Renaissance Texts, Modern Sexualities*. Stanford, Calif.: Stanford University Press, 1992.

Gonzales-Berry, Erlinda, and Chuck Tatum, eds. *Recovering the U.S. Hispanic Literary Heritage*. Vol. 2. Houston: Arte Público, 1996.

González, John M. "Romancing Hegemony: Constructing Racialized Citizenship in María Amparo Ruiz de Burton's *The Squatter and the Don*." In *Recovering the U.S. Hispanic Literary Heritage*, vol. 2, ed. Erlinda Gonzáles-Berry and Chuck Tatum. Houston: Arte Público, 1996. 23–39.

González, Jovita, and Eve Raleigh (pseudonym of Margret Eimer). *Caballero: A Historical Novel*. 1938. Ed. José E. Limón and María Eugenia Cotera. College Station: Texas A&M University Press, 1996.

———. *Dew on the Thorn*. Ed. José E. Limón. 1927–1940. Houston: Arte Público, 1997.

Gordon, Avery F. *Ghostly Matters: Haunting and the Sociological Imagination*. Minneapolis: University of Minnesota Press, 1997.

Grajeda, Ralph F. "Tomás Rivera's Appropriation of the Chicano Past." In *Modern Chicano Writers: A Collection of Critical Essays*, ed. Joseph Sommers and Tomás Ybarra-Frausto. Englewood Cliffs, N.J.: Prentice Hall, 1979. 74–85.

Green, George N. "The Felix Longoria Affair." *Journal of Ethnic Studies* 19 (1991): 23–49.

Grossberg, Lawrence. *We Gotta Get Out of This Place: Popular Conservatism and Postmodern Culture*. New York: Routledge, 1992.

Grosz, Elizabeth. *Volatile Bodies: Toward a Corporeal Feminism*. Bloomington: Indiana University Press, 1994.

Gruesz, Kirsten Silva. *Ambassadors of Culture: The Transamerican Origins of Latino Writing*. Princeton, N.J.: Princeton University Press, 2002.

Gubar, Susan. *Racechanges: White Skin, Black Face in American Culture*. New York: Oxford University Press, 1997.

Habermas, Jürgen. *The New Conservatism: Cultural Criticism and the Historians' Debate*. Ed. and trans. Shierry Weber Nicholsen. Cambridge, Mass.: MIT Press, 1989.

———. *The Structural Transformation of the Public Sphere: An Inquiry into a Category of Bourgeois Society*. Trans. Thomas Burger with Frederick Lawrence. Cambridge, Mass.: MIT Press, 1989.

Hartman, Geoffrey, ed. *Bitburg in Moral and Political Perspective*. Bloomington: Indiana University Press, 1986.

Herrera-Sobek, María. *Reconstructing a Chicano/a Literary Heritage: Hispanic Colonial Literature of the Southwest*. Tucson: University of Arizona Press, 1993.

Hinojosa, Rolando. "Foreword: Redefining American Literature." In *Criticism in the Borderlands: Studies in Chicano Literature, Culture, and Ideology*, ed. Héctor Calderón and José David Saldívar. Durham, N.C.: Duke University Press, 1991. xi–xv.

hooks, bell. "In Our Glory: Photography and Black Life." In *Picturing Us: African American Identity in Photography*, ed. Deborah Willis. New York: New Press, 1994. 42–53.

Hughes, Langston. *The Collected Poems of Langston Hughes.* Ed. Arnold Rampersad and David Roessel. New York: Knopf, 1994.

Hulme, Peter. *Colonial Encounters: Europe and the Native Caribbean, 1492–1797.* New York: Routledge, 1987.

Humphries, Jefferson. *Losing the Text: Readings in Literary Desire.* Athens: University of Georgia Press, 1986.

Ignatiev, Noel. *How the Irish Became White.* New York: Routledge, 1995.

Inda, Jonathan Xavier. "Foreign Bodies: Migrants, Parasites, and the Pathological Nation." *Discourse* 22, no. 3 (fall 2000): 46–62.

Jameson, Fredric. *The Political Unconscious: Narrative as a Socially Symbolic Act.* Ithaca, N.Y.: Cornell University Press, 1981.

Kammen, Michael. *Mystic Chords of Memory: The Transformation of Tradition in American Culture.* New York: Vintage, 1991.

Kanellos, Nicolás. "A Socio-Historic Study of Hispanic Newspapers in the United States." In *Recovering the U.S. Hispanic Literary Heritage,* vol. 1, ed. Ramón A. Gutiérrez and Genaro M. Padilla. Houston: Arte Público, 1993. 107–28.

Kanellos, Nicolás, Kenya Dworkin y Méndez, José B. Fernández, Erlinda González-Berry, Agnes Lugo Ortiz, and Charles Tatum, eds. *Herencia: The Anthology of Hispanic Literature of the United States.* Oxford: Oxford University Press, 2002.

Kilgour, Maggie. *From Communion to Cannibalism: An Anatomy of Metaphors of Incorporation.* Princeton, N.J.: Princeton University Press, 1990.

Lancaster, Roger N., and Micaela di Leonardo. *The Gender Sexuality Reader: Culture, History, Political Economy.* New York: Routledge, 1997.

Larkin, Andrew M. *Modernism and the Other in Stevens, Frost, and Moore.* Gainesville: University Press of Florida, 1996.

Lattin, Vernon E., ed. *Contemporary Chicano Fiction: A Critical Survey.* Binghamton, N.Y.: Bilingual Press/Editorial Bilingüe, 1984.

Leal, Luis. "Mexican American Literature: A Historical Perspective." In *Modern Chicano Writers: A Collection of Essays,* ed. Joseph Sommers and Tomás Ybarra-Frausto. Englewood Cliffs, N.J.: Prentice Hall, 1979. 18–30. First published in *Revista Chicano-Riqueña* 1, no. 1 (1973): 32–44.

Lentricchia, Frank. *Ariel and the Thought Police: Michel Foucault, William James, Wallace Stevens.* Madison: University of Wisconsin Press, 1988.

Leslie, Mrs. Frank. "Eulalia Perez, the Oldest Woman in the World." *Frank Leslie's Illustrated Newspaper,* January 12, 1878.

Lévi-Strauss, Claude. *Tristes tropiques.* Trans. John Weightman and Doreen Weightman. New York: Atheneum, 1967.

Limón, José E. *American Encounters: Greater Mexico, the United States, and the Erotics of Culture.* Boston: Beacon, 1998.

———. *Dancing with the Devil: Society and Cultural Poetics in Mexican-American South Texas.* Madison: University of Wisconsin Press, 1994.

Littell, Robert, Kent Biffle, and Nolan Davis. "Tío Taco Is Dead," *Newsweek,* June 29, 1970, 22–28.

Lomelí, A. Francisco. "Po(l)etics of Reconstructing and/or Appropriating a Literary Past: The Regional Case Model." In *Recovering the U.S. Hispanic Literary Heritage*, vol. 1, ed. Ramón A. Gutiérrez and Genaro M. Padilla. Houston: Arte Público, 1993. 221–40.

Lomelí, A. Francisco, and Donaldo W. Urioste. *Chicano Perspectives in Literature: A Critical and Annotated Bibliography*. Albuquerque, N.M.: Pajarito Publications, 1976.

Looby, Christopher. *Voicing America: Language, Literary Form, and the Origins of the United States*. Chicago: University of Chicago Press, 1996.

López Tijerina, Reies. *They Called Me "King Tiger": My Struggle for the Land and Our Rights*. Trans. and ed. José Angel Gutierrez. Houston: Arte Público, 2000.

Lowe, Lisa. *Immigrant Acts: On Asian American Cultural Politics*. Durham, N.C.: Duke University Press, 1996.

Ludmer, Josefina. *The Corpus Delicti: A Manual of Argentine Fictions*. Trans. Glen S. Close. Pittsburgh: University of Pittsburgh Press, 2004.

MacCannell, Juliet Flower. Introduction to *Thinking Bodies*, ed. Juliet Flower MacCannell and Laura Zakarin. Stanford, Calif.: Stanford University Press, 1994.

Maciel, David R., and Isidro D. Ortiz, eds. *Chicanas/Chicanos at the Crossroads: Social, Economic, and Political Change*. Tucson: University of Arizona Press, 1996.

Maciel, David R., Isidro D. Ortiz, and María Herrera-Sobek, eds. *Chicano Renaissance: Contemporary Cultural Trends*. Tucson: University of Arizona Press, 2000.

Madrid, Arturo. "In Search of the Authentic Pachuco." In *Velvet Barrios: Popular Culture and Chicana/o Sexualities*, ed. Alicia Gaspar de Alba, foreword by Tomás Ybarra Frausto. New York: Palgrave Macmillan, 2003. 17–40.

Madrigal, Iñigo. *Historia de la literatura hispanoamericna*. Vol. 1, *Época colonial*. Madrid: Cátedra, 1982.

Magill, Frank N., ed. *Masterpieces of Latino Literature*. New York: HarperCollins, 1994.

Manrique Cabrera, Francisco. *Historia de la literatura puertorriqueña*. New York: Las Américas, 1956.

Marbán, Jorge. Review of Elías Miguel Muñoz's *The Greatest Performance*. *Chasqui* 23, no. 1 (May 1994): 131–32.

Mariscal, George, ed. *Aztlán and Viet Nam: Chicano and Chicana Experiences of the War*. Berkeley: University of California Press, 1999.

Martin, Emily. "The End of the Body." In *The Gender/Sexuality Reader: Culture, History, Political Economy*, ed. Roger N. Lancaster and Micaela di Leonardo. New York: Routledge, 1997. 543–58.

Martín-Rodríguez, Manuel M. *Life in Search of Readers: Reading (in) Chicano/a Literature*. Albuquerque: University of New Mexico Press, 2003.

———. "Textual and Land Reclamations: The Critical Reception of Early Chicana/o Literature." In *Recovering the U.S. Hispanic Literary Heritage*, vol. 2, ed. Erlinda Gonzáles-Berry and Charles M. Tatum. Houston: Arte Público, 1996.

Maura, Juan Francisco. "Escalvas españolas en el Nuevo Mundo: Una nota histórica." *Colonial Latin American Literary Review* 2 (1993): 188–89.

———. "Veracidad en los *Naufragios*: La técnica narrativa de Alvar Núñez Cabeza de Vaca." *Revista Iberoamericana* 61, nos. 170–71 (January-June 1995): 187–95.

McCracken, Ellen. "Latina Narrative and the Politics of Signification: Articulation, Antagonism, and Populist Rupture." *Crítica: A Journal of Critical Essays* 2, no. 2 (fall 1990): 202–7.

Meier, Matt S., and Feliciano Ribera. *Mexican Americans, American Mexicans: From Conquistadores to Chicanos*. New York: Hill and Wang, 1995.

Metz, Christian. "Photography and Fetish." *October* 34 (fall 1985): 81–90.

Mignolo, Walter. "Cartas, crónicas y relaciones del descubrimiento y la conquista." In *Historia de la literatura hispanoamericna*, vol. 1, *Época colonial*, ed. Luis Iñigo Madrigal. Madrid: Cátedra, 1982. 57–116.

Mitchell, W. J. T. *Picture Theory: Essays on Verbal and Visual Representation*. Chicago: University of Chicago Press, 1994.

Moraga, Cherríe. "An Irrevocable Promise: Staging the Story Xicana." Paper presented at Bryn Mawr College, February 2005.

———. *The Last Generation: Poetry and Prose*. Boston: South End, 1993.

———. *A Xicanadyke Codex of Changing Consciousness*. Forthcoming.

Moraga, Cherríe, and Gloria Anzaldúa, *This Bridge Called My Back: Writings by Radical Women of Color*. New York: Kitchen Table Women of Color Press, 1983.

Morales, Alejandro Morales. *The Brick People*. Houston: Arte Público, 1988.

Morrison, Toni. *Beloved*. New York: Plume, 1987.

Muñoz, Carlos. "The Quest for Paradigm: The Development of Chicano Studies and Intellectuals." In *Latinos and Education: A Critical Reader*, ed. Antonia Darder, Rodolfo D. Torres, and Henry Gutiérrez. New York: Routledge, 1997.

Muñoz, Elías Miguel. *The Greatest Performance*. Houston: Arte Público, 1991.

Nadar, Félix. "Balzac and the Daguerreotype." In *Literature and Photography: Interactions 1840–1990*, ed. Jane M. Rabb. Albuquerque: University of New Mexico Press, 1995. 6–9.

Oboler, Suzanne. *Ethnic Labels, Latino Lives: Identity and the Politics of (Re)Presentation in the United States*. Minneapolis: University of Minnesota Press, 1995.

Olalquiaga, Celeste. *Megalopolis: Contemporary Cultural Sensibilities*. Minneapolis: University of Minnesota Press, 1990.

Ortego, Philip. "The Chicano Renaissance." *Social Casework* 52, no. 5 (May 1971): 294–307.

Ortíz, Ann M. "The Prophetic Structure of the *Naufragios* of Alvar Núñez Cabeza de Vaca." *Journal of the Southeast Council on Latin American Studies* 27 (March 1996): 17–26.

Otero-Warren, Nina. *Old Spain in Our Southwest*. New York: Harcourt Brace, 1936.

Oviedo y Valdés, Gonzalo Fernández de. *Sumario de la natural historia de las Indias*. 1526. Madrid: Historia 16, 1986.

Padilla, Genaro. *My History, Not Yours: The Formation of Mexican American Autobiography.* Madison: University of Wisconsin Press, 1993.

Padilla, Ray. "Apuntes para la documentación de la cultura chicana." *El Grito* 5, no. 2 (winter 1971–72): 3–36.

Paredes, Américo. *George Washington Gomez: A Mexicotexan Novel.* Houston: Arte Público, 1990.

———. *"With His Pistol in His Hand": A Border Ballad and Its Hero.* Austin: University of Texas Press, 1958.

Paredes, Raymund A. "Mexican-American Literature: An Overview." In *Recovering the U.S. Hispanic Literary Heritage,* vol. 1, ed. Ramón A. Gutiérrez and Genaro M. Padilla. Houston: Arte Público, 1993. 37–51.

Pastor Bodmer, Beatriz. *The Armature of Conquest: Spanish Accounts of the Discovery of America, 1492–1589.* Trans. Lydia Longstreth Hunt. Stanford, Calif.: Stanford University Press, 1992.

———. *Discursos narrativos de la conquista: Mitificacción y emergencia.* Hanover, N.H.: Ediciones del Norte, 1983.

Pease, Donald E. "National Identities, Postmodern Artifacts and Postnational Narratives." In *National Identities and Post-Americanist Narratives,* ed. Donald E. Pease. Durham, N.C.: Duke University Press, 1994.

Pedreira, Antonio S. *Insularismo* (1934). Reprinted in *Obras.* Vol. 1. San Juan: Instituto de la Cultura Puertorriqueña, 1970.

Peña, Manuel. "Folksong and Social Change: Two Corridos as Interpretive Sources." *Aztlán* 13 (1982): 13–42.

Pérez, Emma. *The Decolonial Imaginary: Writing Chicanas into History.* Bloomington: Indiana University Press, 1999.

Pérez, Eulalia. *An Old Woman and Her Recollections.* Trans. Ruth Rodríguez. 1957. BANC MSS C-D 139 Translation.

———. *Una vieja y sus recuerdos.* 1877. BANC MSS C-D 139.

Pérez-Torres, Rafael. *Movements in Chicano Poetry: Against Myths, against Margins.* Cambridge: Cambridge University Press, 1995.

Piedra, José. "Loving Columbus." In *Amerindian Images and the Legacy of Columbus,* ed. René Jara and Nicholas Spadaccini. Minneapolis: University of Minnesota Press, 1992. 230–65.

Plath, Sylvia. *Ariel.* New York: Perennial, 1965.

Rabasa, José. *Writing Violence on the Northern Frontier: The Historiography of Sixteenth-Century New Mexico and Florida and the Legacy of Conquest.* Durham, N.C.: Duke University Press, 2000.

Rabb, Jane M. "Notes toward a History of Literature and Photography." In *Literature and Photography: Interactions 1840–1990,* ed. Jane M. Rabb. Albuquerque: University of New Mexico Press, 1995. xxv–lx.

Rehder, Robert. *The Poetry of Wallace Stevens.* New York: St. Martin's, 1988.

Restrepo, Luis Fernando. "Las elegías de varones ilustres de Indias de Juan de

Castellanos y la construcción del Nuevo Reino de Granada." Ph.D. diss., University of Maryland, 1996.

Review of Elías Miguel Muñoz's *The Greatest Performance*. *Kirkus Review*, September 1, 1991.

Ripoll, Carlos. *Conciencia intelectual de América: Antología del ensayo hispanoamericano*. New York: Eliseo Torres and Sons, 1974.

Rivera, Tomás. . . . *y no se lo tragó la tierra/And the Earth Did Not Devour Him*. 1971. Bilingual edition. Trans. Evangelina Vigil-Pinón. Houston: Arte Público, 1992.

Rodríguez del Pino, Salvador. *La novela chicana escrita en español: Cinco autores comprometidos*. Ypsilanti, Mich.: Bilingual Press/Editorial Bilingüe, 1982.

Roediger, David R. *Towards the Abolition of Whiteness: Essays on Race, Politics, and Working-Class History*. New York: Verso, 1994.

Rogin, Michael Paul. *Subversive Genealogy: The Politics and Art of Herman Melville*. New York: Knopf, 1983.

Romano, Octavio Ignacio, ed. *El Espejo—The Mirror: Selected Mexican-American Literature*. Berkeley, Calif.: Quinto Sol, 1969.

Rosaldo, Renato. "Cultural Citizenship, Inequality, and Multiculturalism." In *Latino Cultural Citizenship: Claiming Identity, Space, and Rights*, ed. William V. Flores and Rina Benmayor. Boston: Beacon, 1997.

Rothblatt, Martine. *The Apartheid of Sex: A Manifesto on the Freedom of Gender*. New York: Crown, 1995.

Rubin-Dorsky, Jeffrey. *Adrift in the Old World: The Psychological Pilgrimage of Washington Irving*. Chicago: University of Chicago Press, 1988.

Ruiz de Burton, María Amparo. *Don Quijote de la Mancha: A Comedy in Five Acts, Taken from Cervantes' Novel of That Name*. San Francisco: J. H. Carmany, 1876.

———. *The Squatter and the Don: A Novel Descriptive of Contemporary Occurrences in California*. 1885. Ed. Rosaura Sánchez and Beatrice Pita. Houston: Arte Público, 1992.

———. *Who Would Have Thought It?* 1872. Ed. Rosaura Sánchez and Beatrice Pita. Houston: Arte Público, 1995.

Rulfo, Juan. "Paso del Norte." In *El llano en llamas*. México, D.F.: Fondo de Cultura Económica, 1967. 141–50.

Saldívar, José David. *Border Matters: Remapping American Cultural Studies*. Berkeley: University of California Press, 1997.

Saldívar, Ramón. *Chicano Narrative: The Dialectics of Difference*. Madison: University of Wisconsin Press, 1990.

Salinas, Judy. "The Image of Woman in Chicano Literature." *Revista Chicano-Riqueña* 4, no. 4 (fall 1976): 139–48.

Sánchez, Rosaura. *Telling Identities: The Californio Testimonios*. Minneapolis: University of Minnesota Press, 1995.

Sandoval, Chela. *The Methodology of the Oppressed*. Minneapolis: University of Minnesota Press, 2000.

San Miguel, Guadalupe. "Actors Not Victims: Chicanas/os and the Struggle for Educational Equality." In *Chicanas/Chicanos at the Crossroads: Social, Economic, and Political Change*, ed. David R. Maciel and Isidro D. Ortiz. Tucson: University of Arizona Press, 1996. 159–80.

Sarduy, Severo. *La simulación*. Caracas: Monte Ávila, 1982.

Scarry, Elaine. *The Body in Pain: The Making and Unmaking of the World*. New York: Oxford University Press, 1985.

Schrecker, Ellen. *Many Are the Crimes: McCarthyism in America*. Princeton, N.J.: Princeton University Press, 1998.

Simmons, Marc. *The Last Conquistador: Juan de Oñate and the Settling of the Far Southwest*. Norman: University of Oklahoma Press, 1991.

Sommer, Doris. *Bilingual Aesthetics: A New Sentimental Education*. Durham, N.C.: Duke University Press, 2004.

———. *Foundational Fictions: The National Romances of Latin America*. Berkeley: University of California Press, 1991.

———. *One Master for Another: Populism as Patriarchal Rhetoric in Dominican Novels*. Lanham, Md.: University Press of America, 1983.

———. *Proceed with Caution, When Engaged by Minority Writing in the Americas*. Cambridge, Mass.: Harvard University Press, 1999.

Sommers, Joseph, and Tomás Ybarra-Frausto, eds. *Modern Chicano Writers: A Collection of Essays*. Englewood Cliffs, N.J.: Prentice Hall, 1979.

Spivak, Gayatri Chakravorty. *Outside in the Teaching Machine*. New York: Routledge, 1993.

Stevens, George. *Giant* (1956). Warner Home Video, 1992.

Stevens, Wallace. *The Collected Poems of Wallace Stevens*. New York: Vintage, 1982.

———. *Harmonium*. New York: Knopf, 1933.

———. *Ideas of Order*. New York: Knopf, 1936.

———. *Transport to Summer*. New York: Knopf, 1947.

Stevens, Wallace, and José Rodríguez Feo. *Secretaries of the Moon: The Letters of Wallace Stevens and José Rodríguez Feo*. Ed. Beverly Coyle and Alan Filreis. Durham, N.C.: Duke University Press, 1986.

Streeby, Shelly. *American Sensations: Class, Empire, and the Production of Popular Culture*. Berkeley: University of California Press, 2002.

Sturken, Marita. *Tangled Memories: The Vietnam War, the AIDS Epidemic, and the Politics of Remembering*. Berkeley: University of California Press, 1997.

Suárez, Virgil. "*Greatest Performance*: Two Lost Souls in Violent World." *Miami Herald*, December 24, 1991, 2C.

Tani, Stefano. *The Doomed Detective: The Contribution of the Detective Novel to Postmodern American and Italian Fiction*. Carbondale: Southern Illinois University Press, 1984.

Thoreau, Henry David. *Walden and Civil Disobedience*. New York: Penguin, 1986.

Todorov, Tzvetan. *La conquête de l'Amérique*. Paris: Editions du Seuil, 1982.

————. *The Conquest of America: The Question of the Other.* New York: Harper and Row, 1984.

Tripplett, Cornel Frank. *Conquering the Wilderness; or, New Pictorial History of the Life and Times of the Pioneer Heroes and Heroines of America.* New York and St. Louis: N. D. Thompson, 1883.

Umpierre, Luz María. *Ideología y novela en Puerto Rico.* Madrid: Playor, 1983.

————. "Manifesto: Whose Taboos? Theirs, Yours or Ours." *Letras Femeninas* 22, nos. 1–2 (spring-fall 1996): 263–68.

————. *The Margarita Poems.* Bloomington, Ind.: Third Woman Press, 1987.

————. *Nuevas aproximaciones críticas a la literatura puertorriqueña contemporánea.* Río Piedras, P.R.: Editorial Cultural, 1983.

Villagrá, Gaspar Pérez de. *Historia de la Nueva México.* Bilingual ed. Trans. Miguel Encinias, Alfred Rodríguez, and Joseph P. Sánchez. Albuquerque: University of New Mexico Press, 1992.

————. *A History of New Mexico.* Trans. Gilberto Espinosa. Los Angeles: Quivira Society, 1933.

Villanueva, Tino. *Scene from the Movie Giant.* Willimantic, Conn.: Curbstone, 1993.

Villareal, José Antonio. *Pocho: A Novel about a Young Mexican American Coming of Age in California.* Garden City, N.Y.: Doubleday, 1959; repr., New York: Anchor Books, 1994.

Ward, Geoffrey C. *The West: An Illustrated History.* New York: Little, Brown, 1996.

Watney, Simon. *Practices of Freedom: Selected Writings on HIV/AIDS.* Durham, N.C.: Duke University Press, 1994.

Weber, David, ed. *Foreigners in Their Native Land: Historical Roots of the Mexican Americans.* Albuquerque: University of New Mexico Press, 1973.

————. *Myth and the History of the Hispanic Southwest.* Albuquerque: University of New Mexico Press, 1988.

Yáñez, Agustín. *Al filo del agua.* México, D.F.: Porrúa, 1947.

————. *The Edge of the Storm.* Trans. Ethel Brinton. Austin: University of Texas Press, 1963.

Zacks, Richard. *History Laid Bare: Love, Sex, and Perversity from the Ancient Etruscans to Warren G. Harding.* New York: HarperCollins, 1994.

Index

Padilla, *My History, Not Yours (continued)*
Savage, 37; and photograph, 28; reading doesn't take violence into account,
37; and San Gabriel, 37

Padilla, Ray, and "pre-Chicano Aztlanense
materials," 93

Paredes, Américo, *"With a Pistol in His
Hand . . . ," George Washington Gómez,*
59; "Greater Mexico," 200n5; Latin and
Chicano studies, 59

Paredes, Raymund A., and Mexican American literature, 58

"passing" (racial), 170; "fantasy heritage"
(Carey McWilliams), 57; "passing for
Spain," 56–62, 74, 171. *See also* race
and racism

Pastor Bodmer, Beatriz, *Discursos narrativos de la conquista,* 102–3, 193n19; on
Cabeza de Vaca, 102–4

patriotism: in Chicano literature, 60–63,
67–68; and Cold War patriotic rhetoric,
17, 68; *Earth* as counternarrative of patriotism (Tomás Rivera), 72, 75–87; and
the illusive national embrace, 8, 12–13,
61–63, 67–68; as Latino counterpatriotic crisis identity, 17, 171–72; as
Latino identity modality, 8; in Puerto
Rican literature, 136; as traveling ideology, 68–72. *See also* Freedom Train

Pease, Donald, 131–32

Pedreira, Antonio S., *Insularismo,* 131,
132; corporeal rhetoric, 136; failed
bildungsroman (Arnaldo Cruz-Malavé),
132; paternalistic (Juan G. Gelpí), 136;
Puerto Rico as effeminate "sick body,"
136, 138; Puerto Rico staged history,
196n7. *See also* Puerto Rico

Pérez, Emma, *Decolonial Imaginary,* 129;
"third space," 129

Pérez, Eulalia, *An Old Woman and Her Recollections,* 16, 23, 170; age, 31–32, 34;
birth and origins, 33–34; body as palimpsest of truth claims, 41; as Catholic,
36, 53; choice of maiden name, 33–34;
cooking contest prearranged, 183n27;
and culture disjuncture, 27; and demise
of mission system, 39; as elegy topos,
31–32; as fictional character in *The
Brick People* (Alejandro Morales), 180n4;
and Gold Rush violence, 23; identification with mission system, 40, 41; and
internalized racism, 23; marriage to
Mariné, 38; Mexican-white slippage,
56; as mission elite, 37; "mulatto
body," 35–36; pressure to assimilate,
37; "pure Caucasian," 33–34, 37; at San
Gabriel, 36–38; Savage interview, 27;
"Spanishness," 34–35. *See also* Leslie,
Mrs. Frank

Pérez, Eulalia, engraving, *35;* inscription,
36; spelled "Perrez," 36

Pérez, Eulalia, photograph, 27–28, *29,*
41, 180n4; age given, 31–32; Barthian
reading, 32–33; caption omitted in
Padilla, 181n16; caption and Pérez as
"written in English," 182n22; as
ethnographic text, 28; ignored in
studies; 30–31; inscription, 31–32;
photographic death of Mexican era,
31; pose as topos, 31–32; "spelled
Perz, 31; *studium* and *punctum* function,
32–33

Pérez-Torres, Rafael, *Movements in Chicano
Poetry,* 199n53

Philip III, 118, 194n35

photographs: Anderson, 29–30, 62; disassociating referents identities, 30; as ethnographic medium, 28; ignored in

Squatter and the Don and Ruiz de Burton's biography, 49

Saldívar, Ramón, *Chicano Narrative*, 190n42; *Earth* and generational split, 85

Salinas, Judy, "Image of Woman in Chicano Literature," 191n43

San Gabriel mission, overthrow, 39; Captain Barroso, 39

San Miguel mission: massacre, 42–44; owned by Reed and Ríos, 43, 45; strategic position for gold fields, 45

Sánchez, José, Father, 37, 39–40; control over Pérez's life, 38; death, 39

Sánchez, Luis Rafael, 139

Sánchez, Rosaura (*Telling Identities*), 23, 39, 40–41, 56; and Alta California, 39, 180–81n10; Bancroft narratives as testimonials, 181n11; coercive strategies on Indians, 40; Mexican state, 180–81n11; and mission elite, 37

Sandoval, Chela, *Methodology of the Oppressed*, "third space," 129

Santo Domingo, 108

Sarduy, Severo, *La simulación,* and Baudrillard, 198n37

Savage, Thomas: Ávila de Rios, 42, 45–46; interview with Pérez, 27, 33; photographed body as historical artifact, 28–29; poem, 41

Scarry, Elaine, *The Body in Pain,* 143

Schrecker, Ellen, on HUAC, 71, 189–90n34

Scribner's, 4, 5

Sexuality: *bugarrón* as term from Cuban and Caribbean sexual vernacular, 141, 197n22; Julia de Burgos as symbol of lesbian desire in *Margarita Poems* (Luz María Umpierre), 133, 162; and ethnically marked narrative expression, 142; and gender theory, 146–51; *The Greatest Performance* (Elías Miguel Muñoz), 140–46; and Modernism (Rafael Campo and Wallace Stevens), 151–61; and national identity, 18; and Puerto Rican cultural history, 130–40. *See also* queer

Smith, John, *Generall Historie of Virginia,* 194n36

Sommer, Doris, 11–12; "erotics of politics," 54; *Foundational Fictions,* 11–12; notion of "romance," 12; texts that resist critical reading, 145; Umpierre's bilingual aesthetics, 139

Spain: Mexican independence from, 22; Spanish vs. Mexican identity, 57, 59; and Spanish-American War, 3, 58

Spanish-American War (1898), 3, 58

Spanish literature in U.S., 57–58

Spivak, Gayatri Chakravorty, *Outside in the Teaching Machine,* strategy, 9, 176n9

Stevens, Wallace, 152–60; Cuban things in *Orígenes,* 153; fetishization of things Cuban, 160; "A Word with José Rodríguez Feo," 153–54

Stevens, Wallace, "Academic Discourse at Havana," 154–56; and Darío, 155; defining America by what it is not, 155; reality coterminous with but not subservient to language, 156; relation to British literature (Rehder), 154, 156

Stevens, Wallace, "The Cuban Doctor," 157, 160; and AIDS, 160; and Campo's "The Good Doctor," 157, 60

Stevens, Wallace, and José Rodríguez Feo, *Secretaries of the* Moon, 153

strategic essentialism, 9

Streeby, Shelly, *American Sensations*, 24–25; Mexican-American and Civil War, 24–25
subaltern: bodies, 5–6; body as expendable commodity, 16; Latino body as emancipating itself, 148–49; Mexican American bodies, 6–7, 81; Ruiz de Burton as subaltern (Saldívar), 48, 49; subjects, 175–76n6

Texas, 5; Ferber, and *Giant*, 64–65; Juárez border, 19; Lone Star Republic, 5. *See also* El Paso
thinking through the body, 146–51; Plato and Idea, 146; untenable (Kant), 146–47
Thoreau, Henry David, 191n5
Tinckle, Lon (Dallas critic), and Ferber, 65
"Tío Taco Is Dead." *See* Littell, Robert, Kent Biffle, and Nolan Davis, "Tío Taco Is Dead"
Todorov, Tzvetan, *Conquest of America*, Cabeza de Vaca and ecumenical subject superiority, 103–4, 193n23
Treaty of Guadalupe Hidalgo (1848), 5, 13; Articles 8–10, 26; and Mexican Americans becoming foreigners, 22, 53; in *Squatter and the Don*, 50–53
Tripplett, Cornel Frank, *Conquering the Wilderness*, 52

Umpierre, Luz María: *Margarita Poems*, 19, 130; Amazonic counternarrative to Pedreira, 139; bilingual aesthetics (Doris Sommer), 139; Boricua identity, 132, 140, 162, 172; homocriticism, 130–31; "Manifesto: Whose Taboos?" 135; "mental illness," 135–36; name

association, 131; as re-membering, 130, 140; response to Pedreira, 131, 138–39; "Una Isla Amazónica Libre," 130
Umpierre, Luz María, "Immanence," 131–35; Amerindian nymphomaniac displaced by Amazon, 133; "armies of Amazons" in Ohio, 133; body as "new lady Lazarus," 132; invocation of Julia de Burgos, 133–35; writing as "incestuous romps," 134
Umpierre, Luz María, "The Mar/Garita Poem," 131, 136–39; "dismember the patriarch," 136–38; invented language, 139
U.S. Border Patrol, 61, 76; and illusion of territorial impermeability, 61
Utah, 5, 22

Vespucci, Americo: Amerindian women and hypersexual desire, 132–33; "Letter to Lorenzo Pietro de Medici," 132–33
Vietnam War, 77, 79
Villagrá, Gaspar Pérez de, *Historía de la Nueva México*, 118–23; accepts Cabeza de Vaca's persona, 120–21; Acoma as "fictional," 120; Amerindians barbarous, 121; battle of Acoma Rock, 121; publication history, 194–95n36; self-constituting Spanish subject, 120; truth-bearing claims of historical document, 119
Villanueva, Tino, *Scene from the Movie Giant*, 189n21
Villarreal, José Antonio, *Pocho*, 56, 59–61, 76, 81, 171; and assimilation, 60; and Chicano literature, 59; as "first" popular Latino novel published in English, 56

228

ABOUT THE AUTHOR

Lázaro Lima is Associate Professor of Spanish and Latino Studies at Bryn Mawr College. His website can be found at www.lazarolima.com.